TABLE OF CONTENTS

® Landoll, Inc.
Ashland, Ohio 44805
® The Landoll Apple Logo is a trademark owned by Landoll, Inc.
and is registered with the U.S. Patent and Trademark Office.
No part of this book may be reproduced or copied.
All rights reserved. Made in the U.S.A.
Conforms to ASTM D-4236

© 1996 Merehurst Limited. All Rights Reserved.

Barbecues

Made Easy

Series Consultant: Jenni Fleetwood

GREAT COOKING VALUE

Introduction

There's no more relaxing and enjoyable way to entertain family and friends than with a barbecue. The anticipation begins with the lighting of the fire, and increases as the aroma of char-grilled food fills the air. Whether your preference is for poultry, fish, sausages, steaks or whole roasts cooked to a turn on the rotisserie, you'll find plenty to please within the pages of this book. Vegetarians are catered for too, and the selection of recipes concludes with a sweet surprise.

Written by Antje Grüner

Recipe Notes

Use standard spoon and cup measures. All measures are level unless otherwise stated.

Eggs used are large unless otherwise stated.

Citrus fruit should be washed and dried before grating – use unsprayed fruit where possible.

Use heavy-duty foil for barbecuing, or a double thickness of regular foil. Barbecue cooking times are based upon the food that takes the longest time.

Calorie counts for average-size servings are set down at the end of each recipe, and are rounded up to the nearest whole number.

T-Bone Steaks with Sesame Potatoes

Serves 4

Red wine, rosemary and juniper berries provide a marvelous marinade for tender steaks.

Preparation time: about 40 minutes
Marinating time: 12-15 hours
Barbecuing time: 50-60 minutes plus
20 minutes to par-cook potatoes

2 x 1¼-pound T-bone steaks, trimmed
10 juniper berries
4 cloves garlic, roughly chopped
3 fresh rosemary sprigs or 1 tablespoon dried
  rosemary
1 teaspoon coarsely ground black pepper
2 cups dry red wine
2 tablespoons oil

SESAME POTATOES
4 potatoes, about 7 ounces each
1 teaspoon oil
3 tablespoons sesame seeds
1 cup dairy sour cream

1 Briefly rinse steaks under cold, running water. Drain well and pat dry with paper towels. Using a mortar and pestle, grind juniper berries to a paste. Add garlic. If using fresh rosemary, strip leaves from sprigs. Add fresh or dried rosemary to mortar with pepper. Grind mixture to a paste.

2 Rub paste into T-bones. Arrange in a single layer in a shallow glass or ceramic dish. Pour in wine. Cover and marinate in refrigerator for 12-15 hours.

3 Sesame Potatoes: About 1½ hours before serving, scrub potatoes and place in a saucepan with water to a depth of about 4 inches. Bring water to a boil, cover pan, lower heat and par-cook the potatoes for 20 minutes.

4 Drain potatoes and pat dry with paper towels. Brush with oil, then roll in sesame seeds in a shallow bowl. Wrap potatoes individually in foil, arrange on barbecue grill over hot coals and cook for 50-60 minutes, turning several times.

5 Remove steaks from marinade and pat dry with paper towels. Strain marinade, transferring 2 tablespoons of the herb mixture remaining in the strainer to a small bowl; stir in oil.

6 Grill steaks for 12-15 minutes on each side or until cooked to your liking, brushing with oil and herbs toward the end of cooking. Do not let oil drip onto the coals or flare-ups will occur.

7 Serve steaks with potatoes and sour cream.

Approximate nutritional value per portion:
1000 calories
Protein: 58g
Fat: 60g
Carbohydrate: 34g

T-Bone Steaks with Sesame Potatoes

Ribs in Spicy Sauce

Serves 4

Sticky, spicy ribs make unforgettable finger food.

Preparation time: about 15 minutes
Marinating time: about 6 hours
Barbecuing time: 30-40 minutes

3 pounds meaty country-style ribs,
    separated
¾-inch piece of fresh ginger root
½ cup bitter orange marmalade
1 tablespoon clear honey
2 tablespoons soy sauce
1 tablespoon mustard powder
¼ teaspoon chili powder

1 Briefly rinse ribs under cold, running water. Drain well and pat dry with paper towels.

2 Peel ginger root and dice finely. Place in a bowl and stir in orange marmalade, honey, soy sauce, mustard, and chili powder.

3 Arrange ribs in a single layer in a shallow glass or ceramic dish. Brush with marmalade mixture.
Cover and marinate for 6 hours in the refrigerator.

4 Drain ribs, reserving marinade in a small bowl. Place ribs in a single layer in a roasting pan and cook over hot coals for 30-40 minutes or until golden brown and crisp. During the final few minutes of cooking, baste the ribs constantly with the reserved marinade. Turn frequently.

5 Serve ribs with a little of the basting sauce. Garnish with grilled tomato topped with rosemary, and a grilled green chili, if you like.

TIP

The ribs may be cooked directly on a lightly oiled barbecue grill, but the marmalade marinade may cause the fire to flare. To limit the likelihood of this, raise the barbecue grill and cook the ribs toward the edge of the grill, where the heat is less intense. Turn the ribs frequently and quench any flare-ups with a quick spray of water.

Approximate nutritional value per portion:
620 calories
Protein: 49g
Fat: 33g
Carbohydrate: 31g

Ribs in Spicy Sauce

Kofta Kabobs with Garlic Sauce

Serves 4

A creamy garlic sauce is the perfect foil for these delicious kabobs.

Preparation time: about 1 hour
Barbecuing time: 10-15 minutes

1 pound lean beef, very finely chopped,
   or ground round steak
5 small onions
2 cloves garlic, crushed
1 egg yolk
1 tablespoon barbecue spice
Salt
Freshly ground white pepper
½ red bell pepper
½ green bell pepper

GARLIC SAUCE

1 small cucumber, (about 4 ounces), halved
   and seeded
8-ounce package cream cheese, softened
½ cup dairy sour cream
1 tablespoon olive oil
2 garlic cloves, crushed
2 tablespoons chopped fresh dill

1 Soak 8 wooden skewers in water
for 30 minutes.
Place chopped or ground lean beef in a
bowl. Chop 1 onion very finely and add to
meat with crushed garlic, egg yolk, and
barbecue spice. Add salt and pepper to
taste. Using clean wet hands or the kneading attachment of a hand-held mixer,
knead mixture thoroughly.

2 Remove all white pith and seeds from
pepper halves, rinse briefly under cold
running water, then drain and cut into bite-
size pieces.

3 Cut remaining onions into fourths; set
aside. Divide meat mixture into
8 parts. Using clean wet hands, roll each
piece to a long 'sausage', about
1 inch thick.

4 Drain skewers. Thread 1 piece of green
bell pepper and 1 piece of onion onto
each skewer, then add the meat 'sausage',
another piece of onion and a piece of red
pepper, as in the picture.

5 Grill kofta kabobs on a lightly oiled
barbecue grill over moderately hot
coals for 10-15 minutes or until cooked
through, turning frequently.

6 Make sauce. Chop cucumber finely
and squeeze in a clean dish towel to
remove excess liquid. Mix cream cheese,
sour cream, and olive oil in a bowl. Add
cucumber, garlic, and dill, with salt and
pepper to taste. Stir until well mixed. Serve
with kabobs.

Approximate nutritional value per portion:
500 calories
Protein: 40g
Fat: 32g
Carbohydrate 13g

Kofta Kabobs with Garlic Sauce

Stuffed Pork and Veal Cutlets

Serves 8

Ask the supplier to cut a pocket in each cutlet for dressing.

Preparation time: about 40 minutes
Barbecuing time: 18-20 minutes

PORK CUTLETS
2 ounces Prosciutto
1 bunch Italian parsley
2 tablespoons shredded Gouda cheese
2 teaspoons drained capers
Freshly ground white pepper
Salt
4 pork cutlets, about 7 ounces each

VEAL CUTLETS
1 tomato
2 basil sprigs
4 veal cutlets, about 11 ounces each
Freshly ground black pepper
4 slices mozzarella cheese

1 Soak 16 thin wooden skewers in cold water for 30 minutes.
Prepare pork cutlets: Dice Prosciutto very finely. Rinse parsley briefly under cold water; shake dry, pluck off leaves and chop finely. In a bowl, mix Prosciutto, parsley, and cheese with capers; add plenty of white pepper.

2 Sprinkle a little salt on insides of pockets in pork cutlets: Divide dressing among them and close each cutlet with 2 drained wooden skewers.

3 Prepare veal cutlets. Cut tomato in 4 slices, making sure base of stalk has been removed.

4 Rinse basil briefly under cold water; shake dry, pluck off leaves and shred. Sprinkle a little salt and pepper on inside of pockets in veal cutlets. Fill each pocket with 1 tomato slice, 1 mozzarella slice and a little basil. Close each cutlet with 2 drained wooden skewers.

5 Cook cutlets on a lightly oiled barbecue grill. Pork cutlets will require 7-9 minutes on each side and veal cutlets 9-10 minutes on each side. Turn cutlets frequently, using metal tongs.

TIP
Cutlets must be cooked right through before serving. To test for doneness, pierce the meat close to the bone with a sharp pointed knife. The juices should be clear.

Approximate nutritional value per portion:
420 calories
Protein: 56g
Fat: 22g
Carbohydrate: 1g

Stuffed Pork and Veal Cutlets

Colorful Grilled Kabobs

Serves 4

Bite-size morsels of meat, poultry, fish or shellfish speared for your satisfaction.

Preparation time: about 45 minutes
Barbecuing time: 6-8 minutes per skewer

PORK KABOBS
11 ounces pork tenderloin
8 narrow strips rindless bacon
12 bay leaves
1 cup pitted prunes

SHRIMP KABOBS
8 small raw baby shrimp
12 firm cherry tomatoes
12 stuffed green olives
½ clove garlic, cut in 4 slivers

TURKEY KABOBS
11 ounces turkey breast fillets
1 red bell pepper, cut in squares
2 fresh pineapple slices
4 onions, quartered

FISH KABOBS
12 ounces halibut fillet
2 tablespoons lemon juice
1 cup button mushrooms
4 ounce piece of cucumber
4 onions, quartered

1 Soak 16 wooden skewers in water for 30 minutes.

2 Pork Kabobs: Cut pork tenderloin in 8 slices. Wrap 1 bacon strip around each slice of meat. Drain 4 skewers. Thread each skewer with bay leaves, wrapped pork slices, and prunes.

3 Shrimp Kabobs: Drain 4 skewers. Thread each skewer with shrimp, cherry tomatoes, olives, and a garlic sliver.

4 Turkey Kabobs: Cut turkey fillets into about 12 large cubes of equal size. Cut pineapple into large neat chunks. Drain 4 skewers. Thread skewers with turkey, pepper pieces, pineapple chunks, and onion quarters.

5 Fish Kabobs: Cut halibut in bite-size cubes; drizzle with lemon juice. Wipe mushrooms. Cut cucumber in thick slices. Drain 4 skewers. Thread with fish cubes, mushrooms, cucumber, and onion wedges.

6 Cook skewers on an oiled barbecue grill over a medium heat for 6-8 minutes, turning frequently.

Approximate nutritional value per portion:
740 calories
Protein: 65g
Fat: 34g
Carbohydrate: 34g

Colorful Grilled Kabobs

Spit-barbecued Pork

Serves 8

Tender pork cooks to perfection on an electrically operated spit.

Preparation time: about 15 minutes
Barbecuing time: 2½-3 hours

3½ pound boned shoulder of pork
   with fat
Salt
Freshly ground white pepper
6 fresh mint sprigs

SPICY BASTING SAUCE
4 tablespoons mango chutney
1 tablespoon curry powder
1 tablespoon soy sauce

1 Using a sharp knife and cutting to a depth of about ¼ inch, score pork fat in a diamond pattern. Turn meat over and rub salt and pepper vigorously into lean side.

2 Rinse mint briefly under cold, running water, shake dry and pluck off leaves. Scatter mint leaves over pork.

3 Roll up pork from the widest point and tie neatly at regular intervals with kitchen twine.

4 Spear pork roll on a large rotary spit, using holding forks to hold the meat securely. Roast for 2½ -3 hours.
If cooking on a charcoal-fueled barbecue, add more coals from a feeder fire as required.

5 Spicy Basting Sauce: Purée mango chutney in a blender or food processor.

6 Scrape mango purée into a bowl and stir in curry powder and soy sauce. Using a basting brush, baste the roast continuously with this mixture during the final 30 minutes of the barbecuing time.

7 Serve the pork in slices, garnished with mint and sliced tomato, if you like.

TIP
A crisp salad composed of sliced tomatoes, zucchini, scallions, iceberg lettuce, fresh cucumber, and beansprouts makes a fine accompaniment. Toss with a lemon and oil dressing.

Approximate nutritional value per portion:
640 calories
Protein: 38g
Fat: 51g
Carbohydrate: 11g

Spit-barbecued Pork

Trout with Herbs and Horseradish

Serves 4

Selected fresh herbs complement the delicate flavor of the trout.

Preparation time: about 30 minutes
Barbecuing time: 12-15 minutes

4 ready-to-cook trout
Salt
Freshly ground white pepper
12 Italian parsley sprigs
8 mint sprigs
8 thyme sprigs
4 tarragon sprigs
1 lemon
Few drops of oil

HORSERADISH SAUCE
2 x 3-ounce packages cream cheese,
  softened
$2/3$ cup dairy sour cream
2 teaspoons creamed horseradish sauce
grated zest and juice of 1 lemon
sugar to taste
2 tablespoons scissored fresh chives

1 Make horseradish sauce. Place cream cheese in a bowl. Stir in sour cream and horseradish. Add grated lemon zest and juice, with salt, pepper, and sugar to taste. Stir in scissored chives. Cover bowl and set aside until required.

2 Rinse each trout under cold running water. Pat dry with paper towels. Season the cavity in each trout with salt and pepper.

3 Rinse herbs under cold water; shake dry. Cut lemon in 8 thin slices. Fill each trout with 3 parsley sprigs, 2 each of mint and thyme sprigs, 1 tarragon sprig and 2 lemon slices.

4 Using a pad of paper toweling and a little oil, grease four fish basket grills. Place trout in basket grills and cook over moderately hot coals for 12-15 minutes, turning occasionally. If you do not own any basket grills, wrap each trout individually in lightly oiled foil.

5 Serve the trout on individual plates, with the horseradish sauce.

TIP
To fillet trout at the table, cut the skin along the spine and neatly lift the top fillet away from the bones, freeing it from the head, using your knife and fork. Turn the fish over; repeat the process on the other side.

Approximate nutritional value per portion:
400 calories
Protein: 65g
Fat: 14g
Carbohydrate: 6g

Trout with Herbs and Horseradish

Step-by-step

MARINADES AND BASTES

1 Marinades made with red wine, oil, garlic, and herbs like rosemary and thyme are suitable for beef and lamb. Arrange meat in a single layer in a shallow glass or ceramic dish.

2 Buttermilk or yogurt are suitable for poultry, while beer and hard cider make good marinades for pork. Ensure that meat remains covered with liquid or turn pieces frequently.

3 Use a basting brush or quality paintbrush to ensure items like ribs are well coated.

GRILLING

1 Drain meat carefully; oil-based marinades or sauces dripping onto glowing charcoal will cause flare-ups.

2 Cook meat on lightly oiled grill, turning it when juice starts to ooze from the top. Never pierce flesh or meat will dry out.

3 Baste meat with sauces or marinades toward the end of the barbecuing time.

KABOBS AND FOIL PACKAGES

1 Soak wooden skewers in water for 30 minutes before use to avoid scorching. Metal skewers may be lightly oiled.

2 Cut ingredients into equal-size pieces. Pack them closely, to retain juices.

3 To make a neat foil package for diced vegetables or fruit, line a small bowl with heavy-duty foil, add filling and liquid, then seal foil tightly.

19

Barbecued Beef Olives and Sausages

Serves 4

A little dexterity is needed here, as the skewers for grilling are whittled from green twigs.

Preparation time: about 45 minutes
Barbecuing time: 20-30 minutes

BARBECUED BEEF OLIVES
4 very thin slices beef tenderloin
8 bacon slices, rind removed
2 teaspoons Dijon or whole-grain mustard
1 teaspoon dried marjoram

SAUSAGES
4 firm cherry tomatoes
1 onion, quartered
4 miniature bratwurst or chipolata sausages

1 To make skewers, use strong green twigs from a non-poisonous tree or shrub. Strip off bark. Skewers for Barbecued Beef Olives should be about $\frac{1}{4}$ inch thick; twigs for sausages may be thinner, but should be given a sharpened point. When whittling the twigs, carve away from your body to avoid injury.

2 Barbecued Beef Olives: Spread beef tenderloin slices flat. Lay bacon on top, trimming slices to fit, and spread thinly with mustard. Sprinkle marjoram on top. Wrap each topped slice tightly around one of the thicker skewers, pressing ends together. Grill over hot coals, turning frequently, for 20-30 minutes.

3 Sausages: Spear 1 tomato, 1 piece of onion and 1 sausage on each of the thinner skewers, threading sharpened stick lengthwise through each sausage. Grill sausages on sticks for 8-10 minutes.

TIP
Children will love eating the sausages with ketchup, while adults generally prefer something a bit hotter, like mustard.

Approximate nutritional value per portion:
290 calories
Protein: 24g
Fat: 18g
Carbohydrate: 3g

Barbecued Beef Olives and Sausages

Herring with a Mustard Crust

Serves 4

A crunchy crust and spicy tarragon sauce transform herring into a taste sensation.

Preparation time: about 45 minutes
Barbecuing time: 5-8 minutes

8 ready-to-cook Atlantic herring
Salt
6 scallions
½ cup mustard seeds
4 teaspoons crushed black peppercorns
1 teaspoon oil

TARRAGON SAUCE
½ cup mayonnaise
⅔ cup low-fat yogurt
2-3 tablespoons milk
2 shallots or baby onions, finely chopped
2 tablespoons chopped fresh tarragon
Pinch of sugar
1-2 teaspoons white wine vinegar
Freshly ground white pepper

1 If the supplier has not already done so, fillet the herring. Slit the skin around the head, cutting down to the bone, then make a long slit down the length of the belly of the fish. Turn the fish over, cut side down, and press firmly on the backbone to loosen it. Turn the fish over again and carefully lift out the backbone and other small bones, using kitchen shears to cut through the bones at the head end. Rinse fish under cold running water; pat dry.

2 Sprinkle salt on inside of herring. Cut green section of each scallion in 1-inch lengths. Cut bulbs lengthwise into fourths, then in thin shreds.

3 Fill herring with scallions. Mix mustard seeds and crushed peppercorns in a bowl. Have ready 8 pieces of foil, each large enough to comfortably enclose one of the herring. Brush foil with a little oil.

4 Sprinkle about 1 teaspoon of the mustard and pepper mixture on either side of the filled herring, pressing down lightly to coat.

5 Wrap herring in foil. Cook on a barbecue grill over moderately hot coals for 5-8 minutes or until cooked through, turning occasionally.

6 Tarragon Sauce: Mix mayonnaise, yogur,t and milk in a bowl. Stir in shallots or baby onions, tarragon, sugar, and vinegar, with salt and pepper to taste.

7 Serve herring on individual plates, with tarragon sauce.

Approximate nutritional value per portion:
570 calories
Protein: 36g
Fat: 47g
Carbohydrate: 5g

Herring with a Mustard Crust

Sage Chicken with Tomato Dip

Serves 4

A first-class summer trio: spicy grilled chicken, a light yogurt sauce and a crunchy leaf salad.

Preparation time: about 40 minutes
Barbecuing time: about 30 minutes

4 chicken breasts with bone
2 tablespoons soft cheese with herbs
8 large fresh sage leaves
Salt
Freshly ground white pepper

TOMATO DIP
2 beefsteak tomatoes
2 tablespoons scissored fresh chives
1 cup yogurt-based salad dressing or
   mayonnaise
1 tablespoon ketchup
Pinch of sugar

1 Rinse chicken breasts and pat dry. Carefully ease away skin from each breast and spread the flesh with soft cheese. Press 2 sage leaves into the cheese on each chicken breast, then ease the skin back. Use toothpicks to hold the filling in place. Sprinkle skin with salt and pepper.

2 Tomato Dip: Cut a small cross in rounded end of each tomato. Place in a heatproof bowl and add boiling water to cover. Leave for 1 minute. Remove each tomato in turn with a slotted draining spoon and rinse under cold water. When cool enough to handle, remove skins.

3 Dice tomatoes and place in a bowl. Add chives, salad dressing or mayonnaise, and ketchup and mix lightly. Stir in sugar, with salt and pepper to taste.

4 Grill chicken breasts, bone down, on an oiled barbecue grill over hot coals for 15-20 minutes, then turn them over, move the breasts to the edge of the grill and cook until brown and crisp. Serve with the dip and a salad (see Tip).

TIP
Serve the chicken breasts with a salad composed of mixed leaves (Bibb, Lollo Biondo, and Romaine), mixed with onion rings and cherry tomatoes. For the dressing, mix 2 tablespoons red wine vinegar with salt, pepper and a pinch of sugar in a bowl. Whisk in 4 tablespoons olive oil. Pour over salad and toss lightly.

Approximate nutritional value per portion:
450 calories
Protein: 23g
Fat: 36g
Carbohydrate: 8g

Sage Chicken with Tomato Dip

Lemon Lamb Chops

Serves 4

Tender lamb chops and warm potato salad make a satisfying meal.

Preparation time: about 1½ hours
Marinating time: about 6 hours
Barbecuing time: 15-18 minutes

4 double loin (butterfly) lamb chops
Oil (see method)
6 fresh marjoram sprigs, or 2 teaspoons
   dried marjoram
2 cloves garlic, chopped
grated zest of 1 lemon
1 teaspoon crushed black peppercorns

POTATO SALAD
2 pounds salad potatoes
Salt
½ cup white wine vinegar
2 teaspoons whole-grain mustard
1 teaspoon sugar
1 onion, finely chopped
4 tablespoons chicken stock
6 tablespoons oil
Freshly ground black pepper
8 radishes, sliced
4 tablespoons chopped fresh mixed herbs

1 Rinse lamb chops briefly under cold water; pat dry with paper towels. Brush thinly with oil.

2 If using fresh marjoram, rinse briefly under cold water, shake dry and pluck off leaves. Chop marjoram leaves finely, place in a bowl and add garlic, lemon rind, and crushed peppercorns. Mix well, adding dried marjoram if using.

3 Rub marjoram mixture into lamb chops; arrange in a single layer in a shallow glass or ceramic dish.
Cover and marinate in refrigerator for about 6 hours.

4 About 40 minutes before cooking chops, make potato salad. Scrub potatoes and cook in a saucepan of lightly salted boiling water until tender. Drain. Mix vinegar, mustard, and sugar in a salad bowl. Add chopped onion, then whisk in chicken stock and oil, with salt and pepper to taste. Cut warm potatoes into slices and add to dressing with radishes and herbs. Toss lightly.

5 Drain lamb chops, scraping herb mixture back into dish.
Cook chops on an oiled barbecue grill over moderately hot coals for 7-9 minutes on each side. About 3 minutes before chops are cooked, stir a few drops of oil into reserved spice mixture and use this to baste the chops constantly. Serve chops with potato salad and grilled onion and zucchini slices, if you like.

Approximate nutritional value per portion:
880 calories
Protein: 28g
Fat: 66g
Carbohydrate: 41g

Lemon Lamb Chops

Vegetable Potpourri

Serves 4

Healthy accompaniment or vegetarian treats, these are certain to prove popular.

Preparation time: about 1 hour
Barbecuing time: 10-15 minutes

2 eggplants
4 tablespoons lemon juice
2 tablespoons olive oil
Salt
Freshly ground white pepper
2 cloves garlic, finely chopped

PEPPER AND TOMATO PACKAGES

2 tomatoes
2 small green bell peppers
2 onions, finely chopped
1 cup drained feta cheese cubes in oil
2 teaspoons dried thyme

CORN KABOBS

2 drained freshly cooked or canned
    corn cobs
2 zucchini, thickly sliced
8 shallots or baby onions, peeled
3 tablespoons herb butter

1 Soak 8 wooden skewers in water for 30 minutes.

2 Cut eggplants in half lengthwise. Pierce cut surfaces several times with a fork. Place each half on a piece of foil large enough to enclose it comfortably. Bend foil edges up.

3 Dribble lemon juice and olive oil on eggplants and add salt and pepper to taste. Sprinkle with garlic. Close tops of foil.

4 Place packages on a barbecue grill over moderately hot coals and cook for 10-15 minutes or until tender.

5 Pepper and Tomato Packages: Cut tomatoes into eighths. Cut peppers in squares, removing all white pith and seeds. Mix tomatoes, peppers, onions, feta cheese, and thyme in a bowl. Divide among 4 foil packages. Cook packages on a barbecue grill over moderately hot coals for 8-10 minutes or until vegetables are tender.

6 Corn Kabobs: Drain skewers. Cut corn cobs into 1½-inch rounds. Thread on skewers with zucchini and shallots or baby onoins. Cook on a barbecue grill over moderately hot coals for 6-8 minutes. Turn frequently. Transfer to individual plates; top each kabob with herb butter.

Approximate nutritional value per portion:
260 calories
Protein: 8g
Fat: 18g
Carbohydrate: 13g

Vegetable Potpourri

Stuffed Bell Peppers

Serves 4

Ground beef, rice, pignoli and dried currants make a tasty filling for red peppers.

Preparation time: about 30 minutes
Barbecuing time: 20-30 minutes

2 tablespoons oil
2 tablespoons pignoli (pine nuts)
1 onion, finely chopped
1 tablespoon dried currants
4 tablespoons minced fresh parsley
10 ounces ground round steak
1 egg
Salt
Freshly ground white pepper
2 cups cooked long-grain white rice
4 red bell peppers

1 Heat oil in a skillet over a very low heat. Brown pignoli (pine nuts) gently, Add diced onion, raise heat slightly and sauté until glassy. Transfer mixture to a plate; set aside.

2 Rinse dried currants under hot water, drain and pat dry on paper towels. Mix currants, parsley, ground beef, and egg in a bowl, with salt and pepper to taste. Add rice and pignoli (pine nut) and onion mixture. Using clean wet hands or the kneading attachment of a hand-held mixer, knead mixture thoroughly.

3 Cut a 'lid' from the top of each pepper. Scoop out cores, taking care not to break pepper shells. Rinse shells and lids under cold water; pat dry on paper towels.

4 Fill peppers with meat mixture and top with lids. Cut 4 pieces of foil, each large enough to enclose a filled pepper comfortably. Lightly oil shiny side of foil, place peppers on top and bring up side of foil to make neat secure packages.

5 Place foil packages on barbecue grill over moderately hot coals and grill for 20-30 minutes or until meat filling is cooked through, turning frequently.

TIP
For an unusual, delicious flavor, add 2 tablespoons freshly chopped mint and 2 crushed garlic cloves to meat mixture instead of parsley.

Approximate nutritional value per portion:
430 calories
Protein: 22g
Fat: 27g
Carbohydrate: 27g

Stuffed Bell Peppers

Tested Tips for Better Barbecues

Barbecues come in a wide array of designs and sizes, from small tabletop models to fancy carts which include preparation and serving areas. The majority of barbecues are fueled by charcoal or wood, but electric and gas models are becoming increasingly popular. When buying a barbecue, check that it is easy to handle and stands firm, even on slightly uneven ground.

• Choose the barbecue that suits your family's needs, whether this be a small portable, a brazier or a kettle barbecue. If you are likely to want to cook large roasts over the coals, look for a model with an electrically operated rotary spit.

• Sauced and marinated meats, fish fillets, vegetables, and fruit are best grilled on a solid griddle or in an aluminum grill pan. Alternatively, simply wrap foods in heavy duty foil; they will cook in their own juices.

• Special barbecue utensils make grilling simpler and safer, as they have particularly long handles to prevent burns. Grilling tongs are useful for turning pieces of meat. A new paintbrush with firmly attached bristles makes a good basting brush.

• Protect your hands with oven gloves and always wear a large apron.

• Whole fish can be grilled in special basket grills: these can be closed around the fish to make turning it a very easy matter. Hinged wire grills are ideal for burgers or fish steaks.

• If fat drips into the glowing charcoal, flare-ups are likely to occur. Keep a water spray bottle or water pistol handy to douse flames, but use sparingly.

• Place a small table near the barbecue for plates, barbecue tools, marinades, a water spray bottle, matches, and other essentials.

• Any food that falls onto the coals or embers should be discarded.

GETTING READY TO GRILL

• Pile charcoal briquets up in the center of the fire box. Place solid fire starters among the charcoal and light them. Use a folded newspaper or bellows to blow air into the flames. Never use kerosene or gasoline when lighting the fire - this would be extremely dangerous.

• After 30-40 minutes, when the charcoal is evenly covered with a layer of white ash, spread the coals out, place the lightly oiled grill on top and start grilling.

• To regulate the heat, raise or lower the grill, or change the shape of the fire. Pushing coals together will raise the temperature; separating them will lower it.

• Steaks and cutlets should be grilled at the start while the heat is still fairly intense. Poultry, light meats, fish and vegetables should be laid around the edges of the grill or cooked when temperature has dropped.

Tested Tips for Better Barbecues

◆NOTES◆

◆NOTES◆

Cookies

Made Easy

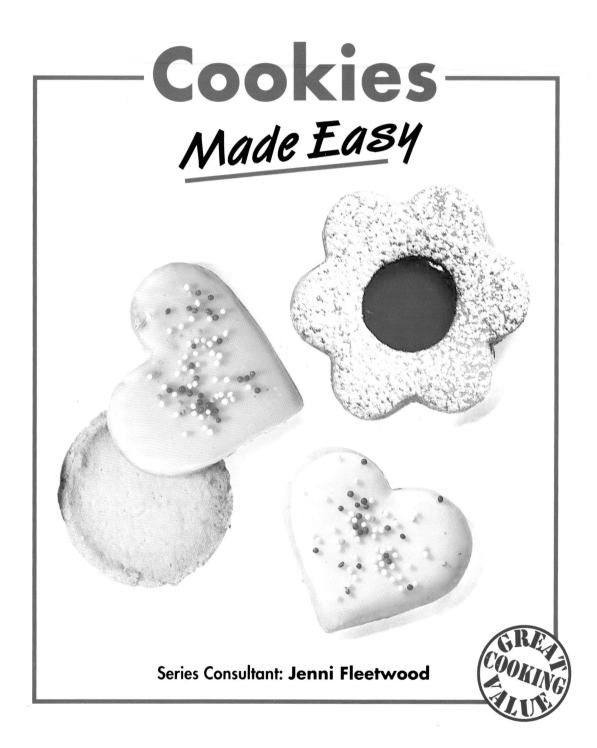

Series Consultant: Jenni Fleetwood

GREAT COOKING VALUE

Introduction

Cookies are easy to bake and great fun to decorate, as the recipes in this book illustrate. Some of the more popular ingredients - used in and on the cookies - are shown here, but the imaginative cook will find many more.

Recipe Notes

All spoon measures are level:
1 tablespoon = 15ml spoon;
1 teaspoon = 5ml spoon.

Follow EITHER metric or imperial measures and NEVER mix in one recipe as they are not interchangeable.

Eggs used are a medium size unless otherwise stated. Citrus fruit should be washed and dried before grating - use unsprayed fruit where possible. Use unsalted butter for preference.

Written by Annette Wolter

Almond Macaroons

Makes about 90

Crisp on the outside, soft in the center, almond macaroons are always popular.

Preparation time: 40 minutes
Baking time: 25-30 minutes per baking sheet

500g (1lb) shelled almonds
375g (12oz/1½ cups) caster sugar
5 egg whites
Rice paper to line baking sheets
Sifted icing sugar for dusting (optional)

1 Preheat oven to 275°F.
Line 4 baking sheets with rice paper. Alternatively, use rice paper discs.

2 Place almonds in a heatproof bowl. Pour over boiling water to cover, then soak for 3 minutes. Drain in a sieve, rinse under cold running water and slip off brown skins. Dry on a clean tea towel.

3 Grind almonds in a nut mill, blender or food processor, tip into a bowl and add sugar. Mix well.

4 In a mixing bowl, whisk egg whites with a whisk or hand-held electric mixer until stiff. Carefully fold in almond mixture with a metal spoon.

5 Using a wet teaspoon take small scoops of almond mixture and transfer to the prepared baking sheets. Allow room for spreading. Alternatively, spoon the mixture onto individual rice paper discs placed on baking sheets.

6 Dry rather than bake the small macaroons in batches on the middle shelf of the oven for 25-30 minutes or until light brown on the outside. Slide rice paper with macaroons onto wire racks to cool.

7 When macaroons are cold, either remove them from the rice paper or trim the rice paper around the base of each. Dust the cookies generously with powdered sugar if liked. Pack in an airtight tin.

Approximate nutritional value per cookie:
50 cal
Protein: 1g
Fat: 3g
Carbohydrate: 6g

Almond Macaroons

Cherry Cookies

Makes about 36

Choose bright red glacé cherries for these delicious cookies.

Preparation time: 40 minutes
Baking time: 15 minutes per baking sheet

155g (5oz) glacé cherries
125g (4oz) butter, softened, plus extra
    for greasing
110g (3½ oz/scant ½ cup) sugar
2 eggs, separated
2 teaspoons grated lemon rind
2 teaspoons lemon juice
Pinch salt
220g (7oz/1¾ cups) plain flour

1 Preheat oven to 350°F.
Grease 3-4 baking sheets and line with non-stick baking paper. Cut cherries into very small pieces, see Tip.

2 Cream butter with sugar in a mixing bowl. Add egg yolks, lemon rind and juice; mix well.

3 In a separate bowl, whisk egg whites until stiff. Whisk in salt.

4 Stir cherries into creamed mixture and heap egg whites on top. Sift flour over egg whites. Mix all ingredients with a wooden spoon until a stiff mixture forms.

5 Using 2 teaspoons scoop small heaps of dough onto the prepared baking sheets, leaving space for spreading. Bake for about 15 minutes or until golden brown, then transfer to a wire rack and allow to cool. Pack in an airtight tin.

TIP
The easiest way to cut up the cherries is with kitchen scissors. Dip them in a mug of boiling water from time to time to remove excess syrup.

Nutritional value per cookie:
74 cal
Protein: 1g
Fat: 3g
Carbohydrate: 11g

Cherry Cookies

Orange Hearts

Makes about 30

These taste delicious, even without icing.

Preparation time: 40 minutes plus standing
Baking time: 10-12 minutes per baking sheet

125g (4oz) butter, softened, plus extra
    for greasing
125g (4oz/½ cup) sugar
Pinch salt
1 egg
grated rind of 1 orange
350g (11oz/2¾ cups) plain flour
1 teaspoon baking powder
110g (3½ oz) plain (dark) chocolate

ICING AND DECORATION
90g (3oz/½ cup) powdered sugar
1-2 tablespoons orange juice
sprinkles

1 Grease 3-4 baking sheets and line with non-stick baking paper.

2 Cream butter with sugar in a mixing bowl. Add salt, egg and orange rind and beat well.

3 Sift flour and baking powder over creamed mixture. Grate chocolate over the top. Quickly mix to a pliable dough, first using a wooden spoon and then clean hands. Shape the dough into a ball, wrap in foil and rest in refrigerator for 1 hour.

4 Preheat oven to 400°F. Divide dough in half. Working with one portion at a time, roll out dough on a floured surface to a thickness of about 5mm (¼ in).

5 Cut out cookies using heart shaped cookie cutters. Arrange on baking sheets, leaving room for spreading.

6 Bake each batch for 10-12 minutes or until golden brown, then transfer to a wire rack to cool.

7 To make icing, sift powdered sugar into a bowl. Stir in enough of the orange juice to make a coating mixture. Cover the cookies with the icing, put sprinkles on top and set aside until completely dry. Pack in an airtight tin.

Nutritional value per cookie:
120 cal
Protein: 2g
Fat: 5g
Carbohydrate: 19g

Orange Hearts

Chocolate Batons

Makes about 50

Tipping the cookies with chocolate isn't as tricky as it looks.

Preparation time: 1 hour, plus standing
Baking time: 10 minutes per baking sheet

220g (7oz/1¾ cups) self-raising flour
50g (2oz/¼ cup) sugar
90g (3oz) butter, plus extra for greasing
1 egg
125g (4oz) chocolate cake covering

1 Grease 4-5 baking sheets and line with non-stick baking paper. Sift flour into a large mixing bowl. Sprinkle sugar over flour.

2 Cut butter into small pieces and rub in to flour. Add egg. Quickly mix to a pliable dough, first using a wooden spoon and then clean hands. Shape the dough into a ball and leave to rest in the covered bowl for about 1 hour.

3 Preheat oven to 400°F. Roll small pieces of dough between floured hands to the thickness of your thumb. Cut into 7.5cm (3in) lengths.

4 Arrange batons on baking sheets, leaving a little room between each.

5 Bake the batons for 10 minutes or until golden brown. Transfer to wire racks to cool.

6 Melt chocolate cake covering in a heatproof bowl over hot water.

7 Dip both ends of each baton in the hot chocolate coating and lay them on a sheet of non-stick baking paper to harden.

8 Pack the batons in an airtight tin, with non-stick baking paper between the layers.

Nutritional value per cookie:
45 cal
Protein: 1g
Fat: 2g
Carbohydrate: 6g

Chocolate Batons

Shortbread Fingers

Makes about 40

A traditional teatime treat.

Preparation time: 40 minutes plus standing
Baking time: 20-25 minutes

315g (10oz) butter, softened (see Tip), plus
 extra for greasing
185g (6oz/¾ cup) sugar
¼ teaspoon salt
500g (1lb/4 cups) plain flour
155g (5oz/⅔ cup) sugar

1 Grease a large baking sheet (about 33
x 23cm/13 x 9in) and line with non-stick
baking paper.

2 Place butter in a mixing bowl. Stir in
sugar and salt. Sift flour on top. Quickly
mix to a pliable dough, first using a wooden
spoon and then clean hands. Shape the
dough into a ball, wrap in foil and rest in
refrigerator for 2 hours.

3 Preheat oven to 375°F.
Place dough on a lightly floured surface. Using a floured rolling pin, roll out
to a rectangle the same size as the
baking sheet and just over 1cm (½ in) thick.

4 Lop dough over rolling pin and fit onto
baking sheet. Prick at regular intervals
with a fork. Bake shortbread for 20-25
minutes or until golden.

5 Remove baking sheet from the oven
and cut shortbread into 2.5 x 7cm
(1 x 2¾ in strips).

6 Sprinkle caster sugar evenly on a
plate. Using a palette knife ease shortbread fingers from tin and carefully turn in
sugar until coated. Cool on a wire rack.
Pack cookies in an airtight tin.

TIP
Soften butter by cutting it into cubes and
placing it in a heatproof bowl over hot
water, or by heating in the microwave on
Defrost for about 45 seconds and leaving to
stand for 1-2 minutes.

Nutritional value per cookie:
140 cal
Protein: 1g
Fat: 7g
Carbohydrate: 18g

Shortbread Fingers

Chocolate Dollars

Makes about 50

For a cookie with a firmer consistency, bake on rice paper.

Preparation time: 45 minutes, plus standing
Baking time: 12-15 minutes per baking sheet

90g (3oz) cocoa powder
220g (7oz) ground almonds
155g (5oz/$\frac{2}{3}$ cup) sugar
Pinch salt
30g (1oz/$\frac{1}{4}$ cup) plain flour
2 eggs
90g (3oz/$\frac{1}{2}$ cup) powdered sugar
butter for greasing

1 Grease 3 baking sheets and line with non-stick baking paper. Mix cocoa powder, ground almonds, sugar, salt and flour in a large bowl.

2 Break in eggs. Stir them into the dry ingredients with a wooden spoon, then use clean hands to knead the mixture to a soft sticky dough. Shape into a ball. Transfer the bowl to the refrigerator and chill for about 1 hour.

3 Preheat oven to 350°F. Measure 2 tablespoons of the powdered sugar into a small bowl. Dip fingers in powdered sugar and pinch off walnut-sized pieces of dough. Place on baking sheets, leaving room for spreading. Bake for 12-15 minutes.

4 Using a palette knife or spatula, transfer cooked biscuits to a wire rack to cool.

5 Sift remaining powdered sugar generously over chocolate dollars. Pack in an airtight tin.

TIP
Use a tea strainer for sifting a small amount of powdered sugar over cookies or a cake.

Nutritional value per cookie:
59 cal
Protein: 2g
Fat: 3g
Carbohydrate: 6g

Chocolate Dollars

Hussar Cookies

Makes about 96

The deliciously tart taste of redcurrant jelly contrasts well with the sugar-dusted cookie.

Preparation time: 1 hour plus standing
Baking time: 12-15 minutes per baking sheet

155g (5oz) butter, softened. plus extra
 for greasing
185g (6oz/¾ cup) sugar
1 teaspoon vanilla extract
Pinch of salt
2 egg yolks
185g (6oz/1½ cups) plain flour
125g (4oz) ground hazelnuts
4 tablespoons powdered sugar
110g (3½ oz) redcurrant jelly

1 Grease 4-5 baking sheets and line with non-stick baking paper. Cream butter with sugar in a mixing bowl. Beat in vanilla extract, salt and egg yolks, adding a little of the flour if the mixture shows signs of curdling.

2 Mix ground hazelnuts and remaining flour in a bowl or on a clean surface. Make a well in the center and add the creamed mixture. Rapidly knead all ingredients together to a smooth dough.

3 Divide dough in half, wrap each portion in foil and rest in refrigerator for 2 hours.

4 Preheat oven to 400°F.
Remove one of the portions of dough and place on a floured surface. With floured hands roll to a sausage shape, about 3cm (1¼ in) thick.

5 Using a sharp knife, cut a slice about 1 cm (½ in) thick and form into a ball. Make a depression in the center with the end of a wooden spoon. Form more cookies in the same way until both portions of dough have been used.

6 Arrange the cookies on the prepared baking sheets and bake for 10-12 minutes. Cool on wire racks.

7 Sift powdered sugar evenly all over cookies (see Tip, page 14).
Using a small spoon, fill the center of each cookie with redcurrant jelly. Allow jelly to dry for a few days before storing cookies in an airtight tin. Place a sheet of non-stick baking paper between the layers to prevent the cookies from sticking together.

TIP
Another way of making these cookies is simply to pinch off small pieces of dough (about 1 teaspoon) and roll them into balls. Bake as above, until golden, making the depressions in the cookies after baking, while the cookies are still soft. Add the jelly as described above.

Nutritional value per cookie:
37 cal
Protein: 0g
Fat: 1g
Carbohydrate: 4g

Hussar Cookies

Simple Cinnamon Stars

Makes about 60

Not to be confused with Christmas cinnamon stars, which are more difficult to make.

Preparation time: 1 hour, plus standing
Baking time: 12-15 minutes per baking sheet

350g (11oz/2¾ cups) plain flour
2 tablespoons ground cinnamon
185g (6oz/1 cup) powdered sugar, sifted
2 eggs, beaten
155g (5oz) butter

GLAZE
1 egg yolk
2 tablespoons rum

1 Grease 4 baking sheets and line with non-stick baking paper. Sift flour onto a clean surface. Make a well in the center.

2 Spoon cinnamon, powdered sugar and eggs into the well.

3 On a board, cut butter into flakes. Distribute around edge of flour. Quickly knead all ingredients together to a pliable dough. Shape the dough into a ball, wrap in foil and rest in refrigerator for 1 hour.

4 Preheat oven to 350°F. Place dough on a lightly floured surface, using a floured rolling pin, roll out to a thickness of just less than 5mm (¼ in). Using a small cutter, cut out star shapes and lay them on the prepared baking sheets.

5 Make the glaze by beating the egg yolk and rum together in a small bowl. Brush the tops of the cookies with the mixture.

6 Bake cookies for 12-15 minutes until golden, then transfer to wire racks to cool before packing in an airtight tin.

Nutritional value per cookie:
55 cal
Protein: 1g
Fat: 3g
Carbohydrate: 7g

Simple Cinnamon Stars

Moroccan Hats

Makes about 40

Delicate meringue-based cookies that melt in the mouth.

Preparation time: 1 hour
Baking time: 15 minutes per baking sheet

125 g (4oz) shelled almonds
60g (2oz) bar of plain (dark) chocolate
1 tablespoon brandy
2 egg whites
125g (4oz/¾ cup) powdered sugar
butter for greasing

1 Preheat oven to 150C (300F/Gas 2). Grease 2-3 baking sheets and line with non-stick baking paper.

2 Grind unblanched almonds in a nut mill or food processor. Tip into a bowl. Grate chocolate finely and add to ground almonds; mix well. Stir in brandy.

3 In a separate bowl, make meringue mixture by whisking egg whites until stiff. Sift powdered sugar over egg whites, a little at a time, and fold in. Set aside 2 tablespoons of meringue mixture.

4 Fold almond and chocolate mixture lightly but evenly into meringue mixture. Do not stir.

5 Using 2 wet teaspoons, separate small heaps of mixture and place on the prepared baking sheets. Leave a little space between each. Spoon a hazelnut-sized blob of the reserved plain meringue onto the center of each cookie.

6 Bake for 15 minutes, then transfer cookies to a wire rack to cool. Pack in an airtight tin.

Nutritional value per cookie:
40 cal
Protein: 1g
Fat: 2g
Carbohydrate: 4g

Moroccan Hats

Ginger Bar Cookies

Makes about 50

America is the home of these flavorsome cookies.

Preparation time: 40 minutes plus standing
Baking time: 15 minutes per baking sheet

6 pieces of drained preserved ginger
  in syrup
155g (5oz) butter plus extra for greasing
7 tablespoons sugar
Pinch salt
½ teaspoon ground ginger
315g (10oz/2½ cups) plain flour
1 egg plus 2 yolks
1 tablespoon water

1 Grease 3 baking sheets and line with non-stick baking paper. Cut half the pieces of preserved ginger into tiny cubes, using scissors or a very sharp knife. Place in a mixing bowl. Dice remaining preserved ginger and set aside for topping.

2 Cut butter into cubes and add it to mixing bowl with sugar, salt and ground ginger. Sift flour over mixture. Rub in butter, then add whole egg and quickly mix to a pliable dough, first using a wooden spoon and then clean hands. Shape the dough into a ball, wrap in foil and rest in refrigerator for 2 hours.

3 Preheat oven to 400°F.
Divide dough into 3 portions. Roll out each portion in turn on a floured surface to a thickness of just less than 5mm (¼ in). Cut dough into 2.5 x 5 cm (1 x 2 inch) bars.

4 Arrange cookies on prepared baking sheets. Beat the egg yolks with the measured water in a small bowl. Brush mixture over cookies, then sprinkle with reserved ginger, pressing pieces down lightly.

5 Bake for 15 minutes, then transfer bars to wire racks to cool. Pack in an airtight tin.

Nutritional value per cookie:
55 cal
Protein: 1g
Fat: 3g
Carbohydrate: 7g

Ginger Bar Cookies

Multi-colored Sugar Cookies

Makes about 80

Perfect for a child's party, these ring cookies may be decorated in a wide variety of ways.

Preparation time: 35 minutes
Baking time: 10-15 minutes per baking sheet

500g (1lb/4 cups) plain flour
250g (8oz/1 cup) sugar
5 egg yolks
4 tablespoons whipping cream
$\frac{1}{2}$ teaspoon vanilla extract
250g (8oz) butter, plus extra for greasing
110g ($3\frac{1}{2}$ oz) sprinkles

1 Preheat oven to 350°F.
Grease 4-5 baking sheets and line with non-stick baking paper.

2 Sift flour into a bowl or onto a clean surface and make a well in the center.
Add sugar, 3 of the egg yolks, half the whipping cream and the vanilla extract.

3 On a board, cut butter into flakes.
Distribute around edge of flour. Quickly knead all ingredients together to a firm pliable dough.

4 Divide dough into 3 portions. Roll out each portion in turn on a lightly floured surface to a thickness of just less than 5mm ($\frac{1}{4}$ in). Using a ring cutter with a scalloped edge, cut out cookies. Arrange cookies on prepared baking sheets.

5 Mix remaining egg yolks with remaining cream in a bowl. Brush each cookie with a little of this mixture, then top with sprinkles.

6 Bake in batches for 10-15 minutes until golden brown, reusing baking sheets as necessary. Transfer to wire racks to cool.

TIP
Use sugar strands or coffee sugar crystals for topping if preferred.

Nutritional value per cookie:
70 cal
Protein: 1g
Fat: 3g
Carbohydrate: 10g

Multi-colored Sugar Cookies

Moorland Crunchies

Makes about 120

Bake a large batch of these cookies - they keep extremely well.

Preparation time: 1 hour plus standing
Baking time: 12-18 minutes per baking sheet

375g (12 oz/3 cups) plain flour
155g (5oz) butter, plus extra for greasing
250g (8oz/1 cup) sugar
1 teaspoon vanilla extract
2-3 tablespoons milk
110g ($3\frac{1}{2}$ oz/scant $\frac{1}{2}$ cup) sugar crystals

1 Sift flour into a mixing bowl. Cut butter into small pieces. Add to flour and rub in until the mixture resembles coarse bread-crumbs. Stir in sugar. Add vanilla extract with enough of the milk to make a pliable dough. Knead well.

2 Divide dough in half and shape each portion into a roll, about 4cm ($1\frac{1}{2}$ in) in diameter. Wrap each roll in foil and chill for at least 12 hours.

3 Preheat oven to 350°F. Lightly grease 4-5 baking sheets and line with non-stick baking paper.

4 Remove one of the rolls of dough from refrigerator. Spread sugar crystals in a shallow bowl and turn the roll in them until well coated. Press the crystals gently into the dough,then, using a very sharp knife, cut into 5mm ($\frac{1}{4}$ in) slices, taking care as the dough has a tendency to crumble. Repeat with remaining roll.

5 Carefully lay the dough slices on the prepared baking sheets. Bake for 12-18 minutes or until golden, checking frequently after 12 minutes. Transfer to wire racks to cool. Reuse baking sheets for further batches if necessary. Pack in an airtight tin.

TIP
The beauty of this recipe is that the rolls of dough may be frozen, ready for slicing and baking when guests arrive unexpectedly.

Nutritional value per cookie:
32 cal
Protein: 0g
Fat: 1g
Carbohydrate: 6g

Moorland Crunchies

Urchins

Makes about 60

The glaze keeps these cookies moist and fresh.

Preparation time: about 1 hour
Baking time: 10-12 minutes per baking sheet

375g (12oz/3 cups) plain flour
125g (4oz/½ cup) sugar
250g (8oz) butter. plus extra for greasing
½ teaspoon vanilla extract

GLAZE
125g (4oz/¾ cup) powdered sugar
2 tablespoons lemon juice

1 Grease 3 baking sheets and line with non-stick baking paper. Sift flour into a bowl or onto a clean surface. make a well in the center and add sugar.

2 On a board. cut butter into flakes. Distribute around edge of flour. Rub in. add vanilla extract. then quickly knead all ingredients together to a pliable dough. Shape the dough into a ball. wrap in foil and rest in refrigerator for 1 hour.

3 Preheat oven to 375°F. Divide dough in half. Using a floured rolling pin. roll out one piece on a lightly floured surface to a thickness of just under 5mm (¼ in). Use a glass with a diameter of 3cm (1¼ in) to cut out circles. Arrange cookie rounds on prepared baking sheets.

4 Bake for 10-12 minutes until golden brown, then transfer to wire racks to cool. Repeat with remaining dough.

5 Make the glaze. Sift powdered sugar into a bowl. Stir in lemon juice and enough warm water to make a smooth coating mixture. Top each cookie with glaze and allow to dry well. Pack in an airtight tin.

TIP
For an extra-special treat sandwich the cookies together in pairs, using strawberry or apricot jam, before adding the topping.

Nutritional value per cookie:
75 cal
Protein: 1g
Fat: 4g
Carbohydrate: 10g

Urchins

Wholewheat Nutties

Makes about 60

The perfect choice for a lunchbox treat.

Preparation time: 40 minutes plus standing
Baking time: 20 minutes per baking sheet

410g (13oz/3¾ cups) wholewheat flour
2 teaspoons baking powder
½ teaspoon ground cinnamon
155g (5oz/1 cup) soft light brown sugar
155g (5oz) ground hazelnuts
200g (6½ oz) butter, plus extra for greasing
2 eggs
40g (1½ oz) hazelnuts, cut in half, for
    decoration

1 Mix flour, baking powder, cinnamon, brown sugar and ground hazelnuts in a large bowl. Stir.

2 On a board, cut butter into flakes. Dot over dry ingredients, rub in, then add eggs to bowl. Quickly mix to a pliable dough, first using a wooden spoon and then clean hands. Knead well.

3 Divide dough into 3 and shape each portion into a roll, about 4cm (1½ in) in diameter. Wrap each roll in foil and rest in the refrigerator for 1 hour.

4 Preheat oven to 350°F. Lightly grease 3 baking sheets and line with non-stick baking paper.

5 Remove one of the rolls of dough from the refrigerator. Using a very sharp knife, cut into 5mm (¼ in) slices and arrange on a baking sheet. Repeat with remaining rolls.

6 Press half a hazelnut into the center of each cookie. **Bake for about 20 minutes** or until golden brown, then transfer to wire racks to cool. Pack in an airtight tin.

Nutritional value per cookie:
80 cal
Protein: 1g
Fat: 5g
Carbohydrate: 8g

Wholewheat Nutties

◆NOTES◆

◆NOTES◆

Burgers
Made Easy

Series Consultant: Sonia Allison

GREAT
COOKING
VALUE

Introduction

Succulent hamburgers must be made with the freshest ground beef, lamb, poultry, fish, or even vegetables if they are to be successful and tempting to eat. All meat patties have every right to demand the best ingredients, whether they happen to be Sweden's Kyottbullar, Berlin's meat burgers or South America's corn lamb burgers, called Bori-Bori. Hamburgers fire the imagination, variations abound as a result, but the same basic principle applies to all; the ground meat must be of excellent quality, as fresh as possible. Ideally, it should be ground at home (that way you know exactly how good it is) or bought from a reputable supplier and used on the day of purchase or deep-frozen immediately it reaches home.

Written by Annette Wolter

Hamburger, The Original

Serves 2

Use the best quality ground beef (round) you can buy for this burger, or grind your own. The better the meat, the better the burger. Sparkling water is used here to add lightness to the burgers.

Preparation time: about 10 minutes
Cooking time: 8 minutes

¾ pound lean ground beef
Salt and pepper to taste
3 tablespoons sparkling water
1 small onion
2 tablespoons butter or oil if
    panfrying
4 hamburger buns, with or without sesame
    seeds
4 teaspoons mild mustard
4 lettuce leaves
4 tablespoons ketchup

1 Put meat into a bowl. Season with salt and pepper. Add water. Work together with 2 forks or knead by hand until smoothly combined.

2 Peel onion, slice thinly and separate slices into rings. Put onto a plate, cover and set aside.

3 Shape the meat mixture into 4 burgers, each about 1-inch thick.

4 To panfry, heat butter or oil in a heavy-based, non-stick skillet over a medium heat until sizzling and hot. Add the burgers, reduce heat slightly and cook for 8 minutes, turning burgers, once at half-time. (see Tip).

5 Cut the buns in half and spread cut sides with mustard. Sandwich together with lettuce, the hot hamburgers, onion rings, and ketchup. Serve with a choice of relishes.

CHEESEBURGERS

Make exactly as previous recipe. Sandwich buns together with lettuce, hamburgers, slices of process cheese (which will soften on the hot burgers), tomato slices, and onion rings. The ketchup can be an optional extra.

TIP
Panfrying is recommended for these burgers because lean beef has little fat and can dry out easily. Broil the burgers if you prefer or grill them on the barbecue.

Nutritional value per portion (burgers panfried):
810 calories
Protein: 54g
Fat: 38g
Carbohydrate: 60g

Hamburger, The Original

Turkey Cheeseburgers

Serves 2

An appetizing variation on the original hamburger. Look for ground turkey in the supermarket.

Preparation time: about 10 minutes
Cooking time: 10 minutes

¾ pound ground turkey
Salt and pepper to taste
½ small onion
6 tablespoons shredded Cheddar or
   Brick cheese
3 tablespoons sparkling water
2 tablespoons butter or oil
   if panfrying

1 Put turkey into a bowl and sprinkle with salt and pepper.

2 Peel onion and finely chop or grate.

3 Add to turkey with cheese and water. Work together with 2 forks or knead by hand until smoothly combined.

4 Shape the turkey mixture into 4 burgers, each about 1-inch thick.

5 To panfry, heat butter or oil in a heavy-based, non-stick skillet over a medium heat until sizzling and hot. Add the burgers, reduce heat slightly and cook for 10 minutes, turning once at half-time.

6 Serve with sliced French bread and a mixed salad.

Tip
Put a little extra shredded cheese on top of the burgers so that it melts to make an attractive garnish, if you like.

**Nutritional value per portion
(burgers panfried):**
600 calories
Protein: 46g
Fat: 44g
Carbohydrate: 2g

Turkey Cheeseburgers

Tropical Chicken Burgers

Serves 2

These delicately spiced burgers are perfect served with long grain rice and a creamy pineapple sauce.

Preparation time: about 10 minutes
Cooking time: about 10 minutes

1 pound skinless boneless chicken breasts
½ teaspoon each salt and mild curry
  powder
1 egg, beaten
2 teaspoons finely chopped preserved
  ginger in syrup
6 tablespoons fresh bread crumbs
2 tablespoons light sesame oil
5 tablespoons pineapple juice
3 tablespoons crème fraîche or
  heavy cream

1 Wash chicken and pat dry with paper towels. Grind or chop finely.

2 Put chicken into bowl with salt, curry powder, egg, ginger, and bread crumbs.

3 Work chicken mixture together with 2 forks or knead by hand until smoothly-combined and shape into 6 small burgers, each about 1-inch thick.

4 Heat oil in a heavy-based, non-stick skillet over a medium heat until sizzling and hot. Add the burgers, reduce heat slightly and cook for 8 minutes, turning once at half-time.

5 Take burgers out of pan, put onto a warm plate and keep hot while making the pineapple sauce.

6 To make sauce, add pineapple juice to pan in which burgers were panfried and bring to a boil, stirring all the time. Remove pan from heat and stir in the crème fraîche or heavy cream.

7 Pour sauce over the burgers and serve, with freshly cooked rice.

Nutritional value per portion:
620 calories
Protein: 59g
Fat: 29g
Carbohydrate: 29g

Tropical Chicken Burgers

Salisbury Burgers

Serves 2

Piquant burgers made with beef, bacon, and green pepper. The flavoring is Worcestershire sauce.

Preparation time: about 20 minutes
Cooking time: 10 minutes

1 slice day-old white bread, crusts removed
½ cup water
¾ pound lean ground beef
Salt and pepper to taste
1 teaspoon Worcestershire sauce
½ small green bell pepper
3 bacon slices, rind removed
2 tablespoons corn oil
1 tablespoon minced fresh parsley
Green pepper strips and fresh parsley sprig
   for garnish

1 Dice bread, put into a bowl, cover with the water and let soak while preparing rest of ingredients.

2 Put beef into a bowl and sprinkle with salt, pepper, and Worcestershire sauce.

3 Remove seeds from pepper and cut away inner white membranes. Finely chop flesh. chop bacon coarsely. Put into a heavy, non-stick skillet with the pepper and 1 tablespoon of the oil. Panfry until bacon is a light golden brown.

4 Lift pepper and bacon out of pan with a slotted draining spoon and add to bowl with meat. Squeeze bread dry, add to meat and work together with 2 forks or knead by hand until smoothly-combined.

5 Shape meat mixture into 4 burgers, each about 1-inch thick.

6 Put remaining oil into pan and heat until sizzling and hot. Add the burgers, reduce heat slightly and panfry for 10 minutes, turning once at half-time.

7 Remove burgers from pan, sprinkle with parsley, garnish and serve.

TIP
Grill or broil the burgers if you prefer.

Nutritional value per panfried portion:
550 calories
Protein: 42g
Fat: 40g
Carbohydrate: 7g

Salisbury Burgers

Swedish Kyottbullar

Serves 2

Almost a national dish, Kyottbullar are generally served with creamed potatoes and either cranberry sauce or a beet and onion salad.

Preparation time: about 20 minutes
Cooking time: about 20 minutes

1 slice day-old white bread, crusts removed
½ cup water
½ small onion
¾ pound lean ground beef
2 tablespoons butter or margarine, softened
Salt and pepper to taste
1 egg, beaten
1 tablespoon corn oil
5 tablespoons hot beef stock
½ cup whipping cream
1 egg yolk

1 Dice bread, put into a bowl, cover with the water and let soak while preparing rest of ingredients.

2 Peel onion and grate or finely chop.

3 Put meat into a bowl and fork in butter or margarine. Add onion, then season with salt and pepper.

4 Squeeze bread dry. Add to meat with egg and work mixture together with 2 forks or knead by hand until smoothly-combined.

5 Shape meat mixture into 4 burgers, each about 1-inch thick.

6 Heat oil over a medium heat until sizzling and hot. Add burgers and cook for 2 minutes, turning once at half-time.

7 Pour stock into pan, reduce heat and partially cover pan. Simmer gently for 15 minutes.

8 Remove burgers to a warm plate and keep hot.

9 Lift pan off heat. Beat together cream and egg yolk, stir into pan juices and re-heat without boiling. Pour over kyottbullar and serve.

Nutritional value per portion:
690 calories
Protein: 46g
Fat: 51g
Carbohydrate: 8g

Swedish Kyottbullar

Austrian Schnitzel Burgers

Serves 2

Although veal is usually used, turkey makes an ideal substitute in these delicious burgers.

Preparation time: about 10 minutes.
Cooking time: about 16 minutes

1 slice day-old white bread, crusts removed
½ cup milk
10 ounces ground turkey
½ teaspoon salt
2 pinches of ground nutmeg
1 egg, beaten
8 leaves of lemon balm, chopped, or
    1 teaspoon finely grated lemon zest
4 tablespoons fresh white bread crumbs
3 tablespoons butter
6 tablespoons hot chicken stock
Lemon juice
Fresh parsley sprig for garnish

1 Dice bread, put into a bowl, cover with the milk and let soak while preparing rest of ingredients.

2 Put turkey into a bowl with salt, nutmeg, egg, and lemon balm or lemon zest.

3 Squeeze bread dry. Add to turkey and work mixture together with 2 forks or knead by hand until smoothly-combined. If necessary, add enough of the bread crumbs to firm-up the burgers.

4 Shape turkey mixture into 6 burgers, each about 1-inch thick.

5 Heat 2 tablespoons of the butter in a heavy-based, non-stick skillet over a medium heat until sizzling and hot.

6 Add the burgers, reduce heat slightly and panfry for 16 minutes, turning once at half-time. Remove burgers from pan and keep hot on a plate.

7 Pour chicken stock into the pan, add lemon juice to taste and bring to a boil. Off heat, add remaining butter in small pieces, stirring until melted.

8 Pour sauce over burgers, garnish and serve with peas and creamed potatoes.

Nutritional value per portion:
780 calories
Protein: 75g
Fat: 29g
Carbohydrate: 49g

Austrian Schnitzel Burgers

Horseradish Burgers

Serves 2

Flavored with horseradish, these burgers are delicious served with tomato salad and crusty brown bread.

Preparation time: about 10 minutes
Cooking time: 10 minutes

10 ounces lean ground beef
Salt and pepper to taste
1 small onion
5 tablespoons porridge oats
2-3 teaspoons bottled creamed
   horseradish sauce
3 tablespoons tomato juice
2 tablespoons corn oil

1 Put beef into a bowl and sprinkle with salt and pepper.

2 Peel onion and either grate or finely chop.

3 Add onion and oats to meat with horseradish. Work together with 2 forks or knead by hand until smoothly combined. Add some, or all, of the tomato juice if mixture seems to be dry.

4 Shape meat mixture into 4 burgers, each about 1-inch thick.

5 Heat oil in a heavy-based, non-stick skillet over a medium heat until sizzling and hot.

6 Add the burgers, reduce heat slightly and panfry for 10 minutes, turning once at half-time.

7 Serve with tomato salad and wholewheat bread.

Nutritional value per portion:
450 calories
Protein: 36g
Fat: 27g
Carbohydrate: 13g

Horseradish Burgers

Step-by-step

CHOPPING MEAT FOR BURGERS

1 Wash meat under cold running water and pat meat dry with paper towels. Trim away excess fat and any gristle. Cut into cubes.

2 Grind meat in a food processor, keeping it fairly coarse.

3 Alternatively, chop meat finely by hand. This gives it a really good texture.

PREPARING AND SHAPING HAMBURGERS

4 Put all ingredients listed into a bowl. Lightly wet clean hands. Knead mixture together with hands until smoothly combined.

5 Divide mixture in 4 and shape into hamburgers, each about about 1-inch thick.

6 Coat burgers with bread crumbs, crushed cornflakes, semolina flour or grated Parmesan cheese (depending on recipe).

PANFRYING THE BURGERS

7 Heat butter or margarine in a heavy-based non-stick skillet over a medium heat until hot, tilting the pan to coat the bottom.

8 Add hamburgers and reduce heat to medium low.

9 Panfry burgers for about 5 minutes, turning once. Allow a little more time for thicker burgers.

Berlin Burgers

Serves 2

In their own home town, the burgers are eaten cold with mustard, brown bread and tomatoes. Marvelous picnic food.

Preparation time: about 25 minutes
Cooking time: about 15 minutes

1 slice day-old white bread, crusts removed
½ cup water
6 ounces lean ground beef
6 ounces lean ground pork
Salt and pepper to taste
1 small onion
2 tablespoons corn oil
1 egg

1 Dice bread, put into a bowl, cover with the water and let soak while preparing rest of ingredients.

2 Put beef and pork into a bowl and sprinkle with salt and pepper.

3 Peel onion and grate or finely chop.

4 Heat 1 tablespoon oil until hot and sizzling over a medium heat in a heavy-based, non-stick skillet. Add the onion and sauté until pale golden. Remove onion from pan with a slotted draining spoon and add to meat.

5 Beat egg until foamy. Add to meat mixture and work together with 2 forks or knead by hand until smoothly combined.

6 Shape meat mixture into 4 burgers, each about 1-inch thick.

7 Pour remaining oil into pan and heat until hot. Add the burgers and lower heat slightly.

8 Fry the burgers for 10 minutes, turning once at half time. Serve hot with suggested accompaniments.

Nutritional value per portion:
600 calories
Protein: 46g
Fat: 44g
Carbohydrate: 2g

Berlin Burgers

Beef Burgers with Ham and Almonds

Serves 2

Flavored with Parmesan cheese and finely ground almonds, these Italian-style burgers make a pleasant change.

Preparation time: about 10 minutes
Cooking time: about 8 minutes

½ pound lean ground beef
Salt and pepper to taste
4 ounces lean cooked ham
6 tablespoons finely ground almonds
1 egg, beaten
6 small celery leaves
4 tablespoons olive oil
4 tablespoons grated Parmesan cheese
4 tablespoons fresh white bread crumbs

1 Put beef into a bowl and sprinkle with salt and pepper.

2 Chop ham fairly finely and add to bowl with almonds and egg.

3 Chop celery leaves. Add to meat mixture and work together with 2 forks or knead by hand until smoothly-combined.

4 Shape meat mixture into 4 burgers, each about 1-inch thick.

5 Brush burgers all over with 1 tablespoon of the oil, then mix the cheese and bread crumbs together in a deep plate, add the burgers and toss until they are well-coated.

6 Heat remaining oil in a heavy-based, non-stick skillet over a medium heat until sizzling and hot.

7 Add the burgers, reduce heat slightly and panfry for 8 minutes, turning once at half-time. Serve with broccoli sprinkled with coarsely chopped hard cooked egg.

Nutritional value per portion:
760 calories
Protein: 47g
Fat: 56g
Carbohydrate: 15g

Beef Burgers with Ham and Almonds

Bori-Bori Burgers

Serves 2

A South American specialty, these burgers combine lamb and corn.

Preparation time: about 10 minutes.
Cooking time: 12 minutes.

¾ pound lean ground lamb
Salt and pepper to taste
2 eggs
1 cup drained canned or cooked frozen
    whole kernel corn
1 tablespoon chopped fresh parsley
½ cup fresh white bread crumbs
2 tablespoons corn oil

1 Put lamb into a bowl and sprinkle with salt and pepper.

2 Beat eggs and add to meat with corn and parsley.

3 Knead mixture lightly with damp hands, adding enough bread crumbs to make mixture hold together.

4 Shape meat mixture into 4 burgers, each about 1-inch thick.

5 Heat oil in a heavy-based, non-stick skillet over a medium heat until sizzling and hot.

6 Add the burgers and panfry for about 10 minutes, turning once at half-time.

7 Serve hot with garlic bread and green salad.

Nutritional value per portion:
760 calories
Protein: 45g
Fat: 47g
Carbohydrate: 39g

Bori-Bori Burgers

Munich Pan Burgers

Serves 2

Made with mixed meats, these simple burgers can be eaten hot or cold and make ideal picnic food.

Preparation time: about 45 minutes
Cooking time: 10 minutes

1 slice day-old white bread, crusts removed
½ cup water
1 onion
¾ pound mixed ground meat such as beef, pork, and turkey
Salt and pepper to taste
1 teaspoon prepared English mustard
1 tablespoon chopped fresh parsley
1 egg, beaten
2 tablespoons corn oil
Fresh parsley for garnish

1 Dice bread, put into a bowl, cover with the water and let soak while preparing rest of ingredients.

2 Peel onion and chop fairly finely.

3 Put meats into a bowl. Add onion, salt, pepper, mustard, parsley, and egg.

4 Squeeze bread dry. Add to bowl and work mixture together with 2 forks or knead by hand until smoothly-combined.

5 Shape meat mixture into 4 burgers, each about 1-inch thick.

6 Heat oil in a heavy-based, non-stick skillet over a medium heat until sizzling and hot.

7 Add the burgers, reduce heat slightly and panfry for 10 minutes, turning once at half time.

8 Garnish and serve with cucumber and potato salad with chives and chopped peeled tomatoes.

Nutritional value per portion:
690 calories
Protein: 41g
Fat: 53g
Carbohydrate: 13g

Munich Pan Burgers

Surf and Turf Burgers

Serves 2

Beef and anchovies work brilliantly together to make very flavorsome burgers.

Preparation time: about 10 minutes
Cooking time: 15 minutes

5 drained canned anchovy fillets in oil
10 ounces lean ground beef
2 tablespoons drained small capers
1 egg, beaten
1 onion
4 tablespoons corn oil
4 tablespoons fresh white bread crumbs
2 tablespoons semolina flour

1 Finely chop anchovies. Put in a bowl with the beef, capers, and egg.

2 Peel onion and chop finely or grate. Sauté in 1 tablespoon of the oil in a heavy-based, non-stick skillet until light golden. Lift onion out of pan with a slotted draining spoon and add to meat mixture.

3 Work together with 2 forks or knead by hand until smoothly-combined, adding bread crumbs to firm-up the burgers, if necessary.

4 Combine any leftover bread crumbs with the semolina flour and tip onto a piece of foil.

5 Shape meat mixture into 4 burgers, each about 1-inch thick.

6 Coat burgers with bread crumb and semolina flour mixture.

7 Pour remaining oil into pan in which onions were sautéed and heat until sizzling and hot.

8 Add the burgers, reduce heat slightly and panfry for 10 minutes, turning once, at half-time.

9 Serve with seeded rolls and a crisp raw zucchini salad.

Nutritional value per portion:
570 calories
Protein: 42g
Fat: 38g
Carbohydrate: 15g

Surf and Turf Burgers

Fish Burgers

Serves 2

Made with fresh fish and flavored with dill, these burgers are delicious with salad, or tucked inside burger buns with a little mayonnaise and crisp lettuce.

Preparation time: about 15 minutes, plus 1½ hours chilling
Cooking time: 10 minutes

1 pound skinned white fish or salmon fillets
1 small onion
1 egg, beaten
3 tablespoons fresh white bread crumbs
1 tablespoon chopped fresh dill
2 tablespoons finely ground almonds
Salt and pepper to taste
1 egg white
3 tablespoons finely crushed cornflakes
3 tablespoons corn oil

1 Wash fish under cold running water and pat dry with paper towels. Cut fish into cubes.

2 Peel onion and cut into eighths. Grind with the fish cubes.

3 Put fish and onion mixture into a bowl with egg, bread crumbs, dill, ground almonds, and salt and pepper. Knead by hand until smoothly combined and mixture holds together.

4 Cover and chill for 1 hour.

5 Shape fish mixture into 4 burgers, each about 1-inch thick.

6 Brush burgers with lightly beaten egg white, coat with the crushed cornflakes. Chill for 30 minutes.

7 Heat oil in a heavy-based, non-stick skillet over a medium heat until sizzling and hot.

8 Add the burgers, reduce heat slightly and panfry for 10 minutes, turning once at half-time.

9 Eat hot or cold with a squeeze of lemon juice, and a tomato and cucumber salad dusted with dill.

Nutritional value per portion:
240 calories
Protein: 9g
Fat: 12g
Carbohydrate: 23g

Fish Burgers

Vegetarian Burgers

Serves 2

Designed especially for non-meat eaters, these burgers are healthy and sustaining.

Preparation time: about 1 hour
Cooking time: about 20 minutes

2 medium potatoes (total weight 10 ounces)
4 ounces celery root
1 carrot
1 onion
1 bunch of fresh chives
1 egg
1 clove garlic
4 tablespoons semolina flour
3 tablespoons corn oil
1 tablespoon sunflower seeds or
   pignoli (pine nuts)
Small knob of butter
Scissored fresh chives for garnish

1 Wash, and peel potatoes. Dice them coarsely. Rinse under cold water then tip into a large saucepan. Cook, covered, in boiling salted water until soft. Drain, then mash in a large bowl while still hot.

2 Peel, wash, and grate celery root and carrot. Peel onion and finely grate or chop. Snip chives into small pieces. Add celery root, carrot, onion, and chives to mashed potatoes.

3 Beat egg until foamy. Add to potato mixture with salt. Peel garlic and crush into vegetable mixture.

4 Draw ingredients together in bowl with 2 forks, adding enough semolina flour for mixture to hold together.

5 Shape vegetable mixture into 4 burgers, each about 1-inch thick.

6 Heat oil in a heavy-based, non-stick skillet over a medium heat until sizzling and hot.

7 Add the burgers, reduce heat very slightly then panfry for 6 minutes, turning once at half-time.

8 Sauté the sunflower seeds or pignoli (pine nuts), in melted butter in a small pan until golden, keeping heat low and stirring all the time.

9 Garnish the burgers with chives and serve with the seeds or nuts.

TIP
Celery root is also called celeriac, knob celery or German celery. It has a delicious flavor.

Nutritional value per portion:
450 calories
Protein: 23g
Fat: 20g
Carbohydrate: 45g

Vegetarian Burgers

◆NOTES◆

◆NOTES◆

Chinese
Dishes
Made Easy

Series Consultant: **Sonia Allison**

GREAT
COOKING
VALUE

Introduction

Vegetables play a very important role in Chinese family meals, often in combination with a relatively small amount of meat or fish. Meals traditionally consist of a two, four or six course 'buffet' served on the dining table to which guests help themselves. The food is presented in serving dishes in multiples of even numbers as this is considered to be lucky. Soup is often included and is served at the end of the meal.

Depending on the region, rice, noodles or steamed bread may be served as accompaniments. Rice wine or tea (or both) are drunk throughout the meal. Dessert spoons and forks may be used instead of chopsticks in Western homes.

One important point: the dishes in this book have been designed to form part of a Chinese meal for up to 6 people; if served solo, most recipes will only serve 2-4.

Recipe Notes

Use standard spoon and cup measures. All measures are level unless otherwise stated.

Eggs used are large unless otherwise stated.

Calorie counts for average-size servings are set down at the end of each recipe, and are rounded up to the nearest whole number.

Written by Xiaohui Wang

Stuffed Zucchini

Si Gua Niang Rou

Serves 4-6 as part of meal

An easy vegetable and pork dish with a tangy sauce.

Preparation time: about 30 minutes

4 ounces lean ground pork
1½ teaspoons cornstarch
Salt
1 egg, beaten
2 zucchini (about 7 ounces each)
⅓ cup water
1½ teaspoons soft light brown sugar
1½ teaspoons light soy sauce
1 teaspoon sesame oil

1 Put ground pork into a mixing bowl. Using a fork, work in about half the cornstarch. Add salt to taste, then gradually stir in the beaten egg.

2 Peel zucchini with a vegetable parer. Using a sharp knife, cut them into four 3-inch lengths, following the step-by-step pictures.

3 Using a teaspoon or melon baller, gently scoop out two-thirds of the seeds from the center of each piece of zucchini, leaving bases intact to keep filling in place.

4 Sprinkle inside of each zucchini 'tube' with a little of the remaining cornstarch. Fill each with pork mixture. Arrange on a lightly oiled heatproof plate.

5 Put a custard cup inside a large saucepan, then pour in sufficient water to come two-thirds of the way up the side of the cup.

6 Carefully stand plate of filled zucchini on top of pan. Bring water to a boil. Cover pan closely and steam zucchini for 12-15 minutes. Cool slightly, cut zucchini in 1-inch rounds and keep hot on a serving platter.

7 Make sauce. Tip remaining cornstarch in a small saucepan. Stir in measured water smoothly with a wooden spoon. Add brown sugar and soy sauce and bring to a boil, stirring constantly. Lower the heat and simmer for 30 seconds. Pour sauce over zucchini then trickle oil over the top. Add garnish, if you like, and serve.

Total energy value:
740 calories

Stuffed Zucchini
Si Gua Niang Rou

Eggplants from North China

Shao Qie zi

Serves 4-6 as part of meal

A striking eggplant combination, packed with garlic.

Preparation time: about 45 minutes

1 pound eggplants
2 scallions
5-6 cloves garlic
3 thin slices of peeled fresh ginger root
3 tablespoons dark soy sauce
2 teaspoons cornstarch
1 teaspoon sugar
¼ cup water
2½ cups corn oil for frying
Salt

1 Put eggplants on cutting board, trim them, then cut each eggplant in ¾-inch rounds with a sharp knife. Score top of each round in a fine trellis.
Cut rounds in fourths or
sixths, depending on diameter of eggplants.

2 Trim scallions and cut in thin slices. Peel garlic and slice thinly. Cut ginger in strips.

3 Pour soy sauce into a small bowl. Add cornstarch, sugar, and measured water. Mix until smooth, then stir in scallions.

4 Pour oil into a medium saucepan or deep fat fryer. Heat until just beginning to sizzle. Add eggplant rounds, a few at a time; fry until golden brown. Using a slotted draining spoon, transfer to a plate lined with paper towels to drain.

5 Spoon 1 tablespoon of oil from pan or fryer into wok or medium-size skillet. Add garlic and ginger and stir-fry until pale gold. Add eggplants and stir in cornstarch mixture. Cook, stirring with a wooden spoon, until sauce boils and thickens. Season to taste with salt. Serve at once.

TIP
To make a more substantial dish, stir-fry 5 ounces ground minced pork or turkey with the garlic and ginger.

Total energy value:
710 calories

Eggplants from North China

Shao Qie zi

Peas and Pork

Wan dou bei Rou

Serves 4-6 as part of meal

Ginger enlivens this quick, trouble-free supper dish.

Preparation time: about 45 minutes

10 ounces pork tenderloin
2 scallions
3 thin slices of peeled fresh ginger root
2 cups frozen peas
1 teaspoon cornstarch
4 tablespoons water
2 tablespoons corn oil
3 tablespoons rice wine or medium
    sherry wine
Salt

1 Trim pork. Put it into a saucepan with just enough water to cover. Bring to a boil, lower the heat and cover. Simmer gently for 30-35 minutes until meat is really tender but not about to fall to pieces. Skim surface of liquid 2-3 times with a tablespoon to remove foam as it rises to the top.

2 Lift pork out of pan, transfer to a cutting board and cut into ½-inch cubes with sharp knife. Set aside 1 cup of the cooking liquid, making up to specified amount with water if necessary.

3 Trim scallions. Chop fairly finely with ginger. Thaw and separate peas. In a small bowl, mix cornstarch smoothly with measured water, stirring with a fork until perfectly smooth.

4 Heat oil in wok or skillet until sizzling. Add chopped scallion and ginger mixture, and pork. Stir-fry briskly for 2 minutes.

5 Pour in reserved liquid, cornstarch mixture and wine or sherry. Add peas. Bring to a boil, stirring, then lower the heat and simmer for 1 minute. Season with salt. Serve at once.

TIP
This stir-fry is equally delicious when made with snow peas or sugarsnaps. Add them with the chopped scallions and omit the frozen peas.

Total energy value:
1000 calories

Peas and Pork
Wan dou bei Rou

Hot and Sour White Cabbage Salad

La Bai Cai Juan

Serves 6-8

A full-flavored cold salad featuring marinated 'cigars' of white cabbage.

Preparation time: about 1 hour
Marinating time: 4 hours

2 pounds white cabbage
1 large red bell pepper
3 scallions
2 dried red chilies
2 thin slices of peeled fresh ginger root
3 tablespoons sesame oil
Salt
2/3 cup hot water
3 tablespoons superfine sugar
2 tablespoons white vinegar

1 Remove tough outer leaves from cabbage. Reserve for coleslaw or cooking. Carefully peel off remaining leaves.

2 Place leaves on cutting board. Using a sharp knife, cut out coarse part of stalk from base of each. Blanch in a large saucepan of boiling water for 2-3 minutes or until leaves are flexible. Drain well.

3 Cut pepper in half, remove inner fibers and seeds, then cut flesh into narrow strips. Blanch in saucepan of boiling water for 2-3 minutes. Drain.

4 Trim scallions and cut each lengthwise into 8 pieces. Cut chilies in very thin rings, discarding fiery seeds at the same time (see Tip). Cut ginger in fine shreds.

5 Make marinade. Heat oil in a wok or skillet until sizzling, add chilies and then quickly stir-fry until light brown. Stir in scallions, add salt to taste, then add ginger. Stir-fry briskly for 1 minute.

6 Pour in hot water, then add sugar and vinegar. Simmer for 2 minutes. Draw wok or skillet off heat; leave to stand.

7 Put a strip of pepper at the base (stalk end) of each leaf. Roll each leaf into a 'cigar'. Arrange in a single layer in a dish, pour over marinade to coat, then cover tightly. Let salad stand at room temperature, covered, for 4 hours before serving.

TIP
Touching your mouth or eyes after handling chilies can cause irritation, so wear rubber or plastic gloves if possible. Alternatively, wash your hands thoroughly immediately after contact.

Energy value per serving:
75 calories

Hot and Sour White Cabbage Salad

La Bai Cai Juan

Shrimp with Snow Peas

Xia Ren Bian Dou

Serves 4-6 as part of meal

A stylish combination for seafood lovers.

Preparation time: about 25 minutes

8 ounces shrimp, in the shell
Salt
1 tablespoon rice wine
1 egg white, lightly beaten
1 teaspoon cornstarch
8 ounces frozen snow peas or the same
    weight of lightly cooked fresh snowpeas
2 tablespoons corn oil

1 Peel and clean shrimp, tip into a strainer then rinse and drain well. Pat shrimp dry on paper towels. Transfer to a mixing bowl and season to taste with salt. Lightly stir in rice wine, beaten egg white and cornstarch. Turn shrimp to coat them thoroughly in the mixture.

2 If using frozen snow peas, rinse them in a strainer and drain well. Drain lightly cooked fresh snow peas and pat dry on paper towels.

3 Heat oil in a wok or skillet. Add shrimp mixture and stir-fry for 1 minute.

4 Add peas to wok or skillet and stir-fry for 2 minutes. Adjust seasoning to taste and serve at once.

If using a wok, preheat it over a moderate heat for about 1 minute before adding the oil. Wait for the oil to heat up before adding the shrimp mixture.

Total energy value:
790 calories

Shrimp with Snow Peas

Xia Ren Bian Dou

Oyster Mushrooms with Garlic

Suan shan ping gu

Serves 4-6 as part of meal

Generously laced with garlic, these oyster mushrooms are quite delicious.

Preparation time; about 20 minutes

1 pound (4 cups) oyster mushrooms
5-6 cloves garlic
2 tablespoons corn oil
Salt
5 tablespoons cold water
1 tablespoon light soy sauce
½ teaspoon cornstarch

1 Thoroughly wash and drain mushrooms. Put on a cutting board. Using a sharp knife, cut out hard pieces of stalk.

2 Bring a saucepan of water to a boil, add mushrooms and blanch them for 1 minute. Drain thoroughly in a strainer, then dry each mushroom thoroughly with paper towels.

3 Leave small mushrooms whole. Break large ones into bite-size pieces with fingers. Peel garlic and slice thinly.

4 Heat oil in a wok or skillet until sizzling. Add garlic and fry over a moderate heat until pale gold. Mix in mushrooms with salt to taste. Stir in 3 tablespoons of the measured water and add the soy sauce.

5 Cook, uncovered, for 3 minutes. In a small bowl, mix cornstarch smoothly with rest of water. Pour into wok or skillet, over mushrooms and garlic. Bring to a boil, stirring constantly. Lower the heat and simmer for 1 minute more. Serve at once.

TIP
This recipe can also be used with button mushrooms. They will probably not need washing but should be thoroughly wiped with a damp sheet of paper toweling.

Total energy value:
310 calories

Oyster Mushrooms with Garlic

Suan shan ping gu

Sweet-sour Mushrooms

Qie zhen mo gu

Serves 4-6 as part of meal

A wonderful way of preparing mushrooms.

Preparation time: about 30 minutes

2 cups button mushrooms
2 scallions
2 tablespoons corn oil
2 thin slices of peeled fresh ginger root
2 tablespoons tomato paste
⅓ cup water
Salt
2 tablespoons superfine sugar
2 tablespoons wine vinegar
1 teaspoon cornstarch

1 Trim mushrooms and put into a saucepan. Add just enough boiling water to cover. Let stand for 1 minute, then drain in a strainer. Pat each mushroom dry with paper towels.

2 Trim scallions and cut into 1-inch lengths.

3 Heat oil in wok or large skillet until sizzling. Add scallions and ginger and stir-fry until pale creamy gold. Mix in tomato paste with ¼ cup of the measured water and salt to taste. Stir in sugar and vinegar. Cook, stirring, until liquid bubbles.

4 Strain liquid into clean pan. In a small bowl, mix cornstarch to a smooth paste with remaining measured water. Stir into pan. Bring to a boil, stirring constantly with a wooden spoon.

5 Add mushrooms, mix well and heat through for 1 minute, stirring. Tip into a dish and serve at once.

TIP
Fresh ginger root can be frozen. When needed, simply shave off the required amount with a vegetable parer or sharp knife, then return the frozen ginger to the freezer. This method makes it very easy to obtain very fine slices of ginger, which thaw instantly when added to hot food.

Total energy value:
380 calories

Sweet-sour Mushrooms

Qie zhen mo gu

Step-by-step

PREPARING AND STEAMING STUFFED ZUCCHINI

1 Peel zucchini. Cut 4 pieces, each about 3 inches in length.

2 Using a melon baller scoop out two-thirds of the seeds from the center of each piece of zucchini, leaving bases intact.

3 Sprinkle inside of each zucchini tube with a little cornstarch then fill with meat mixture.

4 Stand a custard cup, or small bowl upright in a large saucepan which has its own well-fitting lid.

5 Add sufficient hot water to come one third of the way up the side of the cup. Arrange filled zucchini on a lightly oiled heatproof plate and place carefully on top.

6 Bring water to a boil, cover pan securely and steam zucchini for 12-15 minutes or until tender and the filling cooked, topping up the water level with extra boiling water as necessary.

CUTTING MEAT INTO STRIPS

1 Cut a well-chilled and still firm piece of beef into 1/8-inch slices, leaving them joined at the base.

2 After cutting, put slices of meat together again.

3 Holding all the slices together, cut through the layers simultaneously with a sharp knife, so that the meat falls in narrow strips.

Green Beans with Eggs and Pork

Dou Jiao Xü Rou

Serves 4 to 6 as part of meal

Complementary flavors combine to create an appetizing Chinese delicacy.

Preparation time: about 45 minutes

10 Chinese dried mushrooms
12 ounces fresh green beans
2 shallots or green onions, thinly sliced
2 eggs
Salt
6 tablespoons or corn oil
1 teaspoon cornstarch
scant ½ cup water
4 ounces pork tenderloin
3 thin slices of peeled fresh ginger root
2 tablespoons dark soy sauce
1 tablespoon rice wine

1 Put mushrooms into a bowl, cover with hot water and let soak for 15 minutes to soften. Trim beans. Bring a large saucepan of water to a boil, add beans, then lower heat and half cover pan with lid. Simmer for 8 minutes.

2 Tip beans into a strainer and rinse under cold water. Drain thoroughly. Transfer beans to a cutting board and cut on the bias into fairly narrow strips.
Drain mushrooms, pat dry with paper towels and cut into bite-size pieces, removing stalks.

3 Using a fork, beat eggs with salt to taste in a small bowl. Sizzle 2 tablespoons of the oil in a medium-size skillet, add eggs; cook until lightly scrambled. Tip into clean bowl. In second bowl, mix cornstarch smoothly with 3 tablespoons of the water.

4 Put pork on cutting board and slice fairly thinly with sharp knife. Cut each slice into narrow strips.

5 Pour rest of oil into a wok or large skillet. Heat until hot but not smoking. Stir-fry pork strips until they turn creamy white. Mix in ginger, soy sauce, rice wine, and all the remaining water. Adjust the seasoning.

6 Heat through for 1 minute, then stir in mushrooms, beans, shallots or green onions, and scrambled eggs. Heat through for about 1½ minutes, stirring. Pour in cornstarch mixture and bubble briefly until sauce thickens. Simmer for 30 seconds, then serve.

Total energy value:
1000 calories

Green Beans with Eggs and Pork

Dou Jiao Xü Rou

Peppers and Pork

Rou Pian Qing Jiao

Serves 4-6 as part of meal

A colorful dish with a piquant flavor.

Preparation time: about 30 minutes

1 pound mixed bell peppers in green, red
  and yellow
2 scallions
5 ounces pork tenderloin, well-chilled
2 tablespoons dark soy sauce
1 tablespoon rice wine
1 teaspoon cornstarch
3 tablespoons water
2 thin slices of peeled fresh ginger root
Salt
2 tablespoons corn oil

1 On a cutting board, cut peppers in half
with a sharp knife. Remove inner fibers
and seeds then cut flesh into ¾-inch
diamond-shaped pieces ,
at the same time trimming away
some of the inner flesh.

2 Trim scallions and cut into thin slices.

3 Put pork on a cutting board. Cut first
into thin slices, then into narrow strips.
Transfer to a medium-size bowl. Stir in
1 teaspoon of the soy sauce with the rice
wine. Add ½ teaspoon of the cornstarch,
stirring well with a wooden spoon.

4 Mix remaining cornstarch smoothly with
the measured water in a small bowl,
then stir in the remaining soy sauce,
scallions, ginger, and salt to taste.

5 Heat oil in a wok or large skillet until hot
but not smoking. Add pork mixture and
stir-fry until two-thirds cooked. Mix in peppers
and continue to stir-fry for 2 minutes. Pour in
cornstarch mixture and bring to a boil,
stirring. Lower the heat and simmer for
about 1 minute until the sauce thickens.
Adjust the seasoning and serve.

Total energy value:
570 calories

Peppers and Pork
Rou Pian Qing Jiao

Tomato Omelet

Fan Qie Hua Dan

Serves 4-5 as part of meal

This version of an international favorite has just a hint of the Orient.

Preparation time: about 25 minutes

2 tomatoes
2 scallions
3 eggs
Salt and ground black pepper
Pinch of sugar
2 tablespoons corn oil

1 Cut a small cross in each tomato. Put into a bowl. Cover with boiling water, let stand for 1 minute, then rinse under cold water. When cold enough to handle, slide off tomato skins.

2 On a cutting board, cut each tomato in half with a sharp knife. Carefully remove seeds with a teaspoon. Cut remaining flesh into small pieces.

3 Trim scallions and chop fairly finely.

4 Break eggs into a bowl, season to taste with salt, pepper, and sugar, then beat lightly. Stir in scallions.

5 Heat half the oil in a skillet until sizzling. Add tomatoes and stir-fry for 2 minutes. Tip contents of skillet into egg mixture; stir until well mixed.

6 Pour remaining oil into skillet and heat until very hot. Add egg mixture and cook until underside of omelet is golden brown, checking frequently.

7 Turn omelet over carefully with spatula and cook briefly until second side is golden. Tip out onto a plate. Garnish with finely sliced scallion and parsley, if you like. Cut into bite-size pieces for eating.

TIP
To make a more substantial meal, mix the chopped omelet with rice and sautéed mushrooms.

Total energy value:
830 calories

Tomato Omelet

Fan Qie Hua Dan

Celery with Beef

Qin Cai Niu Rou

Serves 4-6 as part of meal

Blanched celery adds crispness and color to this flavorsome stir-fry.

Preparation time: about 30 minutes

5 ounces well-chilled beef tenderloin
2 teaspoons cornstarch
Salt
8 ounces celery
2 tablespoons corn oil
2 tablespoons rice wine
2 tablespoons dark soy sauce
scant ½ cup water

1 Put tenderloin on cutting board. Using a sharp knife, cut first into thin slices, then into narrow strips. Transfer strips to a bowl and stir in 1 teaspoon of the cornstarch and salt to taste. Stir well.

2 Trim celery. Put on clean board and cut into 2-inch lengths. Bring a saucepan of water to a boil. Add celery, half cover pan and simmer for 2 minutes. Drain celery in strainer, rinse under cold water and pat dry on paper towels.

3 Heat oil in wok or skillet until very hot. Add beef strips and stir-fry for about 30 seconds until lightly cooked. Using a slotted spoon, transfer beef to plate.

4 Reheat oil in wok or skillet. Add celery and stir-fry for 2 minutes. Replace beef then add all remaining ingredients. Bring to a boil, stirring constantly until sauce thickens. Lower the heat and simmer for 30 seconds. Serve at once.

TIP
Finely sliced water chestnuts can be used instead of celery, if you prefer. There is no need to blanch them.

Total energy value:
450 calories

Celery with Beef

Qin Cai Niu Rou

Cucumber with Pork

Huang Gua Rou Ding

Serves 4-6 as part of meal

An unusual specialty, with an interesting combination of ingredients.

Preparation time: about 30 minutes

2 scallions
5 ounces well-chilled pork tenderloin
1 egg white
2 teaspoons cornstarch
2 tablespoons light soy sauce
Salt
2 cucumbers (total weight about 10 ounces)
2 tablespoons water
2 tablespoons corn oil
3 thin slices of peeled fresh ginger root
1 tablespoon rice wine or medium
    sherry wine

1 Trim scallions. Place on a cutting board and slice thinly.

2 Cut pork into ¾-inch slices with a sharp knife, then cut slices into ¾-inch cubes.

3 Put pork cubes into medium-size bowl. Beat egg white lightly in a separate bowl. Add half the cornstarch, half the soy sauce, and salt to taste. Mix well.

4 Pour mixture into bowl with pork. Stir until all pork cubes are coated in mixture.

5 On clean board, cut unpeeled cucumber in half lengthwise. Remove seeds carefully with teaspoon. Cut hollowed-out cucumber halves into small dice. Tip into a strainer and sprinkle with salt.

6 Place strainer over a large mixing bowl until most of the watery liquid has drained from the cucumber. In a small bowl, mix remaining cornstarch smoothly with measured water.

7 Heat oil in a wok or skillet until sizzling. Add pork and stir-fry for 2 minutes. Add cucumber, scallions and ginger and stir-fry for 3 minutes more. Stir in remaining soy sauce, cornstarch mixture and rice wine or sherry. Bring to a boil, lower the heat and simmer for 1 minute. Adjust seasoning to taste, then serve.

Total energy value:
570 calories

Cucumber with Pork

Huang Gua Rou Ding

Eggplant Pockets

Zha Qie Jia

Serves 4-6 as part of meal

A mouth-watering dip and dunk combination which makes a wonderful hot snack.

Preparation time: about 40 minutes

1 pound eggplants
2 scallions
3 thin slices of peeled fresh ginger root
5 ounces lean ground pork
2 teaspoons light soy sauce
1 teaspoon rice wine or medium sherry wine
1 teaspoon sesame oil
1¼ cups cornstarch
Salt
3 eggs, well-beaten
1¼ cups corn oil for frying
Equal quantities of coarse salt and coarsely-ground black pepper, lightly mixed, for dipping

1 Using a sharp knife, trim all the eggplants Put on cutting board and cut into ¾-inch thick rounds. Following step-by-step pictures, slit a pocket in each, leaving each round joined at bottom to keep filling in.

2 Trim scallions, removing most of the green ends. Chop white parts with the ginger, then put into a mixing bowl. Add pork, soy sauce, rice wine or sherry, sesame oil and 1 teaspoon of the cornstarch. Add salt to taste and mix well.

3 Tip 7 tablespoons of the remaining corn-starch into a second bowl. Gradually beat in eggs to make a smooth batter. Season to taste with salt.

4 Fill eggplant pockets with meat mixture. Coat with remaining cornstarch then dip into the egg batter, turning slices over twice with 2 spoons.

5 Heat corn oil in wok or skillet until hot. Add eggplant pockets, 2-3 at a time, and fry them until well-browned and crisp. Allow 5-8 minutes, turning over at least twice in the oil.

6 Using a slotted draining spoon, transfer eggplant pockets to a plate lined with paper towels. Drain well. Put the bowl containing the salt and pepper on the center of a platter, arrange the eggplant pockets around the rim and serve at once.

Total energy value:
2100 calories

Eggplant Pockets

Zha Qie Jia

•NOTES•

◆NOTES◆

Decorating
Cakes
Made Easy

Series Consultant: **Sonia Allison**

GREAT COOKING VALUE

Introduction

Cake decorating is one of the most satisfying art forms. Not only is it an enjoyable pastime, but you - and your guests - get to eat the results. This book aims to show how familiar and easily obtained ingredients can be used with a variety of bought trimmings to turn the simplest cakes into mini masterpieces.

All the designs are based upon two basic cakes, a fatless sponge and a Victoria sandwich. Both are baked in springform tins and are deeper than usual to allow for layering. These popular cakes can be decorated quickly and easily for any occasion, from birthdays and tea parties to family lunches and glamorous celebration dinners.

Recipe Notes

All spoon measures are level:
1 tablespoon = 15ml spoon;
1 teaspoon = 5ml spoon.

Follow EITHER metric or imperial measures and NEVER mix in one recipe as they are not interchangeable.

Eggs used are a medium unless otherwise stated.

Written by Ulrich Kuhn-Hein

Feathered Effect

A classic and elegant icing design.

Decorating time: about 35 minutes

1 ready-prepared deep Victoria Sandwich
   Cake
110g (3½ oz) apricot jam
315g (10oz) plain (dark) chocolate
110g (3½ oz) white chocolate

SPECIAL EQUIPMENT
Pastry brush
Palette knife
Piping bag fitted with small writing tube
Sharp knife or skewer

1 Stand cake on a wire rack.

2 Brush top and sides of cake to remove excess crumbs. Heat apricot jam in a small saucepan; sieve into a bowl. Brush jam generously all over cake to anchor any remaining crumbs and prevent them from working their way into the icing. Leave to stand for 1 hour.

3 Break up both kinds of chocolate and melt separately in heatproof bowls over saucepans of barely simmering water. Stir occasionally.

4 Spoon plain (dark) chocolate over cake, spreading it evenly over top and sides with the palette knife.

5 Spoon white chocolate into the prepared piping bag. Pipe evenly-spaced parallel lines on top of cake.

6 Give cake a quarter turn, then draw the tip of a sharp knife or skewer through lines, first in one direction, then the other, to create the feathery effect. Leave cake until chocolate has set before moving.

TIP
When decorating any cake, turn it upside down first to create a flat surface.

Feathered Effect

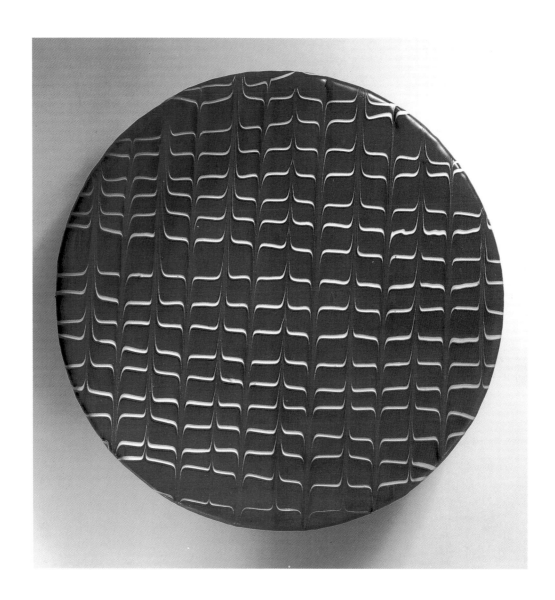

Caraque and Pistachio Topping

Make this decoration from melted chocolate or cheat by using chocolate flake bars.

Decorating time: about 40 minutes

1 ready-prepared deep Victoria Sandwich
   Cake
2 teaspoons powdered gelatine
2 tablespoons water
470 ml (15fl oz/scant 2 cups) chilled heavy
   cream
1 teaspoon vanilla flavoring
110g (3½ oz) plain (dark) bitter chocolate
4 teaspoons chopped pistachio nuts

SPECIAL EQUIPMENT
Palette knife
Large non-serrated knife

1 Stand cake on wire rack.

2 Sprinkle gelatine over measured water in a small heatproof bowl. Leave to soften for 2-3 minutes. Stand bowl in a small saucepan of hot water and stir until dissolved. Set aside to cool.

3 Pour cream into a large bowl. Using a whisk or hand-held electric mixer, whip until thick. Gently fold in cooled gelatine and vanilla flavoring.

4 Spread flavored cream smoothly over top and sides of cake with the palette knife then refrigerate while preparing chocolate decoration.

5 Break up chocolate and put into a small heatproof bowl.

6 Stand the bowl over a saucepan of barely simmering water. Leave until melted, stirring 2-3 times. Pour onto a clean ceramic or marble surface and spread out smoothly with clean palette knife. Leave until set.

7 Holding blade of knife at an acute angle to chocolate, draw it across to shave chocolate into curls and flakes. Arrange these on center of cake as illustrated opposite. Add a border of pistachio nuts.

TIP
If using flake bars, break each in half then cut lengthwise into strips.

Caraque and Pistachio Topping

Fruit and Alaska Meringue

A cheerful red berry fruit and meringue topping enhances a plain sponge cake.

Decorating time: about 1 hour

1 ready-prepared deep Victoria Sandwich
   Cake
3 tablespoons sweet sherry or orange juice
185g (6oz) redcurrant jelly
500g (1lb) prepared berry fruits: raspberries,
   sliced strawberries, blackberries, logan-
   berries, redcurrants
3 egg whites
¼ teaspoon lemon juice
90g (3oz/⅓ cup) sugar
spray of redcurrants for decoration
   (optional)

SPECIAL EQUIPMENT
Large piping bag fitted with star-shaped
   tube

1 Preheat oven to 450°F.
Stand cake on a wire rack and moisten
with sherry or orange juice.

2 Slowly heat redcurrant jelly in a small
saucepan. As soon as it melts, remove
pan from heat. Gently stir in fruit.

3 Spoon jelly mixture evenly over top of
cake, transfer to a flat baking sheet and
chill in the refrigerator until jelly topping
begins to set.

4 To make meringue, beat egg whites
with lemon juice in a large mixing bowl
until stiff, using a whisk or hand-held electric
mixer. Gradually add sugar, continuing to
beat until meringue is shiny and thick.

5 As soon as meringue stands in peaks
when whisk or beaters are lifted out of
bowl, spoon into prepared piping bag. Pipe
a basket weave of lines over top of cake as
illustrated opposite, so that fruit just shows
through. Finally, pipe on a meringue border.

6 Place cake, on baking sheet, in hot
oven for 1-1½ minutes until meringue just
begins to turn golden. Decorate with the
redcurrants, if using.

7 Cut cake into portions and serve
straight away.

TIPS
If preferred, brown meringue briefly under a
very hot grill. Do not freeze leftover cake as
meringue will weep.

Fruit and Alaska Meringue

Trellis

A simple decoration made from cocoa powder and powdered sugar adds a dramatic touch to a cake filled with crème fraîche.

Decorating time: about 50 minutes

1 ready-prepared deep Victoria Sandwich
   Cake
300ml (10fl oz/1¼ cups) crème fraîche
2 tablespoons liquid coffee or
   Kahlua
60g (2oz) flaked almonds, lightly toasted
Powdered sugar
Cocoa powder

SPECIAL EQUIPMENT
Large serrated knife
Palette knife
Fine mesh sieve
8 strips of greaseproof paper, each
   measuring 30 x 2.5cm (12 x 1 in)

1 Cut cake in half horizontally with the serrated knife. Stand both halves, crumb side uppermost, on a wire rack.

2 Spoon crème fraîche into a small bowl, add coffee or Kahlua and stir gently with a fork until well mixed.

3 Use about two-thirds of flavored crème fraîche to fill cake, then spread remainder over top and sides with the palette knife. Decorate sides with toasted flaked almonds.

4 Using the fine sieve, sift a thick even layer of powdered sugar over top of cake. Arrange the greaseproof paper strips on top in a trellis pattern, taking care not to disturb powdered sugar.

5 Sift cocoa powder thickly over top of cake, then gently lift off paper strips to reveal design as illustrated opposite.

TIP
As an alternative, place a paper doiley lightly on top of the icing sugar before sifting over the cocoa powder. Remove the doiley carefully and a lacy pattern will emerge.

Trellis

Miniature Carrots with Pistachios

Almond paste carrots and pistachios make a novel topping for a sponge cake covered with white glacé icing.

Decorating time: about 1 hour

1 ready-prepared deep Sponge Cake
110g (3½ oz) apricot jam
1 egg white
1 teaspoon lemon juice
350g (11oz/2 cups) powdered sugar
220g (7oz) light-colored almond paste,
    bought or homemade
Orange food coloring
75g (2½ oz) blanched pistachio nuts, peeled

SPECIAL EQUIPMENT
Pastry brush
Palette knife

1 Stand cake on a wire rack. Brush top and sides of cake to remove excess crumbs. Heat apricot jam in a small saucepan; sieve into a bowl. Brush jam generously all over cake.

2 Using a whisk or hand-held electric mixer, whisk egg white with lemon juice in a mixing bowl until foamy. Gradually sift in 250g (8oz) of the powdered sugar, beating to make a smooth, fairly thick and spreadable icing. If necessary, sift in some of the remaining powdered sugar to achieve the correct consistency.

3 Spread icing evenly over top and sides of cake with the palette knife and leave to set while preparing carrots.

4 On a clean surface, knead rest of powdered sugar into almond paste. Using your hands, work in sufficient food coloring to turn the mixture orange. Divide into 12 even-sized pieces, shape into carrots and ridge each horizontally with a fork. Set aside 12 pistachio nuts; chop the rest.

5 Decorate sides and center of cake with chopped pistachios. Arrange carrots on cake as illustrated opposite, pressing a whole pistachio in the top of each to resemble ends of stalks.

Miniature Carrots with Pistachios

Raspberries and Cream Criss-cross

The freshest flavors of summer combined in a delectable cake.

Decorating time: about 45 minutes

500g (1lb) firm fresh raspberries, hulled
1 ready-prepared deep Sponge Cake
200g (6½ oz) seedless raspberry jam,
    warmed but not melted
470ml (15fl oz/scant 2 cups) heavy
    cream
1 tablespoon sugar
1 tablespoon cold milk

SPECIAL EQUIPMENT
Large serrated knife
Pastry brush
Piping bag fitted with star-shaped tube

1 Put raspberries in colander and rinse gently under cold running water. Drain thoroughly.

2 Cut cake in half horizontally with the serrated knife. Stand both halves, crumb side uppermost, on a wire rack.

3 Using two thirds of the jam and about one third of the raspberries, sandwich cake halves together again. Brush top with rest of jam.

4 Pour cream into a mixing bowl. Add sugar and milk, then whip with a whisk or hand-held electric mixer until thick.

5 Transfer cream to prepared piping bag and pipe criss-cross lines over top of cake. Finally, fill gaps with whole raspberries.

6 Transfer cake to a platter and chill lightly before serving.

TIP
When piping the cream, keep up an even pressure on the bag so that lines remain straight and of equal thickness.

Raspberries and Cream Criss-cross

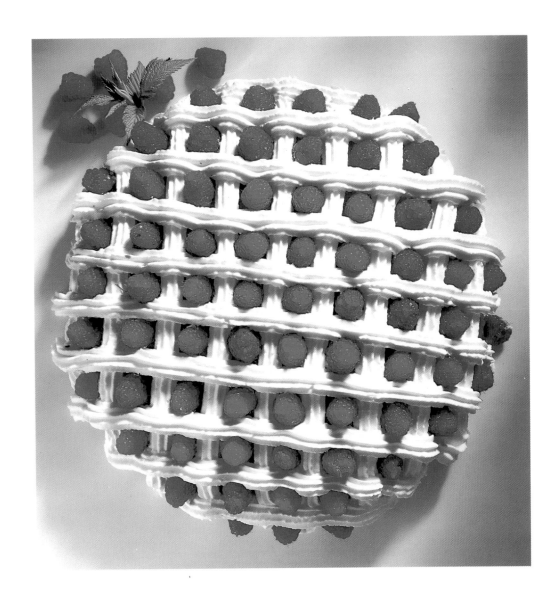

Birthday Cake

A simple cake which children will enjoy decorating.

Decorating time: about 50 minutes

1 ready-prepared deep Victoria Sandwich
   Cake
315g (10oz) light-colored almond paste,
   bought or homemade
110g ($3\frac{1}{2}$ oz/$\frac{2}{3}$ cup) powdered sugar, sifted,
   plus extra for dusting
Blue food coloring
1 egg white
36 small sugar flowers in assorted colors
birthday numeral or numerals, bought or
   see Tip

SPECIAL EQUIPMENT
Pastry brush
Rolling pin
Small sharp knife

1 Stand cake on a wire rack.

2 On a clean surface, mix almond paste
with powdered sugar, kneading it in
well. Transfer to a mixing bowl, make a well
in the center and add a few drops of food
coloring. Work this in well, adding a few extra
drops until the desired color is achieved.

3 Whisk egg white lightly in a small bowl;
using the pastry brush, coat top and
sides of cake.

4 Using the rolling pin, roll out colored
almond paste on surface dusted with
powdered sugar. Cut a round large enough
to cover top of cake.

5 Lop round over rolling pin, place in position on cake and press down gently.

6 Press remaining almond paste into a
ball, knead briefly, then roll out on
sugared surface. Cut one or two strips, large
enough to go around sides of cake. Press
firmly in position.

7 Brush underside of each sugar flower
with rest of egg white. Arrange on top
of cake as illustrated right. Fix numeral and
extra flowers in position in center of cake
in the same way.

TIP
Icing may be used for the birthday
numeral(s) if preferred. Alternatively, roll a
piece of plain almond paste to a long thin
sausage and mould it to the shape of the
number or numbers required.

Birthday Cake

Chocolate Cream Dream Cake

A chance to be creative and produce an eye-catching centerpiece.

Decorating time: about 1 hour

1 ready-prepared deep Victoria Sandwich
  Cake
110g (3½ oz) strawberry jam
315g (10oz) milk chocolate
13 firm strawberries with stalks, washed and
  thoroughly dried
110g (3½ oz) plain (dark) chocolate
12 rose leaves or similar non-poisonous
  leaves
155ml (5fl oz) heavy cream
1 tablespoon milk

SPECIAL EQUIPMENT
Pastry brush
Palette knife
Piping bag fitted with large star-shaped
  tube

1 Stand cake on a wire rack. Brush top
and sides to remove excess crumbs.
Heat jam in a small saucepan; sieve into a
bowl. Brush jam generously all over cake
with the pastry brush.

2 Break up milk chocolate and place in a
heatproof bowl over a saucepan of
barely simmering water. Stir frequently
until melted.

3 Spread about two thirds of the melted
chocolate over top and sides of cake
with the palette knife. Leave until almost set,
then mark into 12 portions with back of knife.
Meanwhile dip 12 of the strawberries into
remaining milk chocolate until half covered.

4 Leave half-dipped strawberries on a
piece of greaseproof paper or foil until
chocolate is firm.

5 Melt plain (dark) chocolate as for milk
chocolate, standing second heatproof
bowl over same pan of water. Using clean
pastry brush, brush melted chocolate over
tops of leaves; set aside on a piece of
greaseproof paper or foil until chocolate is
firm. Very carefully peel leaves away from
chocolate.

6 In a large bowl, whip cream with milk
until thick, using a whisk or hand-held
electric mixer. Transfer to prepared piping
bag and pipe 12 swirls around edge of
cake. Decorate with half-dipped strawberries and chocolate leaves as illustrated right.
Place the plain strawberry in the center.

TIP
To be on the safe side, make more chocolate leaves than you need in case of break-
ages.

Chocolate Cream Dream Cake

Pastel Perfection

Coconut combines with crisp meringues to provide plenty of contrast in flavor and texture.

Preparation and cooking time for meringues: 1-1½ hours
Decorating time: about 35-40 minutes

2 egg whites
Squeeze of lemon juice
125g (4oz/¾ cup) powdered sugar, sifted
1 teaspoon cornflour
Red, green and yellow food colorings
1 ready-prepared deep Victoria Sandwich Cake
155ml (5fl oz/⅔ cup) heavy cream
1 tablespoon milk
90g (3oz/1 cup) desiccated coconut
Lemon curd (see method)

SPECIAL EQUIPMENT
3 piping bags fitted with star-shaped tubes
Palette knife

1 Make meringues first. Preheat oven to 240°F. Beat egg whites with lemon juice in a large mixing bowl until stiff, using a balloon whisk or hand-held electric mixer.

2 Gradually add powdered sugar, continuing to beat until meringue is shiny and thick and stands in peaks when whisk or beaters are lifted out of bowl. Using a metal spoon, fold in cornflour smoothly.

3 Divide meringue mixture equally between 3 bowls. Tint one bowl pale pink with a few drops of red food coloring, one bowl pale green and remaining meringue pale yellow.

4 Line a baking sheet with non-stick baking paper. Do not grease. Pipe or spoon 12 mounds of meringue mixture in alternate colors onto prepared sheet. Bake for 1½ -2 hours until meringues are crisp and dry, carefully turning them over once towards the end of baking time. Cool completely on wire rack.

5 To complete decoration, whip cream and milk together in a bowl until thick. Spread around sides of cake with the palette knife. Spread coconut on a piece of foil. With one hand on top of cake and the other underneath, carefully turn cake on its side and roll in coconut until sides are evenly covered. Reserve remaining coconut.

6 Spread top of cake smoothly with lemon curd then dust lightly with remaining coconut. Finally add a border of meringues.

TIP
Extra meringues may be stored in an airtight tin.

Pastel Perfection

Decorated with Diamonds

A clever idea for a simple decoration made with a heated skewer.

Decorating time: about 30 minutes

1 ready-prepared deep Victoria Sandwich
  Cake
250g (8oz) seedless raspberry jam
110g (3½ oz) walnuts, finely chopped
200g (6¼ oz/generous 1 cup) powdered sugar

SPECIAL EQUIPMENT
Large serrated knife
Pastry brush
Large metal skewer measuring about 25cm
(10 in) in length

1 Cut cake in half horizontally with the
serrated knife. Sandwich together with
two-thirds of jam.

2 Brush top and sides of cake to remove
excess crumbs. Warm remainder of jam
in a small saucepan until just melted. Brush
evenly over top and sides of cake with the
pastry brush.

3 Spread chopped walnuts on a piece of
foil. With one hand on top of cake and
the other underneath, carefully turn cake on
its side and roll in nuts until sides are evenly
covered. Sift powdered sugar thickly over
the top.

4 Using oven gloves and holding the
skewer securely by its ring, heat it over a
gas flame or under a grill until very hot. Lay it
on top of cake, first one way and then the
other, to form large diamonds by partially
caramelizing sugar. Reheat skewer
frequently.

TIPS
When heating the skewer, keep hands
protected with oven gloves at all times.
A heated skewer may be used to create a
variety of designs - try a tic-tac-toe effect,
if preferred, filling the squares with whole
walnuts to echo the decoration on the
sides of the cake.

Decorated with Diamonds

Hearts and Flowers

The perfect way to celebrate St Valentine's Day.

Decorating time: about 45 minutes

1 ready-prepared deep Sponge Cake
280g (9oz) can mandarin oranges
300ml (10fl oz/1¼ cups) heavy
   cream
2 tablespoons milk
2 tablespoons sugar
155g (5oz) cream cheese
Yellow food coloring
5 tablespoons orange jelly marmalade
About 1 tablespoon each powdered sugar
   and cocoa powder
110g (3½ oz) chocolate vermicelli
   (chocolate sprinkles)

SPECIAL EQUIPMENT
Large serrated knife
Small heart-shaped biscuit cutter
Palette knife

1 Using the serrated knife, remove thin slice from top of cake. Place slice on a clean surface and cut out 12 hearts with cutter. Keep trimmings for trifle.

2 Carefully cut rest of cake in half horizontally; set aside on a wire rack.
Drain mandarins, reserving syrup for adding to drinks or sauces.

3 In a mixing bowl, whip cream with milk and sugar until thick, using a whisk or hand-held electric mixer. Slowly and gently fork in cream cheese and mix until smooth. Tint pale yellow with food coloring.

4 Warm marmalade in a small saucepan until almost melted. To assemble cake, spread the bottom layer with 3 tablespoons of the marmalade, two thirds of the mandarin oranges and one third of the whipped cream. Replace top layer. Using the palette knife, spread remaining cream smoothly over top and sides.

5 Brush remaining marmalade over heart-shaped cut-outs then dust half with a little sifted powdered sugar and half with sifted cocoa powder.

6 Spread chocolate vermicelli (sprinkles) on a piece of foil. With one hand on top of cake and the other underneath, carefully turn cake on its side and roll in vermicelli until sides are evenly covered.

7 Arrange hearts in a border around top of cake then mound rest of mandarins in center. Chill lightly before serving.

Hearts and Flowers

Pastry Lattice

A crisp pastry topping transforms a cake into a light, melt-in-the-mouth jam tart.

Decorating time: about 45 minutes

1 ready-prepared deep Victoria Sandwich
  cake
220g (7oz) red jam, warmed but not melted
280g (9oz) shortcrust pastry, thawed if frozen
1 egg, beaten
About 1 tablespoon sugar

SPECIAL EQUIPMENT
Round-topped knife
Rolling pin
Pastry wheel
Pastry brush

1 Preheat oven to 400°F. Stand cake on
wire rack. Cover top completely with
jam, spreading it smoothly with the round-
topped knife.

2 Roll out pastry fairly thinly on floured
surface then cut into fairly narrow strips
with the pastry wheel.

3 Brush each pastry strip with water and
arrange in a lattice design on top of
cake, making sure pastry comes down
the sides.

4 Brush pastry lattice with egg then, using
a teaspoon, carefully sprinkle with
sugar. Transfer cake to baking sheet.

5 Bake for about 10 minutes or until pastry
turns a warm gold. Cool before cutting
and serving.

TIPS
Use apricot or cherry jam if preferred. A variety of pastry toppings could be used - for a romantic occasion roll out pastry to same size as top of cake and cut out hearts, using a small cutter. Lop pastry over rolling pin and place carefully on top of jam.

Pastry Lattice

Little Angels

Rich chocolate icing and pastry angels make this a cake for special occasions.

Decorating time: about 1 hour

1 ready-prepared deep Sponge Cake
250g (8oz) apricot jam
440g (14oz) plain (dark) chocolate
200g (7oz) sugar
5 tablespoons water
12 tiny pastry puffs
    using half the mixture given in recipe
300ml (10fl oz/1¼ cups) heavy cream
1 tablespoon milk
2 tablespoons sugar
1 tablespoon chopped pistachio nuts

SPECIAL EQUIPMENT
Large serrated knife
Palette knife
Skewer
Piping bag fitted with star-shaped tube

1 Using serrated knife, cut cake carefully into 3 layers. Stand layers , crumb side uppermost, on a wire rack.

2 Melt jam in a small saucepan over low heat. Sieve into a bowl, then spread the jam over 2 of the cake layers. Sandwich cake layers together again and leave on wire rack.

3 Break up chocolate and put into a small heatproof bowl over a saucepan of barely simmering water. Leave until melted, stirring 2-3 times.

4 Pour chocolate over cake. Working swiftly, spread smoothly over top and sides with the palette knife. Leave until chocolate is cold and almost set then mark into 12 equal portions with back of knife.

5 Heat sugar and measured water in a small heavy-bottomed saucepan until sugar melts, then boil until mixture forms a caramel. Using the skewer, dip cold buns in caramel; set on wire rack to cool.

6 In a large bowl, whip cream with milk and sugar until thick, using a whisk or hand-held electric mixer. Place in prepared piping bag.

7 When caramel on buns has set, carefully fill them with cream. Stand buns in a circle around top of cake then pipe on cream `robes' as illustrated opposite. Finally sprinkle pistachio nuts over center of cake.

Little Angels

Pumpkin Party Cake

A realistic-looking cake covered with two-tone almond paste. Make the Pumpkin for a child's birthday or to celebrate Halloween.

Decorating time: about 1 hour

2 ready-prepared deep Victoria Sandwich
    Cakes , using 1½ times the
    quantity listed and baking the mixture in
    two 20cm (8 inch) round tins
220g (7oz) seedless raspberry jam
500g (1lb) almond paste, tinted yellow
    with food coloring
110g (3½ oz) almond paste, tinted green
    with food coloring
Sifted powdered sugar

SPECIAL EQUIPMENT
Large serrated knife
Pastry brush
Rolling pin
Round-topped knife

1 Using the serrated knife, cut both cakes in half horizontally. Use about half the jam to sandwich all 4 layers together. Melt remaining jam in a small saucepan and brush evenly over top and sides of cake with pastry brush.

2 Roll out yellow almond paste on surface dusted with sifted powdered sugar. Place carefully over cake, completely covering top and sides and paste so that cake takes on pumpkin shape.

3 With the side of your hand, press indentations on top of cake to resemble the ridges on a real pumpkin. Transfer the cake to a platter.

4 Roll out green almond paste on surface dusted with sifted powdered sugar. Using the round-topped knife, cut out 7-8 leaves. Score in the vein lines then arrange on top of cake as illustrated opposite.

TIP
It is all too easy to add too much coloring when tinting almond paste. To avoid this, break off a small piece of the paste, put it in a cup and work in a few drops of coloring. Then knead the colored paste into the larger portion. Repeat as often as necessary to achieve the desired depth of color.

Pumpkin Party Cake

Step-by step

MAKING PASTRY BUNS (PUFFS)

1 For 24 buns, have ready 155g (5oz/1¼ cups) strong plain flour sifted with pinch of salt, 300 ml (10fl oz/1¼ cups) water, 125g (4oz) butter or margarine and 4 eggs. Preheat oven to 400°F.

2 Sift flour and salt into a bowl. Heat measured water and butter or margarine gently in a saucepan until fat melts. Bring to a fast boil. Tip in flour mixture in one go.

3 Stir briskly over moderate heat until mixture forms a ball in center of pan, leaving sides clean. Transfer to a mixing bowl.

4 With kneading attachment of hand-held electric mixer, beat in 1 egg at a time to make a smooth and shiny paste.

5 Transfer paste to piping bag fitted with plain tube. Pipe 24 mounds onto a large baking sheet lined with non-stick paper. Bake for 10 minutes, then at 350°F for 25-30 minutes more, until buns are golden.

6 Make a slit in the base of each bun to allow steam to escape. Cool on a rack.

MELTING CHOCOLATE

1 Break up chocolate and put into a small heatproof bowl over a saucepan of barely simmering water. Melt, stirring 2-3 times.

2 If you have a confectionery thermometer, temperature should be 32.2C (90C).

3 Spread melted chocolate evenly over top and sides of cake with a palette knife. Leave to set.

Step-by step

SPONGE CAKE

1 Preheat oven to 350°F. Grease and base line a 10 in. springform tin. Grease lining; dust sides with flour. Have ready 5 eggs, 155g (5oz/²⁄₃ cup) sugar, 1 teaspoon vanilla extract, 90g (3oz/³⁄₄ cup) plain flour, 60g (2oz/¹⁄₂ cup) cornflour and ¹⁄₄ teaspoon baking powder. Grated lemon rind is optional.

2 Separate eggs. In a bowl, beat yolks with sugar until thick and creamy. Stir in vanilla.

3 Whisk egg whites in separate bowl until very stiff. Gradually fold into yolk mixture.

4 Sift dry ingredients over top of mixture; fold them in. Add rind if using.

5 Pour gently into prepared tin. Level top.

6 Bake for 25 minutes until top is golden brown and springs back when lightly pressed.

VICTORIA SANDWICH CAKE

1 Preheat oven and prepare tin as for Sponge Cake above. Have ready 250g (8oz) softened cubed butter or margarine, 250g (8oz/1 cup) sugar, 250g (8oz/2 cups) selfraising flour sifted with 2 teaspoons baking powder, and 4 eggs. Grated lemon rind may be added.

2 Beat all ingredients together for 3 minutes in a mixing bowl, using a hand-held electric mixer, adding a little milk if mixture is very thick.

3 Spread mixture evenly in prepared tin and bake for 40-45 minutes or until risen, cooked through and golden.

◆NOTES◆

◆NOTES◆

Desserts

Made Easy

Series
Consultant:
Sonia Allison

GREAT
COOKING
VALUE

Introduction

Luscious cold desserts, created from fresh ingredients, are always a success, and throughout this book there are delicious confections made from fruit, ice cream, gelatin, chocolate, yogurt, cream, and lady fingers. Many of the recipes are subtly spiced or include favorite ingredients such as vanilla, coconut, lemon zest, mint, nuts, and cherries. There are recipes suitable for all members of the family, plus a selection of more sophisticated desserts with company in mind.

Recipe Notes

Use standard spoon and cup measures. All measures are level unless otherwise stated.

Eggs used are large unless otherwise stated. Always buy eggs fresh from a reputable supplier. Desserts made from raw eggs should not be served to the very young, the sick, the elderly, or pregnant women.

Calorie counts for average-size servings are set down at the end of each recipe, and are rounded up to the nearest whole number.

Written By Annette Wolter

Berry Pudding with Snowballs

Serves 4

A brilliantly colored mix of fresh berries, decorated with snowballs made from beaten egg whites.

Preparation time: about 40 minutes
Cooking time: 15 minutes
Cooling time: 1½-2 hours

1½ pounds mixed fresh berries including pitted red cherries
⅔ cup red wine or apple juice
3 tablespoons superfine sugar

SNOW BALLS
4 egg whites
Dash of lemon juice
2 tablespoons superfine sugar
2 quarts water

1 Rinse fruit gently under cold running water and leave in strainer to drain.

2 Bring wine or apple juice and sugar to a boil in a large shallow saucepan, stirring the mixture frequently.

3 Add fruit to saucepan and poach, uncovered, over a low heat for 5 minutes. Switch heat off and leave pan until fruit has cooled. If fruit seems to be lacking in juice, add 2 or 3 tablespoons water. Transfer to bowl, cover and chill.

4 To make snowballs, beat egg whites with squeeze of lemon until stiff. Gradually beat in sugar and continue to whisk until whites become thick and glossy.

5 Bring the water to a gentle boil in large shallow pan. Drop in tablespoon of egg white mixture and cook for 10 seconds, turning snowball over carefully after this time. The egg white should float to the top of the water. Repeat the process with the remaining egg whites, cooking no more than six snowballs at a time.

6 Lift snowballs out of pan with slotted draining spoon and put onto folded dish towel to drain. Serve immediately, on top of fruit.

Nutritional value per portion:
175 calories
Protein: 6g
Fat: 1g
Carbohydrate: 30g

Berry Pudding with Snowballs

Peach Melba

Serves 4

Quick and easy to prepare, this dessert is everyone's favorite.

Preparation time: about 50 minutes

4 or 8 drained canned peach halves,
  depending on size

RASPBERRY SAUCE
3 cups fresh or thawed frozen raspberries
1 cup powdered sugar
4 tablespoons water
1 teaspoon vanilla extract
$1\frac{1}{2}$ teaspoons arrowroot
1 tablespoon water
1 teaspoon lemon juice
2 tablespoons Kirsch or Cointreau

TO SERVE
4 scoops of vanilla ice cream
$\frac{1}{2}$ cup whipping cream, whipped until thick

1 Drain peaches on paper towels and set aside.

2 To make sauce, put raspberries, powdered sugar and 4 tablespoon water into a saucepan and slowly bring to a boil. Reduce heat and simmer, uncovered, for 3 minutes. Remove pan from heat and stir in vanilla extract.

3 Rub sauce through a fine strainer directly into a clean saucepan. Mix arrowroot with water and lemon juice until smooth, then stir into raspberry sauce in pan.

4 Bring sauce to a boil, lower heat and simmer until sauce comes to a boil again and thickens, stirring constantly. Simmer sauce for 1 minute then cool to lukewarm. Stir in liqueur, cover and set aside until completely cold.

5 To assemble, put peach halves onto 4 plates with slices of ice cream. Surround with raspberry sauce and pipe a whirl of cream onto each.

TIP
If you have difficulty locating arrowroot, use cornstarch instead. The sauce will not be as clear, but will taste just as good.

Nutritional value per portion:
310 calories
Protein: 4g
Fat: 7g
Carbohydrate: 57g

Peach Melba

Fruit Salad with Yogurt Sauce

Serves 4

This refreshing fruit salad makes an excellent appetizer or dessert.

Preparation time: about 30 minutes

1 medium Honeydew melon
2 kiwi fruit
2 cups strawberries
1 tablespoon lemon juice
10 lemon balm or mint leaves

DRESSING

2 tablespoons clear honey
⅔ cup plain yogurt
1 teaspoon lemon juice

1 Cut melon in half and remove seeds. Using melon baller or teaspoon, scoop flesh into large bowl.

2 Peel kiwi fruit, cut in half lengthwise and cut each half into thin slices.

3 Rinse strawberries and slice or cut in half, depending on size. Add kiwi fruit, strawberries, and lemon juice to melon in bowl. Mix Gently.

4 For dressing, combine honey, yogurt, and lemon juice.

5 Spoon fruit salad into dishes, top with yogurt dressing and decorate with lemon balm leaves.

TIPS

Use raspberries instead of strawberries and orange slices instead of kiwi fruit.
If liked, add 1 cup seedless green grapes to the fruit salad.

Nutritional value per portion:
125 calories
Protein: 3g
Fat: 2g
Carbohydrate: 24g

Fruit Salad with Yogurt Sauce

Chocolate Mousse

Serves 4

One of the most popular desserts of all time.

Preparation time: about 40 minutes
Setting time: 3 hours

4 squares (4 ounces) dark chocolate
1 tablespoon butter
3 eggs, at room temperature
4 tablespoons powdered sugar, sifted
Dash of lemon juice
⅔ cup whipping cream

1 Chop chocolate and put into bowl set over saucepan of gently simmering water. Add butter and stir until melted.

2 Separate eggs into two bowls.

3 Add half the sugar to egg yolks and beat until thick and creamy. Gradually beat into melted chocolate. Remove bowl from saucepan.

4 Whisk egg whites until stiff. Gradually whisk in remaining sugar and continue whisking until mixture is thick, glossy and stands in firm peaks when beaters are lifted.

5 Using a large metal spoon, fold egg whites gently into chocolate mixture.

6 Whip cream until thick then gradually fold into chocolate mixture.

7 When mixture is smooth and evenly combined, transfer it to 4 individual serving dishes. Chill for about 3 hours or until the chocolate mouse has set.

TIP
You can flavor the mousse to taste with coffee extract or alcohol by adding it to the chocolate and butter as it melts.

Nutritional value per portion:
325 calories
Protein: 6g
Fat: 24g
Carbohydrate: 22g

Chocolate Mousse

Strawberry Mold with Advokaat

Serves 4

Swirls of strawberry cream with a touch of sophistication.

Preparation time: about 20 minutes
Standing time: 4 hours

4 tablespoons cornstarch
1½ cups milk
½ cup strawberry purée (sieved)
1 tablespoon currant jelly, melted
2 tablespoons superfine sugar, plus extra for
  sprinkling
⅔ cup whipping cream
4 tablespoons advokaat or egg flip

1 Put cornstarch in a small bowl. Add a little of the milk and mix to a smooth thin paste, stirring with a wooden spoon.

2 Pour into a saucepan and add remaining milk, strawberry purée, currant jelly and superfine sugar.

3 Cook until mixtures comes to a boil and thickens, stirring constantly.

4 Simmer for 1 minute over a low heat then gradually add cream.

5 Rinse 4 individual dessert molds or 1 large mold with cold water. Fill with cornstarch mix, then sprinkle top with a little sugar to prevent a skin from forming. Cool, cover and chill for 3 hours or until set.

6 Unmold each dessert on a serving plate and spoon over advokaat or egg flip.

TIPS

1 Lightly sweetened light cream may be poured over the mold instead of the advokaat.
2 If you have no suitable molds, set in glass dessert dishes or wine glasses and do not unmold.

Nutritional value per portion:
245 calories
Protein: 9g
Fat: 3g
Carbohydrate: 41g

Strawberry Mold with Advokaat

Easy Lemon Mousse Ring

Serves 4

A perfect summer dessert.

Preparation time: about 40 minutes
Standing time: 4-6 hours

1 packet lemon flavored gelatin
2 eggs
Finely grated zest of 1 lemon
2 tablespoons lemon juice
2 tablespoons superfine sugar
$\frac{2}{3}$ cup whipping cream

DECORATION
2 tablespoons chopped candied peel,
  preserved ginger or angelica

1 Put gelatin powder in liquid measure. Make up to 1¾ cups with boiling water and stir until melted. Alternatively, melt gelatin with water in a saucepan over a low heat.

2 Cool mixture, cover and chill until just beginning to thicken. The consistency should be like that of unbeaten egg whites.

3 Separate eggs. Beat egg yolks into setting gelatin with lemon zest and juice, using a ballon whisk.

4 Beat egg whites until stiff then gradually whisk in 1 tablespoon sugar and continue beating until mixture is thick, glossy and stands in firm peaks when beaters are lifted. Whip cream separately until thick.

5 Using a large metal spoon dipped in warm water, fold cream and beaten egg whites alternately into lemon gelatin mixture until smooth and well combined.

6 Spoon mixture into wetted ring mold, cover and chill for 4-6 hours until set. Unmold mousse onto serving plate and decorate with candied peel, ginger or angelica.

Nutritional value per portion:
305 calories
Protein: 7g
Fat: 15g
Carbohydrate: 37g

Easy Lemon Mousse Ring

Tutti Frutti Salad with Vanilla Sauce

Serves 4

A colorful dish of summer fruits served with a smooth vanilla sauce.

Preparation time: about 45 minutes

6 large ripe apricots
1 cup red cherries
1 eating apple
1 tablespoon lemon juice
1 tablespoon clear honey
1 chocolate flake bar or chocolate sprinkles

VANILLA SAUCE
1 egg
1 teaspoon vanilla extract
1 tablespoon superfine sugar
1 tablespoon cornstarch
1 tablespoon cold water
1 ¼ cups milk

1 Wash apricots and wipe dry with paper towels. Cut in half and remove pits. Cut flesh into slices and put in mixing bowl.

2 Wash and pit cherries. Add to bowl with apricots.

3 Peel, quarter and core apple and cut flesh into small pieces. Add to bowl of apricots and cherries, then stir in lemon juice and honey. Cover and set aside.

4 Separate egg, putting white into bowl and yolk into saucepan.

5 Stand saucepan over low heat then mix in vanilla extract and sugar. Stir cornstarch with cold water until smooth, then stir into pan and whisk until foaming. Gradually beat in milk.

6 Cook sauce until egg yolk mixture comes to a boil and thickens, stirring constantly. Simmer for 1 minute then remove pan from heat.

7 Whisk egg white until stiff and fold into sauce with large metal spoon.

8 Divide fruit salad equally among 4 dishes. Top with sauce and add 2 pieces of chocolate flake bar to each. Alternatively, top with chocolate sprinkles.

Nutritional value per portion:
220 calories
Protein: 5g
Fat: 5g
Carbohydrate: 38g

Tutti Frutti Salad with Vanilla Sauce

Step-by-step

Preparing Orange or Grapefruit Sections

1 Peel orange or grapefruit, removing all traces of white pith.

2 Hold whole fruit in one hand and, using sharp knife, cut out fruit sections from in between tough membranes.

3 Each section should be in one piece, free from pith and membrane.

Filling and Using a Pastry Bag

4 Fit star-shaped or plain tip inside plastic, cloth or paper pastry bag. The size of tip can be small, medium or large according to the type of decoration required.

5 Stand pastry bag in glass or pitcher for support. Fold back top of bag over rim of glass or pitcher. Spoon in cream or frosting.

6 Lift up top of bag and twist tightly just above mixture inside. Pipe by squeezing bag. Refer to piped decorations inside back book cover.

Making Meringues

7 Separate the eggs into a large, clean, grease-free bowl, making sure that none of the egg yolk gets into the white.

8 Whisk the whites with a pinch of salt, using electric beaters, until the whites are stiff and dry when the beaters are removed.

9 Whisk in the sugar, a spoonful at a time. Whisk well between each addition to make a stiff, shiny meringue, ready for shaping and baking.

1

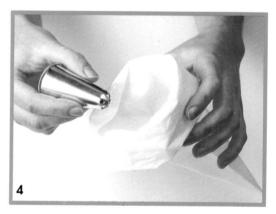

4

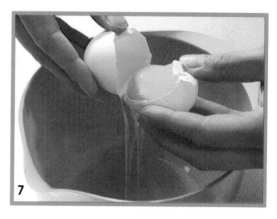

7

Tiramisu

Serves 4

A new version of a great Italian invention. The name means tonic or pick-me-up.

Preparation time: about 30 minutes
Cooling time: 3 hours

2 eggs
¼ cup superfine sugar
1 cup mascarpone cheese, at room
   temperature
Pinch of salt
1 cup cold espresso, made from instant
   coffee and water
16 lady fingers

DECORATION
Unsweetened cocoa powder

1 Separate eggs, putting whites into one bowl and yolks into another.

2 Add sugar to yolks and beat until thick, creamy and very pale in color.

3 Put mascarpone cheese in a bowl and mix in egg yolk mixture. Whisk egg whites with salt until stiff, then fold into cheese and egg mixture with large metal spoon.

4 Pour coffee into shallow dish. Cut 8 lady fingers in half and dip briefly into coffee until soft on outside but still firm in the center.

5 Arrange coffee-soaked lady fingers over the bottom of a shallow dish and cover smoothly with half the mascarpone mixture.

6 Cut remaining lady fingers in half, dip in coffee as before and arrange on top of mascapone.

7 Spoon remaining mascapone on top and dust with sifted unsweeted cocoa powder.

TIP
Flavor espresso by stirring in about 2 tablespoons rum or brandy, if you like.

Nutritional value per portion:
335 calories
Protein: 11g
Fat: 20g
Carbohydrate: 26g

Tiramisu

Raspberry Cornstarch Pudding

Serves 4

Children will love this deep pink cornstarch pudding.

Preparation time: about 40 minutes
Standing time: 4 hours

4 tablespoons cornstarch
1¾ cups milk
¼ cup raspberry purée (sieved)
2 tablespoons superfine sugar
1 tablespoon Framboise or Grenadine
  (optional)
⅔ cup plain yogurt
Red food coloring (optional)

DECORATION
Slices of fresh or canned fruit
1 teaspoon chopped pistachios or walnuts

1 Put the cornstarch in a small bowl. Add a little of the cold milk and mix to a thin, smooth paste.

2 Pour into a saucepan and add all the remaining milk and sugar, then bring to a boil, stirring constantly Simmer for 1 minute until thick. Stir in Framboise or Grenadine and let cool for 5 minutes, then gradually beat in yogurt, with coloring, if used.

3 Spoon cornstarch pudding in to wetted mold or 4 individual dessert molds. Sprinkle tops with sugar to prevent a skin from forming, then cool and cover.

4 Chill cornstarch pudding for 4 hours until set. Unmold and decorate with fruit and chopped nuts.

TIP
To obtain the raspberry purée tip the contents of a 10-ounce can of raspberries in syrup into a blender and whizz to a purée. Rub through a fine strainer to remove the seeds. Use ¼ cup of the purée in the pudding and serve the rest as a sauce, if you like

Nutritional value per portion:
95 calories
Protein: 5g
Fat: 3g
Carbohydrate: 12g

Raspberry Cornstarch Pudding

Double Chocolate Pudding with Cream

Serves 4

An irresistible molded chocolate dessert, perfect for Company.

Preparation time: about 25 minutes
Standing time: 4 hours

4 tablespoons cornstarch
2¼ cups light cream
2 tablespoons superfine sugar
3 squares (3 ounces) dark chocolate,
    shredded
½ teaspoon vanilla extract

DECORATION
⅔ cup whipping cream
1 tablespoon chopped pistachios
Almond cookies (optional)

1 Put cornstarch in a small bowl. Stir in a little of the light cream to form a smooth paste.

2 Pour into a saucepan and stir in the remaining cream. Cook until mixture comes to a boil and thickens, stirring all the time, then lower the heat and simmer for 1 minute.

3 Remove pan from heat and add sugar and shredded chocolate. Stir until both have melted. Add vanilla extract.

4 Spoon cornstarch pudding into wetted mold. Cool, cover and chill for 4 hours until set.

5 Unmold onto a serving plate. Whip cream until thick, pipe a border around edge of chocolate pudding and sprinkle with nuts. Pipe a swirl of cream in the center and top with an almond cookie if you like.

Nutritional value per portion:
415 calories
Protein: 8g
Fat: 23g
Carbohydrate: 45g

Double Chocolate Pudding with Cream

Russian Lemon Cream

Serves 4

A luscious lemon-flavored dessert.

Preparation time: about 30 minutes
Standing time: 4 hours

14-ounce can sweetened condensed milk
1 cup plain yogurt
Finely grated zest and juice of 2 lemons
2 egg whites
1 tablespoon superfine sugar

DECORATION
1 lemon
Mint leaves

1 Spoon condensed milk into mixing bowl and gradually beat in yogurt, grated lemon zest and juice. Stir thoroughly until well combined.

2 Whisk egg whites until stiff. Gradually add sugar and continue whisking until mixture is glossy and stands in firm peaks when beaters are lifted.

3 Using a large metal spoon, fold egg whites gently and lightly into condensed milk and lemon mixture.

4 Spoon mousse into 4 dishes and chill for 4 hours.

5 Thinly slice lemon and use to decorate mousses, with mint leaves.

TIPS
1 Use lime slices instead of lemon for the decoration.
2 1-2 tablespoons of orange flower water, added with the lemon rind and juice, gives the dessert a slightly exotic and perfumed flavor.

Nutritional value per portion:
310 calories
Protein: 8g
Fat: 16g
Carbohydrate: 27g

Russian Lemon Cream

Pears Hélène

Serves 4

Quick and easy to prepare, this classic dessert makes an ideal midweek treat.

Preparation time: about 20 minutes
Cooking time: 10 minutes

8 canned pear halves in syrup
2 tablespoons pear syrup from can
1 tablespoon water
½ teaspoon vanilla extract
4 squares (4 ounces) dark chocolate
⅔ cup whipping cream
8 slices or scoops of vanilla ice cream

1 Drain pears thoroughly on paper towels.

2 To make sauce, pour syrup into heavy-based saucepan. Add water and vanilla extract. Chop chocolate and add.

3 Cook over a moderate heat until the chocolate has melted, stirring frequently. Set aside to cool.

4 Whip cream until thick then gradually add cooled chocolate sauce.

5 Arrange pears and ice cream on 4 dessert plates.

6 Spoon over chocolate sauce and serve at once.

Nutritional value per portion:
490 calories
Protein: 6g
Fat: 27g
Carbohydrate: 46g

Pears Hélène

Vanilla Fluff with Fruit

Serves 4

Light and airy, this dessert makes a perfect end to a heavy meal.

Preparation time: about 30 minutes

4 cups firm strawberries
2 eggs
4 tablespoons superfine sugar
2 cups skim milk soft cheese
Pinch of salt
⅔ cup whipping cream
1 teaspoon vanilla extract
Grated zest and juice of 1 small orange
⅓ cup chopped hazelnuts

1 Hull strawberries, tip into strainer and wash gently under cold running water. Drain thoroughly. Reserve a fourth of the strawberries and slice the remainder.

2 Separate eggs, putting yolks into one bowl and whites into another.

3 Add 3 tablespoons of the sugar to egg yolks and beat until thick, foamy and pale in color. Gradually beat soft cheese into egg yolks.

4 Whisk egg whites with pinch of salt until stiff. Gradually add remaining sugar and continue whisking until mixture is thick, glossy and stands in firm peaks when the beaters are lifted.

5 Using a large metal spoon, fold egg whites into cheese mixture alternately with strawberries.

6 Whip cream until thick. Stir in vanilla extract and orange juice and fold into cheese mixture.

7 Spoon into serving dish and sprinkle with orange zest. Decorate with nuts and remaining strawberries.

Nutritional value per portion:
400 calories
Protein: 24g
Fat: 22g
Carbohydrate: 26g

Vanilla Fluff with Fruit

Currant and Fruit Cake Dessert

Serves 4

Red currants are combined with rich fruit cake in this simple-to-make dessert.

Preparation time: about 50 minutes
Standing time: 1½ hours

2 cups red currants
⅓ cup water
½ cup superfine sugar
8 ounces rich dark fruit cake
1 tablespoon rum
⅔ cup whipping cream
1 cup skim milk soft cheese
4 tablespoons powdered sugar, sifted
1 chocolate flake bar or chocolate sprinkles

1 Wash currants, remove stalks and put three-fourths of the fruit into a saucepan.

2 Add water, bring to a boil, then lower heat and cover. Simmer gently for 10 minutes or until currants are soft.

3 Add sugar to currants and stir until dissolved. Crumble cake into small pieces and add to fruit in saucepan. Let stand for 30 minutes, then stir in rum.

4 Transfer to serving dish. Cover and chill for 30 minutes.

5 Meanwhile, whip cream until thick, then combine with soft cheese, mixing well.

6 Sweeten with powdered sugar and spoon over top of dessert.

7 Arrange remaining red currants around edge of dessert then decorate with pieces of flake bar. Alternatively, top with chocolate sprinkles.

8 Chill for 30 minutes more, then spoon onto plates to serve.

Nutritional value per portion:
480 calories
Protein: 21g
Fat: 11g
Carbohydrate: 67g

Currant and Fruit Cake Dessert

•NOTES•

◆NOTES◆

Garnishes

Made Easy

Series Consultant: **Sonia Allison**

Introduction

Good-looking and beautifully-garnished food is a visual feast, and clever decorations, created in the main from fruit and vegetables, make everything you serve extra special. Once you get the hang of cutting, twisting and twirling, you should gain confidence, but remember practice makes perfect.

Written by Ulrich Kuhn-Hein

Tomato Rose

An elegant and classic decoration, perfect for all savory dishes.

Preparation time: about 5 minutes

FOR ONE TOMATO ROSE
1 large firm tomato, with a smooth, deep red skin

EQUIPMENT
1 small and very sharp kitchen knife and/or sharp vegetable parer

1 Wash tomato thoroughly and wipe dry. Avoid tomatoes with blemishes on the skin as this will spoil the appearance of the finished rose.

2 Carefully remove stalk, then make a small slit in the same spot.

3 Beginning at the slit, start peeling the tomato like an apple with knife or vegetable parer. Work slowly and cut skin as thinly as possible without allowing it to break. If skin is too thick, it will be hard to roll.

4 With skin side out, roll one end of the peel round a finger. Lift off and continue to roll until you have what looks like a rosebud. The appearance of the rose is sometimes more attractive if it is turned upside down.

VARIATION
Instead of a tomato, use the peel of a lemon, orange or lime. You can also make an apple peel rose but it must be sprinkled with lemon juice to avoid browning.

TIP
The rose is more for aesthetics than eating, but the remaining skinned tomato can be used for cooking or added to salads.

Tomato Rose

Zucchini Accordion

Quick to do and very impressive.

Preparation time: about 20 minutes

FOR 1 ACCORDION
1 slender zucchini
Salt
Freshly ground pepper
Juice of ½ lemon
1 tablespoon virgin olive oil

EQUIPMENT
1 small sharp kitchen knife
1 long wooden or metal skewer

1 Choose a zucchini which is straight and no thicker than 1¾-inches in diameter. This makes cutting easier and also helps to prevent the accordion from breaking.

2 Wash the zucchini thoroughly, then slice off both ends evenly with the knife.

3 Starting at one end, carefully push skewer lengthwise through the center of the zucchini , using a twisting action. Holding the top of the skewer with one hand, cut and turn the zucchini at the same time with the other hand, making the slices as even as possible.

4 Continue until the whole zucchini has been cut, then gently ease out the skewer from the center.

5 Open out the accordion on a plate, sprinkle with salt, pepper and lemon juice and leave for 15 minutes so that excess juices from the zucchini are drawn out. This makes it less brittle and easier to handle.

6 Gently lift accordion onto paper towels and leave to drain before using to garnish cold, savory dishes.

VARIATION
Instead of zucchini, use Japanese daikon. For a very pretty effect, twist together two spirals of green and yellow zucchini.

Zucchini Accordion

Radish Crown

*An attractive garnish which makes a pleasant change
from usual vandyke radish.*

Preparation time: about 30 minutes

FOR 10 CROWNS
10 radishes

EQUIPMENT
1 small sharp kitchen knife
1 small bowl

1 Remove and discard radish leaves if necessary. Trim each radish. Cut a thin sliver off the bottom of each so that it stands upright without falling over.

2 Using a sharp knife, cut a small wedge out of the top of each radish.

3 Repeat twice more to give you what looks like a six-pointed star.

4 Starting at the top, make six petals by cutting two-thirds of the way down each radish, working between points of star as shown in the picture. Repeat the process with the remaining radishes.

5 Drop the radishes into a bowl of ice water and chill for 10 minutes. This makes the petals open out and also crisps the radishes. Do not let them soak as they might lose both taste and color.

VARIATIONS
To make chrysanthemum radishes, cut a sliver off the bottom of each so that they stand up straight. Starting at the top, cut downward into thin slices. Give radishes a quarter turn and cut downward again as before, taking care not to slice through to bottoms. Drop radishes into bowl of ice water, leave for 2 minutes then drain. For picture, see inside of back cover.

Radish Crown

Cucumber Variations

Cucumber makes a versatile garnish for cold savory dishes.

Preparation time: about 15 minutes

FOR TWO FANS AND ONE BUNDLE
1 medium cucumber

EQUIPMENT
1 kitchen knife
1 cutting board

1 Wash cucumber thoroughly and wipe dry with paper towels. Cut cucumber into 3 pieces.

2 Cut each piece in half lengthwise. Place on board, cut sides down.

3 To make fan with tail end of cucumber, cut into thin slices lengthwise, almost to top, and open out.

4 To make a short, curvy fan, cut second portion of cucumber into thin parallel slices widthwise as shown on top right of picture. Make sure you don't cut right through to the top edge so that they are joined along the top. Spread out as shown on the top left of picture.

5 To make cucumber bundle, cut last portion of cucumber lengthwise into long, thinnish slices.

6 Lay each slice down flat and make nicks, fairly close together, from outside edge to center cutting about halfway down. Do not cut right through from one side to the other, or bundle will fall apart.

7 Roll up and hold the cucumber bundle in place with toothpick.

VARIATION
Use young and small zucchini instead of cucumber.

Cucumber Variations

Meat Platter

Serves 6

*A selection of cold cuts looks extra special
with some pretty garnishes.*

Preparation time: about 45 minutes

1½ pounds cold cuts

GARNISH
Zucchini Accordion
Radish Crowns
Cucumber Fans
Tomato Roses
Cucumber Bundle

DRESSING
1 package fresh mixed herbs
1 egg yolk
1 tablespoon spicy yellow mustard
Salt to taste
Freshly ground pepper to taste
Juice of ½ lemon
½ cup corn oil
1 tablespoon light cream

1 Arrange the cold cuts around the
outside of a large platter.

2 Arrange the zucchini accordion, the
radish crowns, tomato roses, and
cucumber fans on the platter.

3 To make the dressing: wash and dry the
herbs and chop coarsely. Spoon into
blender. Add the egg yolk, mustard, salt,
pepper, lemon juice, oil, and cream. Blend
until smooth. Pour into a bowl.

4 Arrange the bowl in the center of the
platter. Add a cucumber bundle and a
radish crown and serve at once.

Scallion or Green Onion Tassels

An impressive garnish which is easy to prepare.

Preparation time: about 30 minutes

FOR ONE TASSEL
1 thick scallion or green onion

EQUIPMENT
1 small vegetable knife
1 cutting board
1 bowl

1 Wash scallion or green onion thoroughly under cold running water.

2 Trim scallion or green onion, leaving on a generous length of green leaf. Put scallion or green onion on to cutting board.

3 Using the knife, slit the green part of the scallion or green onion just up to the white bulb. Do this several times to make fairly narrow strips. Repeat the splitting, first giving the scallion or green onion a quarter turn.

4 Soak scallion or green onion in cold water for about 20 minutes or until the green leaves curl.

5 Remove from water and shake dry.

TIP
Young, slender Spring leeks can also be used for tassels. They are usually tender and clean.

Scallion or Green Onion Tassels

Ways with Lemons

A fish dish would not be the same without a beautiful lemon garnish.

Preparation time: about 10 minutes

FOR 8 LOOPS AND 2-3 BUTTERFLIES
2 medium-size lemons

EQUIPMENT
1 small vegetable knife
1 cutting board

1 Choose firm, bright yellow lemons with unblemished skin.

2 Thoroughly wash and dry lemons.

3 For loops, cut one lemon in half lengthwise, then cut each half into 4 sections.

4 Gently cut flesh away from each section, leaving it joined at the top by about ½ inch. Carefully ease skin away from flesh then fold skin under flesh section to form a loop. Repeat with remaining sections. See top right of picture.

5 For butterflies, cut off top and bottom of lemon then slice fruit thinly into a spiral, following the method used for the zucchini accordion, but without using a skewer.

6 Cut spiral into 2 or 3 pieces, depending on size of lemon, and twist into butterfly shapes as shown on bottom right of picture.

Ways with Lemons

Stuffed Eggs

Attractively garnished, stuffed eggs make an appealing centerpiece for any buffet table.

Preparation time: about 30 minutes

FOR 12 EGG HALVES
6 eggs
1 tablespoon soft cream cheese
Salt to taste
Freshly ground pepper to taste
2 radishes
1 package fresh parsley
1 tablespoon ketchup
4 sprigs of fresh dill
12 cooked shelled shrimp
2 teaspoons mock caviar or fish roe
small drained pickled red or green chilies
kiwi fruit

EQUIPMENT
1 kitchen knife
1 cutting board
3 small bowls
pastry bag fitted with star-shape tip
1 balloon whisk

1 Hard cook the eggs in boiling water for 9 minutes. Drain, cover with cold water and leave for 15 minutes. Drain again and shell. Cut each egg in half lengthwise and spoon yolks into a bowl. Mash finely. Cut a thin sliver off the bottom of each egg white half to stop it tilting over to one side.

2 Add cream cheese to yolks and mix in well. Season with salt and pepper. Spoon one-third of the mixture into the pastry bag and pipe into 4 egg white halves.

3 Trim radishes. Wash and dry then cut in thin slices. Arrange in rings on top of the 4 filled egg halves. Add a sprig of parsley to center of each.

4 Divide remaining egg mixture among the two bowls. Add ketchup to one and mix in well. Chop remaining parsley. Add to egg mixture in second bowl, working it in well to add flavor and color.

5 Spoon or pipe the tomato-colored yolk mixture into 4 egg white halves. Repeat with parsley-flavored yolks, using up remaining 4 whites. Wash dill and gently wipe dry with paper towels. Garnish parsley egg halves with shrimp, caviar, and dill.

6 Garnish tomato egg halves with whole chilies and half a peeled slice of kiwi fruit. Cover if not serving immediately.

Stuffed Eggs

Apple Chevrons

*With a little practice you will be able to prepare this
elegant garnish in minutes.*

Preparation time: about 15 minutes

FOR 4 CHEVRONS
1 red apple
Juice of ½ lemon

EQUIPMENT
1 very sharp kitchen knife
Cutting board

1 Use shiny, red apples which are firm
and unblemished.

2 Wash apples and wipe dry with paper
towels. Cut into fourths, then trim top
and bottom to remove any hard pieces.

3 Remove core from each apple quarter,
cutting across flesh to make a flat
surface so that apple quarter will stand
securely when it is turned over.

4 Place quarter of apple on cutting
board with skin side facing up and cut
a small V-shaped wedge from center.
Reserve.

5 Continue to cut out slender, but increasingly larger, V-shaped wedges from
apple quarter as shown in picture. Aim to
cut out four wedges in total.

6 Sprinkle flesh with lemon juice to
prevent browning. Reassemble wedges
to form a feather or chevron design. Space
them a little as shown on left of picture.

Apple Chevrons

Cheese Platter

Serves 6

Preparation time: about 1 hour

FOR CHEESE PLATTER

4 different kinds of cheese such as Gruyère, Emmental, Gouda, Cheddar, Monterey Jack, Jarlsberg, Brie, or Camembert.

CHEESE CREAM

½ cup pot cheese
3-ounce package cream cheese, softened
2 tablespoons whipping cream or dairy sour cream
Salt and freshly ground pepper to taste

GARNISH

1 Scallion or Green Onion Tassel
3 or 4 Stuffed Egg halves
2 radishes
Fresh parsley sprig
2 Tomato Roses
1 Apple Chevron

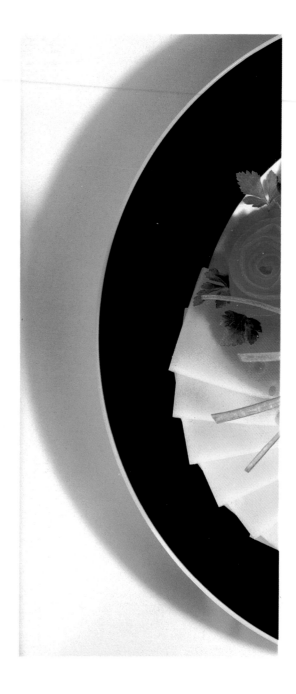

1 Unwrap cheeses and let them come to room temperature.

2 Prepare cheese cream. Mix pot cheese with cream cheese, cream, salt, and pepper. Spoon mixture into a small bowl.

3 Stand cheese cream in the center of a large platter and surround with sliced cheeses as shown in picture. Place scallion or green onion tassel in center of cheese cream. Top egg halves with rings of sliced radishes and parsley. Add tomato roses and garnish with parsley. Add apple chevron to platter as shown.

4 Serve with crisp rolls or assorted breads.

Orange Shapes

Colorful decorations for both sweet or savory dishes.

Preparation time: about 10 minutes

MAKES 4-5 KNOTS AND 2 TWISTS
2 medium-size oranges, preferably a
seedless variety

EQUIPMENT
1 medium-size kitchen knife
1 cutting board

1 Choose thin-skinned and unblemished
oranges. If necessary, buy 3 or 4 smaller
oranges if they are the right type.

2 Rub oranges clean under cold running
water. Wipe dry, then cut a thin slice off
top and bottom of each piece of fruit.

3 For knots, cut one orange into ¼-inch
thick slices. Make a nick through skin.
Cut flesh away from peel three-fourths of
the way around each slice.

4 Tie peel carefully into a loose knot and
rest on orange flesh, see bottom right of
picture. Use to decorate beverages and
desserts or use as a garnish for fish dishes.

5 To make orange twists, prepare oranges
as in step 2.

6 Cut orange into slices, then slit each
slice from center to outer edge.

7 Twist one slice into an S-shape, then
twist second slice over the top to form a
double twist.

TIP
If orange flesh breaks when preparing the
orange knots, cut thicker slices.

Orange Shapes

Chocolate Magic

*Chocolate-coated fruits and leaves are just a few of the tempting ways
of using chocolate as a decoration.*

Preparation time: about 30 minutes

TO COVER 10 LEAVES AND 10 STRAWBERRIES
5 squares (5 ounces) dark chocolate
10 rose or fresh bay leaves
10 medium-size strawberries

EQUIPMENT
1 small saucepan
1 heatproof bowl
1 tablespoon
1 fork

1 Break up chocolate and melt in bowl set over pan of gently simmering water. Stir from time to time, making sure that no water comes into direct contact with the chocolate.

2 Carefully wash and dry rose or bay leaves. Using a pastry brush, cover bottom of each leaf with melted chocolate.

3 Carefully transfer leaves to a piece of plastic wrap or foil and leave to dry in a cool place. When chocolate has completely set, gently peel away leaves. Use chocolate leaves for decorating cakes, ice creams, sherbets, mousses, and pastries.

4 To make chocolate-covered strawberries, choose firm, top quality fruit.

5 Leave stalks in place, then gently wash and dry each strawberry. Using a fork, dip fruit into melted chocolate until well coated. Dry as leaves in step 3.

TIP
Instead of strawberries, use walnut or pecan halves.

Chocolate Magic

Feathered Designs

A classic garnish for desserts, much used by top chefs.

Preparation time: about 30 minutes

FOR 4 PLATES
1 pound ripe apricots
1½ cups powdered sugar, sifted
1½ cups fresh or thawed frozen raspberries
2 teaspoons raspberry or apricot liqueur

EQUIPMENT
1 small knife
1 pastry bag made from non-stick baking
  parchment
1 wooden skewer or toothpick

1 To peel apricots, put into bowl and cover with boiling water. Let stand for 5 minutes. Drain and rinse under cold water, then peel off skins. Cut apricots in half, remove pits and put flesh into blender or food processor with half the powdered sugar. Blend to a smooth purée. Spoon into a clean bowl.

2 Gently wash raspberries (this is not necessary if frozen raspberries are being used) and blend to a smooth purée with remaining sugar and liqueur. Press through a fine strainer to remove seeds.

3 Cover dessert plates evenly with apricot sauce, tilting them a little to ensure sauce completely covers centers of plates.

4 Transfer raspberry purée to pastry bag and pipe rings of raspberry mixture through tiny hole in tip of pastry bag on top of apricot sauce, spacing lines out evenly and looking at picture for guidance.

5 Draw wooden skewer or toothpick in lines from center of plate to outer edge. Reverse procedure, working from outer edge to center to make snowflake design, see bottom right of picture.

Feathered Designs

Melon Vandyke

*An attractive way of presenting melon, especially when filled
with a colorful fruit salad.*

Preparation time: about 15 minutes

FOR 2 MELON BASKETS
1 medium-size Honeydew melon

FILLING
Fresh mixed fruit salad or sherbet
Mint leaves for decoration

EQUIPMENT
1 sharp kitchen knife
1 cutting board
1 tablespoon

1 When choosing a melon, press it gently on the top. If ripe, it will yield slightly to pressure and will have a lovely fragrant smell. Avoid melons which are hard and underripe.

2 Wash and dry melon, put onto cutting board then cut a thin slice away from top and bottom so that the halves will stand upright without falling over.

3 Place melon on its side and cut a deep vandyke pattern through the skin and flesh, slowly turning the fruit all the time and trying to keep cuts as even as possible.

4 Separate melon by carefully twisting and pulling two halves apart. Remove seeds with spoon.

5 Fill melon shell with lightly chilled fruit salad or scoops of sherbet. To serve, spoon fruit salad or sherbet and melon flesh onto plates and decorate with mint leaves.

Melon Vandyke

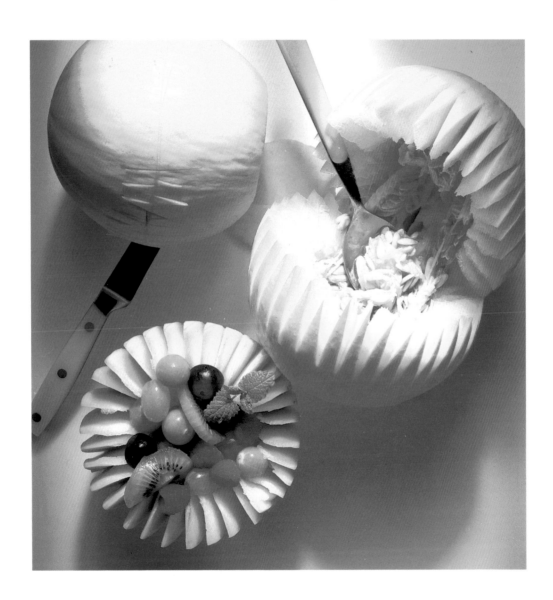

Dessert Spectacular

A magnificent array of mouth-watering desserts.

Preparation time: about 1¼ hours

½ Vandyke Melon, filled
    with 5 or 6 scoops of assorted ice cream
    or sherbet. Choose complementary
    flavors, but avoid mint, which can be
    overpowering.
Several chocolate-covered leaves
Chocolate-covered grapes, cherries, and
    strawberries
1 orange knot
1 orange twist
1 plate feathered with apricot and rasp-
    berry purée

1 Stand the filled melon half on the left of a large oval platter.

2 Add chocolate-covered leaves and fruit and orange knots to platter as shown in picture.

3 Top plate with feathered design with a selection of chocolate-covered fruits, some cut in half.

TIPS
Dip fruits and leaves into the apricot and raspberry purée before eating.
Scoop ice cream, sherbet and melon flesh onto plates before serving.

•NOTES•

•NOTES•

Ice Cream

Made Easy

Series
Consultant:
Jenni Fleetwood

GREAT
COOKING
VALUE

Introduction

For sheer indulgence, a bowl of homemade ice cream takes a lot of beating (as does the ice cream itself). For the creamiest results it is important that the ice crystals are broken up as soon as they form. This is easily achieved in an ice cream maker, but you don't need sophisticated equipment to make excellent ice cream - just patience and a firm wrist or hand-held electric mixer.

Use only top quality ingredients and remember to transfer firm ice cream to the refrigerator 30 minutes before serving to allow it to soften and 'ripen'. Alternatively, soften hard ice cream by warming it briefly in a microwave. Never refreeze ice cream after doing this.

Recipe Notes

All spoon measures are level:
1 tablespoon = 15ml spoon:
1 teaspoon = 5ml spoon.

Follow EITHER metric or Imperial measures and NEVER mix in one recipe as they are not interchangeable.

Eggs used are a medium unless otherwise stated.

Use unsalted butter for preference.

Freezing times listed in recipes refer to ice creams prepared in a home freezer; if using a freestanding ice cream maker. refer to your handbook for timing.

Written by Marey Kurz

Honey and Lime Ice Cream

Serves 6-8

Sophisticated ice cream with a hint of honey.

Preparation time: about 20 minutes plus cooling
Freezing time: 7-8 hours

Grated rind and juice of 2 limes, see Tip
4 tablespoons water
60g (2oz/¼ cup) preserving sugar
4 tablespoons pale creamy honey
250ml (8fl oz/1 cup) heavy cream

DECORATION
Lime slices
Mint leaves
Small spray of fresh flowers

1 Combine grated lime rind, measured water and preserving sugar in a saucepan. Stir over moderate heat until sugar has dissolved, then bring to the boil without further stirring.

2 When syrup boils, stir in lime juice and honey until dissolved. Boil for 30 seconds, then remove pan from heat. Cover with a clean cloth and set aside for 1 hour to cool and thicken. Unless using a free-standing ice cream maker, turn freezer to coldest setting.

3 Whip cream in a bowl until thick, then carefully fold in cooled honey mixture. Immediately transfer the mixture to a deep 1 litre (1¾ pt/4 cup) polythene freezer container.

4 Freeze mixture for 2 hours or until ice crystals have formed around the edges and mixture has started to solidify. Remove from the freezer and beat ice cream until smooth.

5 Cover ice cream and return to freezer. Repeat the beating process twice more, then leave ice cream until solid. Return freezer to normal setting.

6 Before serving ice cream, soften it in the refrigerator or microwave. Serve in scoops on individual plates, decorated with lime slices, mint leaves and fresh flowers.

TIP
When grating any citrus fruit, work over a sheet of greaseproof paper. Use a pastry brush to remove all the rind from the grater, then use the same brush to sweep the rind from the paper into the bowl or saucepan.

Approximate nutritional value per portion:
130 cal
Protein: 1g
Fat: 6g
Carbohydrate: 12g

Honey and Lime Ice Cream

Berry Sorbet

Serves 4

The ultimate refreshment for hot summer days.

Preparation time: about 20 minutes plus standing and cooling
Freezing time: 5-6 hours

315g (10oz) prepared berry fruits:
  redcurrants, blackcurrants, raspberries,
  blackberries, blueberries, strawberries
60g (2oz/¼ cup) sugar
1-2 tablespoons lemon juice
125ml (4fl oz/½ cup) water
60g (2oz/¼ cup) preserving sugar
Grated rind of ½ lemon
2 teaspoons raspberry brandy or liqueur
  (optional)

DECORATION
Mint sprig
Small spray of fresh redcurrants
Wafers

1 Wash berries if necessary, drain and place in a small bowl. Sprinkle with caster sugar. Drizzle with lemon juice, stir lightly, then cover bowl and set aside for 30 minutes. Stir occasionally.

2 Combine measured water, preserving sugar and lemon rind in a saucepan. Stir over moderate heat until sugar has dissolved, then bring to the boil without further stirring. Boil for 1 minute, then allow to cool for at least 30 minutes.

3 Purée fruit mixture in a blender or food processor, then rub through a sieve placed over a bowl. Add raspberry brandy or liqueur, if using.

4 Unless using a free-standing ice cream maker, turn freezer to coldest setting. Spoon ice cream mixture into a deep 500ml (16fl oz/2 cup) polythene freezer container.

5 Freeze mixture for 2 hours or until ice crystals have formed around the edges and mixture has started to solidify. Remove from the freezer and beat ice cream until perfectly smooth.

6 Cover ice cream and return it to freezer. Repeat the beating process twice more, then leave ice cream until solid. Return freezer to normal setting.

7 Before serving ice cream, soften it in the refrigerator or microwave. Serve in scoops or pipe in a large swirl in a glass serving dish. Decorate with redcurrants and serve with wafers.

Approximate nutritional value per portion:
130 cal
Protein: 2g
Fat: 2g
Carbohydrate: 30g

Berry Sorbet

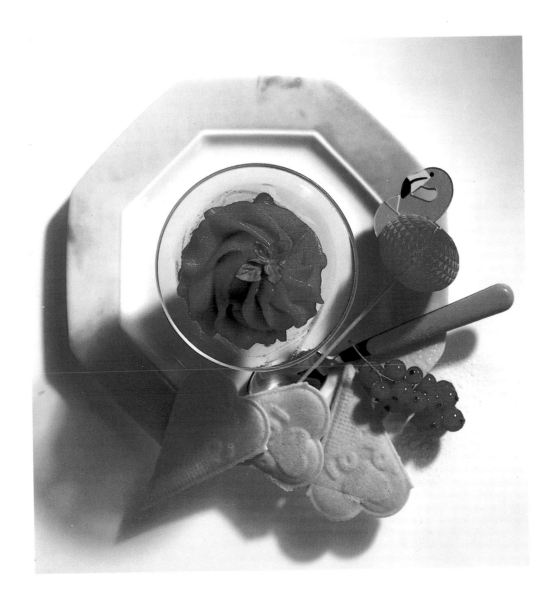

Peanut Ice Cream

Serves 6

All the creaminess of peanut butter and chocolate in a frozen taste sensation.

Preparation time: about 15 minutes plus cooling
Freezing time: 5-6 hours

60g (2oz) crunchy peanut butter
60g (2oz) white chocolate
4 tablespoons pale creamy honey
4 tablespoons orange juice
1 tablespoon lemon juice
2 teaspoons orange liqueur or to taste
250ml (8fl oz/1 cup) heavy cream

DECORATION
Whipped cream
Chopped peanuts

1 Spoon peanut butter into a heatproof bowl which fits over a saucepan, or into a bowl suitable for the microwave. Break chocolate into squares and add to bowl with honey and orange juice.

2 Stand bowl over a pan of gently simmering water. Stir constantly until ingredients melt to form a smooth sauce. Alternatively, heat mixture in microwave on Full Power for 60-90 seconds, then whisk until smooth.

3 Set melted mixture aside until cool, stirring occasionally, then stir in lemon juice with liqueur.

4 In a separate bowl, whip cream until stiff. Stir 1 tablespoon of the whipped cream into the peanut mixture to lighten it, then carefully fold in the remainder.

5 Unless using a free-standing ice cream maker, turn freezer to coldest setting. Spoon ice cream mixture into a deep 600ml (1pt/2½ cup) polythene freezer container.

6 Freeze mixture for 5-6 hours or until solid. It will not be necessary to beat the ice cream during the freezing process. Return freezer to normal setting.

7 Before serving ice cream, soften it in the refrigerator or microwave. Serve in scoops, with whipped cream and chopped peanuts.

NOTE
Peanuts can cause a severe allergic reaction in susceptible individuals. Always advise guests when peanuts are used in a recipe.

Approximate nutritional value per portion:
330 cal
Protein: 5g
Fat: 26g
Carbohydrate: 22g

Peanut Ice Cream

Rum Tortoni

Serves 6

A delicious ice cream based on an Italian meringue mix.

Preparation time: about 25 minutes
Freezing time: 6-7 hours

1 teaspoon powdered gelatine
1 tablespoon water
125ml (4fl oz/$^1/_2$ cup) milk
60g (2oz) unsalted butter, diced
$^1/_2$ teaspoon vanilla flavoring
3 egg whites
90g (3oz/$^1/_2$ cup) powdered sugar, sifted
1 teaspoon lemon juice
125g (4oz) hazelnut biscuits or macaroons,
    crumbed
1 tablespoon white rum or 1 teaspoon rum
    flavoring

1 Sprinkle gelatine over measured water in a small bowl. Leave to soften for 2-3 minutes.

2 Combine milk, butter and vanilla flavoring or vanilla sugar in a saucepan over gentle heat. Stir until milk is warm and butter has melted, then remove pan from the heat and stir in gelatine until completely dissolved. Allow to cool, whisking mixture occasionally.

3 Beat egg whites in a large mixing bowl until stiff, using a whisk or hand-held electric mixer. Gradually add icing sugar, continuing to beat until meringue is shiny and thick and stands in peaks when whisk or beaters are lifted out of bowl. Add lemon juice and whisk for 30 seconds more.

4 Whisk cooled milk mixture. Gradually fold it into stiffly beaten egg whites.

5 Unless using a free-standing ice cream maker, turn freezer to coldest setting. Spoon ice cream mixture into a deep 1 litre (1¾ pt/4 cup) polythene freezer container.

6 Freeze mixture for 2 hours or until ice crystals have formed around the edges and mixture has started to solidify. Remove from the freezer and beat ice cream until smooth. Fold in biscuit crumbs and rum or rum flavouring.

7 Cover ice cream and return it to freezer. Leave until solid. Return freezer to normal setting.

8 Before serving ice cream, soften it in the refrigerator or microwave. Serve in scoops, with cocktail cherries and wafers.

Approximate nutritional value per portion:
257 cal
Protein: 4g
Fat: 13.5g
Carbohydrate: 30g

Rum Tortoni

Yogurt Ice Cream with Berries

Serves 10

White chocolate and whipping cream give this ice cream great taste appeal.

Preparation time: about 30 minutes plus cooling
Freezing time: 7-8 hours

250g (8oz) prepared berry fruits: redcurrants, blackcurrants, blackberries, strawberries, blueberries
60g (2oz/¼ cup) sugar
60ml (2fl oz/¼ cup) water
1 tablespoon lemon juice
315g (10oz) full cream Greek yogurt
110g (3½ oz) white chocolate, broken into squares
250ml (8fl oz/1 cup) heavy cream
1 tablespoon powdered sugar

1 Cut large strawberries in half or quarters. Set aside a quarter of the fruit for decoration.

2 Place remaining berries in a saucepan with preserving sugar, measured water and lemon juice. Simmer until fruit is soft, then press mixture through a sieve into a bowl. Set aside to cool.

3 Spoon about one third of the yogurt into a heatproof bowl which fits over a saucepan. Add chocolate.

4 Place bowl over hot water, stirring until ingredients melt to form a smooth sauce - this will take about 10 minutes. Whisk in remaining yogurt.

5 In a bowl, whip cream with powdered sugar until stiff; carefully fold into yogurt and chocolate mixture.

6 Unless using a free-standing ice cream maker, turn freezer to coldest setting. Spoon ice cream mixture into a deep 1 litre (1¾ pt/4 cup) polythene freezer container.

7 Freeze mixture for 2 hours or until ice crystals have formed around the edges and mixture has started to solidify. Remove from the freezer and beat ice cream until smooth. Swirl in fruit purée mixture to give a marbled effect.

8 Cover ice cream and return to freezer for 5-6 hours or until solid. Return freezer to normal setting.

9 Before serving ice cream, soften it in the refrigerator or microwave. Serve in scoops with reserved fruit and dessert biscuits.

Approximate nutritional value per portion:
160 cal
Protein: 2g
Fat: 10g
Carbohydrate: 14g

Yogurt Ice Cream with Berries

Nectarine Ice Cream

Serves 4

This delicately flavoured fruit ice cream is at its best when freshly made.

Preparation time: about 20 minutes
Freezing time: 5-6 hours

¹/₃ vanilla bean
125ml (4fl oz/¹/₂ cup) water
60g (2oz/¹/₄ cup) sugar
4 tablespoons pale creamy honey
250g/8 oz ripe nectarines
2 tablespoons lemon juice
250ml (8fl oz/1 cup) heavy cream
Whipped cream and nectarine slices to
   decorate

1 Using a sharp knife, slit vanilla bean lengthwise. Place in a saucepan with measured water and sugar. Heat gently, uncovered, for 5 minutes. Remove vanilla bean, scraping out pith into sugar solution. Add honey and stir until dissolved. Set aside to cool.

2 Place nectarines in a heatproof bowl. Pour over boiling water to cover. Set aside for 1-2 minutes, then drain and rinse under cold water. Cut a cross in the top of each fruit and slip off skins. Chop flesh into large chunks.

3 Purée nectarine chunks with cooled sugar solution and lemon juice in a blender or food processor. Add cream and blend again until thoroughly mixed.

4 Unless using a free-standing ice cream maker, turn freezer to coldest setting. Spoon ice cream mixture into a deep 600ml (1pt/2¹/₂ cup) polythene freezer container.

5 Freeze mixture for 2 hours or until ice crystals have formed around the edges and mixture has started to solidify. Remove from the freezer and beat ice cream until smooth.

6 Cover ice cream and return it to freezer. Repeat the beating process twice more, then leave ice cream until solid. Return freezer to normal setting. If using a fast-freeze ice cream maker, freeze mixture for 20 minutes, then transfer to a polythene tub and place in the freezer for 10 minutes.

7 Before serving ice cream, soften it in the refrigerator or microwave. Serve in scoops, decorated with whipped cream and nectarine slices.

Approximate nutritional value per portion:
290 cal
Protein: 2g
Fat: 16g
Carbohydrate: 32g

Nectarine Ice Cream

Marble Ice Cream Cake

Serves 12

This delicious ice cream cake can be stored in the freezer for up to a week.

Preparation time: about 40 minutes
Freezing time: 8-9 hours

4 eggs
125g (4 oz/³/₄ cup) powdered sugar
1 teaspoon vanilla flavoring or 4 teaspoons
    vanilla sugar
375 ml (12fl oz/1¹/₂ cups) heavy
    cream
110g (3¹/₂ oz) plain (dark) chocolate
60 ml (2fl oz/¹/₄ cup) milk

1 Rinse a 1 kg (2lb) loaf tin with cold water, drain and place in freezer until required. Turn freezer to coldest setting.

2 Place 2 of the eggs in a mixing bowl. Sift in half the powdered sugar. Add half the vanilla flavoring or vanilla sugar. Using a hand-held electric mixer whisk the mixture for about 5 minutes until pale and creamy.

3 Whip half the cream with 1 tablespoon of the remaining powdered sugar until stiff. Fold into egg mixture lightly but thoroughly, then spread evenly in loaf tin. Cover and freeze for 2 hours.

4 Break chocolate into squares and place in a heatproof bowl which fits over a saucepan, or in a bowl suitable for use in the microwave. Add milk. Stand bowl over a pan of gently simmering water. Stir constantly until chocolate melts into milk. Alternatively, heat mixture in microwave on Full Power for 60 seconds, then whisk until smooth. Cool.

5 In a bowl, whisk remaining eggs with 3 tablespoons of the remaining powdered sugar and the remaining vanilla flavoring or sugar until pale and creamy. Stir in cooled chocolate mixture.

6 Whip remaining cream with rest of icing sugar until stiff. Fold into chocolate mixture lightly but thoroughly, then spread over partially frozen ice cream in tin. Using a fork and a spiral action, whirl both mixtures together. Smooth surface, cover and freeze ice cream cake for a further 6-7 hours, preferably overnight. Return freezer to normal setting.

7 Serve in slices, decorated with cherries, if liked.

Approximate nutritional value per portion:
220 cal
Protein: 4g
Fat: 16g
Carbohydrate: 16g

Marble Ice Cream Cake

Cocochoc Ice Cream

Serves 8

Rich cubes of melt-in-the-mouth ice cream.

Preparation time: about 25 minutes
Freezing time: 12-18 hours

60g (2oz) creamed coconut, broken into
    cubes
60g (2oz) plain (dark) chocolate, broken
    into squares
2 eggs, separated
60g (2oz/⅓ cup) powdered sugar, sifted
2 teaspoons orange or almond liqueur

1 Turn freezer to coldest setting.
Combine creamed coconut and
chocolate in a heatproof bowl which fits
over a saucepan.

2 Stand bowl over a pan of gently
simmering water. Stir frequently until
ingredients melt to form a smooth sauce.
Allow chocolate mixture to cool but do not
let it solidify. Stir frequently while cooling.

3 In a bowl, whisk egg whites with 1
tablespoon of the powdered sugar
until stiff.

4 Place egg yolks in a separate bowl,
add remaining powdered sugar and
liqueur and whisk until pale and thick. Stir in
chocolate mixture, 1 or 2 tablespoons at a
time, until mixture is smooth, creamy and
evenly colored.

5 Beat in 2 tablespoons of the stiffly
beaten egg whites to lighten the
mixture, then fold in the rest.

6 Pour mixture into a shallow 23cm (7in)
square freezer container. Cover and
freeze for at least 12 hours or until mixture is
firm enough to slice. Return freezer to
normal setting.

7 Cut ice cream into cubes. Arrange five
cubes on each dessert plate, decorate
with whipped cream and chocolate
caraque and serve.

TIP
To make chocolate caraque, pour melted
chocolate onto a clean ceramic or marble
surface and spread out smoothly with clean
palette knife. Leave until set, then, holding
blade of knife at an acute angle to chocolate, draw it across to shave chocolate into
curls and flakes.

Approximate nutritional value per portion:
120 cal
Protein: 3g
Fat: 6g
Carbohydrate: 13g

Cocochoc Ice Cream

Mozart Ice

Serves 8

This symphony of flavors will ensure a special meal ends on a high note.

Preparation time: about 30 minutes
Freezing time: 7-8 hours

110g (3½ oz) chocolate and hazelnut
    spread
2 eggs, beaten
30g (1oz) ground hazelnuts
1 teaspoon lemon juice
1 tablespoon almond liqueur
300ml (10fl oz/1¼ cups) heavy
    cream
60g (2oz/⅓ cup) powdered sugar
Whipped cream and grated chocolate
    to decorate

1 Spoon chocolate and hazelnut spread into a heatproof bowl which fits over a saucepan. Stand bowl over a pan of gently simmering water and stir constantly until melted. Whisk until smooth.

2 Allow chocolate mixture to cool slightly, then stir in beaten eggs, a little at a time, so that mixture remains smooth.

3 Place ground hazelnuts in a bowl. Stir in lemon juice and liqueur, then stir into chocolate mixture.

4 Whip cream with powdered sugar until stiff. Gradually fold in hazelnut mixture.

5 Unless using a free-standing ice cream maker, turn freezer to coldest setting. Spoon ice cream mixture into to a deep 1 litre (1¾ pt/4 cup) polythene freezer container.

6 Freeze mixture for 2 hours or until ice crystals have formed around the edges and mixture has started to solidify. Remove from the freezer and beat until smooth.

7 Cover ice cream and return to freezer until solid. Return freezer to normal setting.

8 Before serving ice cream, soften it in the refrigerator or microwave. Serve in scoops, decorated with whipped cream and grated chocolate. Offer dessert biscuits, if liked.

Approximate nutritional value per portion:
314 cal
Protein: 4g
Fat: 25g
Carbohydrate: 18g

Mozart Ice

Pineapple Ice Cream

Serves 8

Tiny chunks of fresh pineapple make this ice cream particularly fruity. For the best flavor it should be eaten within a day or two of freezing.

Preparation time: about 20 minutes
Freezing time: about 8 hours

1 fresh pineapple, about 750g (1½ lb)
2 tablespoons lemon juice
100g (3½ oz) white chocolate
60ml (2fl oz/¼ cup) milk
250 ml (8fl oz/1 cup) heavy cream
3 tablespoons powdered sugar. sifted
Mint leaves and quartered baby pineapples
   to serve

1 Remove leaves from pineapple and cut off peel thickly, removing any eyes. Cut flesh away from the hard core lengthwise, then slice into very thin strips. Cut each strip into tiny chunks.

2 Place pineapple chunks and any juice in a bowl. Pour in lemon juice and stir to coat. Cover and set aside.

3 Break chocolate into squares and place in a heatproof bowl which fits over a saucepan, or into a bowl suitable for use in the microwave. Add milk. Stand bowl over a pan of gently simmering water. Stir constantly until ingredients melt to form a smooth sauce. Alternatively, heat mixture in microwave on Full Power for 60-90 seconds, then whisk until smooth. Cool, stirring.

4 Whip cream with powdered sugar until thick. Stir about 2 tablespoons of the cream into the chocolate mixture, then fold in the remainder, Finally, fold in pineapple chunks with juice.

5 Unless using a free-standing ice cream maker, turn freezer to coldest setting. Spoon ice cream mixture into a deep 750ml (1¼ pt/3 cup) polythene freezer container.

6 Freeze mixture for 2 hours or until ice crystals have formed around the edges and mixture has started to solidify. Remove from the freezer and beat until smooth.

7 Cover ice cream and return to freezer. Repeat the beating process twice more, then leave ice cream until solid. Return freezer to normal setting.

8 Before serving ice cream, soften it in the refrigerator or microwave. Serve in scoops, decorated with mint sprigs and quartered baby pineapples.

Approximate nutritional value per portion:
105 cal
Protein: 2g
Fat: 2g
Carbohydrate: 13g

Pineapple Ice Cream

Ginger Ice Cream

Serves 8

Go for the burn or chill out with this marvellous combination of ginger and ice cream!

Preparation time: about 25 minutes
Freezing time: 6-7 hours

300ml (10fl oz/1¼ cup) heavy cream
2 tablespoons brandy
4 eggs, separated
155g (5oz/1 cup) powdered sugar
3 tablespoons chopped preserved ginger
1 quantity Bitter Chocolate Sauce

1 Whip cream with brandy in a bowl until soft peaks form. In a separate bowl, beat egg whites until stiff, using a whisk or hand-held electric mixer. Gradually add powdered sugar, continuing to beat until mixture is shiny and thick and stands in peaks when whisk or beaters are lifted out of bowl.

2 Beat egg yolks in a third bowl until frothy, then fold in stiffly beaten egg whites. Fold in brandy-flavored whipped cream with metal spoon.

3 Unless using a free-standing ice cream maker, turn freezer to coldest setting. Spoon ice cream mixture into a deep 750ml (1¼ pt/3 cup) polythene freezer container.

4 Freeze mixture for 2 hours or until ice crystals have formed around the edges and mixture has started to solidify. Remove from the freezer and beat ice cream until smooth.

5 Cover ice cream and return it to freezer. When the ice cream is on the verge of freezing, fold in chopped ginger, then return to freezer again until solid. Return freezer to normal setting.

6 Before serving ice cream, soften it in the refrigerator or microwave. Spoon a pool of Bitter Chocolate Sauce on 8 dessert plates and center a scoop of ice cream on top. Serve with wafers.

Approximate nutritional value per portion:
385 cal
Protein: 4g
Fat: 30g
Carbohydrate: 27g

Ginger Ice Cream

Light Fantastic

Serves 4

Creating an ice cream which is low in calories yet tastes terrific is easy when you follow this simple recipe. Serve as soon as possible after freezing.

Preparation time: about 15 minutes
Freezing time: 5-6 hours

2 teaspoons powdered gelatine
2 tablespoons water
125 ml (4fl oz/½ cup) milk
2 tablespoons sugar
Vanilla flavoring to taste
1 teaspoon liquid sweetener
Pinch saffron powder
1 small ripe banana
2 tablespoons lemon juice
125 ml (4fl oz/½ cup) buttermilk
1 egg white

1 Sprinkle gelatine over measured water in a small heatproof bowl. Leave to soften for 2-3 minutes.

2 Combine milk, sugar and vanilla flavoring in a saucepan. Heat gently, stirring until sugar has dissolved. Bring to the boil, then remove from the heat. Whisk in gelatine mixture until completely dissolved, then whisk in liquid sweetener and saffron.

3 Slice banana into a blender or food processor. Add lemon juice, buttermilk and milk mixture. Process until smooth.

4 Whisk egg white in a bowl until stiff. Fold in banana mixture. Unless using a free-standing ice cream maker, turn freezer to coldest setting. Spoon ice cream mixture into a deep 500ml (16fl oz/2 cup) polythene freezer container.

5 Freeze mixture for 2 hours or until ice crystals have formed around the edges and mixture has started to solidify. Remove from the freezer and beat ice cream until smooth.

6 Cover ice cream and return to freezer. Repeat the beating process twice more, then leave the ice cream until solid. Return freezer to normal setting.

7 Before serving ice cream, soften it in the refrigerator or microwave. Serve in scoops, decorated with sliced banana, if liked.

Approximate nutritional value per portion:
38 cal
Protein: 2g
Fat: 1g
Carbohydrate: 4g

Light Fantastic

•NOTES•

◆NOTES◆

Kids Cooking

Made Easy

Series Consultant: **Sonia Allison**

GREAT COOKING VALUE

Introduction

Cooking is fun – and easy too – with the help of this little book and the guidance of an adult. All that is needed to get started are the utensils shown here, plus a set of measuring spoons and a liquid measure, the ingredients listed in your chosen recipe, and a large sprinkling of enthusiasm. There are lots of tasty recipes to try like Favorite Spaghetti, Campfire Potatoes, Yummy Chocolate Fruit Kabobs and Apple Crunchies.

Now a word of advice. Read through each recipe from start to finish before you begin, and gather together all the utensils and ingredients you will need. This way, you will not forget anything important.

Use standard spoon and cup measures, making sure they are level.

Written by Martina Reigl

Rise and Shine Breakfast

Serves 2

Guaranteed to get you jumping out of bed.

Time to make: 15 minutes

INGREDIENTS

2 tablespoons porridge oats
2 teaspoons unsalted peanuts, chopped
  (See Note)
2 teaspoons raisins
2 teaspoons clear honey
1 apple
1 banana
$\frac{2}{3}$ cup Greek-style yogurt

UTENSILS

Measuring spoons
2 small cereal bowls
1 teaspoon
1 cutting board
1 small knife

1 Put 1 tablespoon of porridge oats into each cereal bowl.

2 Add 1 teaspoon of nuts, raisins, and honey to each bowl.

3 Wash apple and wipe it dry. Carefully cut apple in fourths with a small knife on cutting board, then remove core from each. Slice pieces of apple thinly. Add half the slices to each bowl.

4 Peel banana and cut in slices on board. Add to the bowls, making sure each bowl has the same amount.

5 Divide the yogurt among the bowls. Mix well and breakfast is ready!

NOTE

Some people are allergic to peanuts, so always check before you add peanuts to a recipe.

TIPS

Try adding strawberries and cherries as well as the apple and banana.
If you want to surprise your parents over the weekend with breakfast, double all the ingredients given above.

Rise and Shine Breakfast

Tough Guy Egg Scramble

Serves 2

A super weekend breakfast for you and the family.

Time to make: 20 minutes

INGREDIENTS

Small bunch of fresh chives
2 large green lettuce leaves
4 eggs
4 tablespoons milk
4 pinches of salt
1 tablespoon soft margarine
2 large slices of whole-wheat bread

UTENSILS

1 cutting board
1 small knife
Mixing bowl
Measuring spoons
1 hand whisk
1 medium-size saucepan
1 wooden spoon
Oven gloves or pot holders
2 plates

1 Wash chives and shake dry. Put onto board and chop into small pieces with knife. Wash lettuce leaves and shake dry.

2 Crack eggs into bowl. Pour in milk. Add salt. Using hand whisk, beat mixture until frothy.

3 Place saucepan on one of the burners on top of the stove. Add margarine to pan and melt over a low heat. Pour in beaten eggs and milk. Lower heat. Using wooden spoon, cook and stir eggs until they thicken and just begin to set.

4 With oven gloves or pot holders, carefully move pan away from heat and switch off heat. Give eggs a gentle stir one more time with wooden spoon to make creamy pieces of set egg that cooks call scrambled egg. The mixture should be saucy and not too dry.

5 Put bread slices (or toast, if you prefer) onto 2 plates. Cover each one with a lettuce leaf. Spoon the scrambled egg on top. Sprinkle with chives.

TIP

Another way of cutting up chives is to use clean kitchen shears.

Tough Guy Egg Scramble

Magic Pancakes

Serves 2

These are made with mushrooms and are full of flavor.

Time to make: 30 minutes

INGREDIENTS

4 eggs
3 tablespoons milk
2 teaspoons all-purpose flour
4 pinches of salt
8 mushrooms, shaped like shallow cups
2 tablespoons margarine

UTENSILS

1 mixing bowl
Measuring spoons
1 hand whisk
Paper towels
1 cutting board
1 small knife
1 large skillet
Saucepan lid (see step 7, page 34)
1 wooden spoon
Oven gloves or pot holders
Slotted draining spoon
2 plates

1 Crack eggs into mixing bowl. Spoon in the milk, flour, and salt. Beat ingredients together with hand whisk until mixture is smooth and frothy.

2 Rinse mushrooms under cold water and pat dry with paper towels. Put mushrooms onto cutting board. Carefully cut in fairly thin slices with knife. Melt half the margarine in the skillet over a medium heat.

3 Add mushrooms and sauté until golden brown, stirring them all the time with the wooden spoon and holding the handle of the skillet with oven gloves or pot holders. Lift mushrooms out of pan with slotted draining spoon. Add to bowl with egg mixture.

4 With oven gloves or pot holders, return pan to heat and add rest of margarine. When margarine has melted and is just beginning to sizzle, carefully pour in the egg and mushroom mixture.

5 Cook egg mixture over a medium heat until underneath part and edges are set. Turn pancake over, with the help of the saucepan lid.

6 Put pan back over heat and slide pancake back into the skillet. Cook until second side of pancake is well done, dry and golden brown. Slide out onto plate. Switch off heat. Cut pancake into 2 halves. Put second half onto second plate. Eat pancake straight away with bread or rolls and butter. Cut up tomatoes are delicious with the pancake.

Magic Pancakes

Salad Cooler

Serves 2

A quick, colorful and refreshing salad for hot summer days.

Time to make: 20 minutes

INGREDIENTS
2 medium-size tomatoes
1 small cucumber
4 fresh parsley sprigs
½ medium-size lemon
⅔ cup plain yogurt
2 pinches of salt
1 tablespoon corn oil
2-ounce piece of feta or Muenster cheese

UTENSILS
Paper towels
1 cutting board
1 small knife
1 large bowl
1 lemon squeezer
1 small bowl
Measuring spoons
1 hand whisk
2 large plates

1 Pull stalks out of tomatoes and throw away. Rinse tomatoes and cucumber under cold water and wipe dry with paper towels. Put cucumber onto cutting board, then carefully cut off the ends with knife. Carefully cut cucumber in thin slices. Carefully cut tomatoes in fourths, then cut each wedge in thin slices. Put cucumber and tomatoes into the large bowl.

2 Rinse parsley under cold running water and shake dry over kitchen sink. Put onto cutting board and carefully cut into tiny pieces. Throw away the stalks. Sqeeze juice from lemon half with a lemon squeezer.

3 Put yogurt into second bowl. Add pinches of salt, lemon juice, two-thirds of the parsley, and the oil.

4 Beat yogurt mixture with hand whisk until all ingredients are mixed together.

5 Cut cheese into little squares on cutting board. Divide the tomato and cucumber mixture among 2 plates and sprinkle with rest of the chopped parsley. Spoon yogurt mixture onto center of salads. Dot with cheese as shown in picture. Eat with rolls and butter.

Salad Cooler

Rice Feast

Serves 2

Rice cooked with peas and cheese makes a tasty treat.

Time to make: 40 minutes

INGREDIENTS

6 heaping tablespoons frozen peas
2 cups water
1 teaspoon salt
8 tablespoons easy-cook long-grain
   white rice
1 tablespoon butter or margarine
2 pinches of salt
4 tablespoons shredded Cheddar cheese
   or Monterey Jack
2 teaspoons chopped parsley

UTENSILS

Measuring spoons
1 large plate
Liquid measure
1 large saucepanwith its lid
1 fork
Oven gloves or pot holders

1 Spoon peas onto a large plate.

2 Measure the water in the liquid measure and pour into saucepan. Add 1 teaspoon salt. Place saucepan onto one of the burners on top of the stove and bring the water to a boil. Carefully spoon rice into water and stir with fork.

3 Lower heat, cover saucepan with lid and cook rice, without peeping, for 10-15 minutes or for the time it says on the package.

4 Using oven gloves or pot holders, take the pan off the heat, holding the handle firmly.

5 Add butter or margarine, peas, and pinches of salt to saucepan. Stir with fork until ingredients are mixed together. Cover pan and put back on the stove, over a low heat.

6 Cook rice mixture gently for 5 minutes. Stir in two-thirds of cheese with fork. Switch off heat. Spoon rice and peas onto 2 plates. Sprinkle with rest of cheese and the chopped parsley. Serve hot.

Rice Feast

Campfire Potatoes

Serves 2

Baked with salt and herbs, these potatoes are great for dunking.

Time to make: 1 hour

INGREDIENTS

6 small potatoes
2 tablespoons corn oil
1 teaspoon salt
1 teaspoon dried rosemary
Small bunch of fresh chives
8 tablespoons softened cream cheese
5 tablespoons milk

UTENSILS

1 vegetable brush
1 cutting board
1 knife
Measuring spoons
1 roasting pan
1 pastry brush
1 small bowl
Serving bowl for dip
Oven gloves or pot holders
1 heatproof pad or saucepan stand
2 plates

1 Ask an adult to help you switch the oven to 400°F. Clean potatoes by scrubbing them with a vegetable brush under cold running water. Put onto cutting board. Carefully cut each potato in half lengthwise with a small knife.

2 Pour 1 tablespoon oil into roasting pan and spread evenly over side of pan with pastry brush. Arrange potato halves in pan, cut sides up and skin sides down. Drizzle another tablespoon oil over cut sides of potatoes and brush with a pastry brush.

3 Sprinkle potatoes evenly with salt and rosemary. Carefully put into preheated oven and bake for 30-40 minutes or until cooked.

4 Meanwhile, rinse chives and shake dry. Put onto cutting board and cut in small pieces. Spoon cream cheese into small bowl. Beat in the milk and salt to taste. Stir thoroughly until well mixed to make dip. Lastly stir in chives, keeping back a spoonful. Spoon mixture into serving bowl and sprinkle spoonful of chives on top.

5 Using oven gloves or pot holders, carefully take pan of potatoes out of oven and stand on heatproof pad or saucepan stand. Let pan cool slightly for 1 minute. Switch off oven. Put potato halves onto 2 plates and serve with dip.

Campfire Potatoes

Favorite Spaghetti

Serves 2

Spaghetti mixed with tomatoes and cheese makes the perfect dish for when you are very hungry.

Time to make: 40 minutes

INGREDIENTS

8-ounce can of tomatoes
2 tablespoons corn oil
2 teaspoons fresh chopped basil or 1
    teaspoon dried basil
2 pinches of salt and 1 teaspoon salt
8 ounces spaghetti
2 tablespoons grated Parmesan cheese

UTENSILS

1 can opener
1 strainer
1 small bowl
1 plate
1 small knife
1 small saucepan and lid
Measuring spoons
1 wooden spoon
1 large saucepan
Oven gloves or pot holders
2 plates

1 Ask an adult to help you open can of tomatoes. Place strainer over small bowl and tip tomatoes into strainer so that the juice goes into the bowl. Tip tomatoes onto plate and carefully cut in small pieces with knife.

2 Place small saucepan on one of the burners on top of the stove. Switch the heat to medium and pour in 1 tablespoon oil. Add cut-up tomatoes, basil, and both pinches of salt. Cover pan with lid. Cook tomatoes for 15 minutes. Stir with wooden spoon every 5 minutes. Switch off heat.

3 Two-thirds fill large saucepan with water. Add teaspoon of salt. Place pan on one of the burners on the top of the stove. Switch the heat to high, cover the pan with lid and bring water to a boil. Carefully lift off lid with oven gloves or pot holders.

4 Add spaghetti to boiling water. As the ends soften, push spaghetti into the water. Stir with wooden spoon to stop pasta sticking together. Lower heat under saucepan. Cook spaghetti for 10 minutes. Take pan off heat and switch off heat. Remember to hold handle with oven gloves or pot holders. Ask an adult to hold strainer over sink and help you drain spaghetti through strainer. Take great care not to burn yourself.

5 Divide spaghetti among 2 plates. Top each with cooked tomatoes. Lastly, sprinkle with Parmesan. Add a fresh basil sprig, if you like, and serve hot.

Favorite Spaghetti

Step-by-step

THE ELECTRIC STOVE

1 Each switch works a different burner, sometimes indicated by colored dots.

2 There may be numbers on the switches. The higher the number, the hotter the burner will become.

3 When cooking is finished, switch off the heat. Remove pan with pot holders.

THE OVEN

4 Every oven has a large roasting pan and rack. For most cooking purposes, you will need the pan without the rack.

5 There are usually 4 or 5 shelves in the oven, on which the pan sits. For recipes in this book, use the center shelf.

6 Every oven has a temperature control switch. The higher the temperature, the hotter the oven. The stove in the picture shows °C, but your cooker will probably show °F. Remember to switch off the oven when you have finished cooking.

ELECTRIC HAND MIXER

7 Always handle the mixer with dry hands.

8 Most electric mixers have 2 whisks and 2 kneading hooks.

9 Fit the whisks into the 2 holes under the front of the mixer. Fix into a socket and switch on before using. Switch off and unplug when you've finished.

Always ask an adult to watch over you when using electrical equipment.

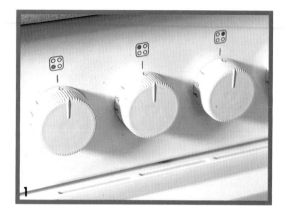

1

4

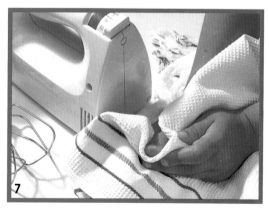

7

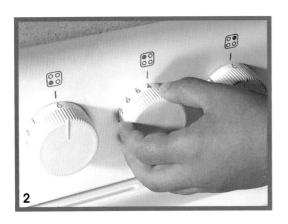

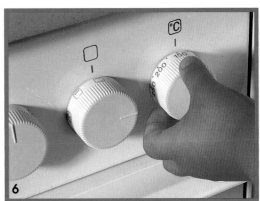

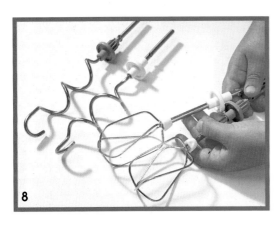

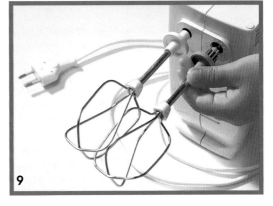

Banana Express

Serves 2

Quick and easy to make when you get home from school.

Time to make: 20 minutes

INGREDIENTS

4 slices of whole-wheat bread
Some butter or margarine for spreading
4 slices of cooked ham
½ lemon
2 bananas
4 slices process cheese
a few fresh chives

UTENSILS

1 toaster
1 cutting board
1 small knife
1 lemon squeezer
1 cookie sheet
Oven gloves or pot holders
1 heatproof pad
1 turner
2 plates

1 Toast bread in toaster. Put onto the cutting board. Spread evenly with butter or margarine.

2 Ask an adult to help you switch the oven to 400°F. Arrange ham on cutting board and carefully cut each slice in half. Put ham on top of toast.

3 Squeeze juice from lemon with lemon squeezer. Peel bananas. Put onto cutting board. Carefully cut in slices. Put equal amounts of bananas onto slices of toast, on top of ham. Sprinkle with lemon juice.

4 Cover bananas completely with slices of process cheese.

5 Arrange covered toast slices on cookie sheet. Carefully place cookie sheet in oven and cook toasts until cheese has melted, checking after 3 minutes. Melting the cheese should not take more than about 5 minutes.

6 Using oven gloves or pot holders, carefully take the cookie sheet out of the oven. Stand it on top of the stove or on a heatproof pad. Switch off oven. With the help of a turner, lift the toasts onto 2 plates. Carefully cut chives into small pieces with a small knife on cutting board. Sprinkle chives over toasts. Eat straight away.

Banana Express

Tomatoes in Bed

Serves 2

These taste yummy served with bread and butter.

Time to make: 30 minutes

INGREDIENTS

2 large tomatoes
4 pinches of salt
5 tablespoons corn oil
1 teaspoon dried basil
4 tablespoons dry bread crumbs (these are
 sold already dried in tubs or packages)
1 tablespoon grated Parmesan cheese

UTENSILS

paper towels
1 cutting board
1 knife
Measuring spoons
1 heatproof dish
1 pastry brush
1 mixing bowl
Oven gloves or pot holders
1 heatproof pad
2 plates

1 Ask an adult to help you switch the oven to 400°F. Pull stalks out of tomatoes and throw away. Wash tomatoes. Wipe dry with paper towels. Put tomatoes onto cutting board. Cut each one in half around the center. Sprinkle tomatoes with 2 pinches of salt.

2 Pour 1 tablespoon oil into heatproof dish. Brush it over bottom and side with pastry brush. Put tomatoes into dish, cut sides up and skin sides down.

3 Tip basil into mixing bowl. Add bread crumbs, 2 pinches of salt and all the remaining oil. Stir to mix.

4 Cover tomatoes carefully with bread crumb mixture, sprinkling it over with spoon and gently pressing it down with your fingertips.

5 Sprinkle cheese over tomatoes. Using oven gloves or pot holders, carefully put dish into oven.

6 Cook tomatoes for 12 minutes. Using oven gloves or pot holders again, carefully take dish out of oven. Put onto heatproof pad. Turn off oven. Using spoon, lift tomatoes onto the 2 plates. Eat while still hot.

Tomatoes in Bed

Captains and Pirates

Serves 2

Cheese slices make a super sauce for fish sticks.

Time to make: 15 minutes

INGREDIENTS
10 frozen fish sticks
3 tablespoons corn oil
5 slices of process cheese
Small bunch of fresh parsley

UTENSILS
1 large plate
1 large skillet
Measuring spoons
1 turner
1 cutting board
1 small knife
1 heatproof dish
1 pastry brush
Oven gloves or pot holders
2 plates

1 Ask an adult to help you switch oven to 425°F. Put the frozen fish sticks onto large plate.

2 Put skillet on one of the burners on the top of the stove. switch heat to medium and add 2 tablespoons of oil to skillet. Heat the oil for a few seconds. Add all the fish sticks and cook for 3 minutes. Turn over with turner. Lower heat and cook sticks for 3 minutes more.

3 Take pan off heat, then switch off heat. Put cheese slices onto cutting board. Cut each slice in half.

4 Pour last tablespoon of oil into heat-proof dish. Brush over bottom and side with pastry brush. Fill with layers of fish sticks and cheese.

5 Using oven gloves or pot holders, carefully put dish into oven. Cook for about 5 minutes, until cheese melts. Rinse parsley and shake dry. Put onto cutting board and carefully cut into small pieces with knife.

6 Again using oven gloves or pot holders, take dish of fish sticks and cheese out of oven. Switch off oven. Sprinkle fish sticks with parsley and spoon out onto 2 plates. Serve with peas.

Captains and Pirates

Cherry Bread Pudding

Serves 2

Serve this pudding with vanilla ice cream.

Time to make: 1 hour

INGREDIENTS

2 white bread rolls
2 cups milk
2 tablespoons sugar
2 tablespoons chopped peanuts (unsalted
  ones are best, but see Note on page 4)
1 egg
16-ounce can pitted cherries
1 tablespoon butter or margarine, softened

UTENSILS

1 cutting board
1 knife
1 large bowl
Measuring spoons
Liquid measure
1 mixing bowl
1 hand whisk
1 strainer
1 small bowl
1 heatproof dish
1 pastry brush
1 wooden spoon
Oven gloves or pot holders
1 heatproof pad
2 plates

1 Put rolls onto cutting board. Carefully cut in slices the width of one finger. Tip into large bowl.

2 Pour milk into mixing bowl. Add sugar and nuts. Break in egg. Beat mixture with hand whisk.

3 Ask an adult to help you switch the oven to 425°F. Pour egg mixture onto sliced bread rolls. Stand strainer over small bowl and pour in cherries. Keep the can juice for beverages.

4 Put butter or margarine into heatproof dish. Spread over bottom and side with pastry brush.

5 Add cherries to bread mixture. Using wooden spoon, beat thoroughly until well mixed. Spoon into heatproof dish and smooth top. Using oven gloves or pot holders, carefully put dish into oven.

6 Cook pudding for 40 minutes. Carefully take out of oven with oven gloves or pot holders. Stand on heatproof pad. Switch off oven. Spoon equal amounts onto 2 plates and serve.

TIP
For a snowy effect, sprinkle the pudding with powdered sugar before spooning it onto plates and eating.

Cherry Bread Pudding

Choco Fruit Sticks

Serves 2

These fruit sticks are great fun to make.

1 **Time to make:** 15 minutes

INGREDIENTS
12 strawberries
1 banana
Juice of ½ lemon
8 seedless green grapes
4 squares (4 ounces) semisweet chocolate

UTENSILS
1 strainer
1 cutting board
1 small knife
4 wooden skewers
1 serving plate
1 small heatproof bowl
1 medium-size saucepan
1 wooden spoon
1 small spoon

1 Put strawberries into strainer. Rinse under cold running water. Leave to drain. Hull the fruit (pull out stalks).

2 Peel banana. Put onto cutting board. Carefully cut into 8 pieces. Sprinkle all over with lemon juice to stop them from turning brown.

3 Thread strawberries, banana pieces, and grapes alternately onto the 4 wooden skewers. Put on 2 plates.

4 Unwrap chocolate. Break into small bowl. Stand bowl over medium-size saucepan containing gently simmering water. Make sure the water does not get into the bowl of chocolate or it will get very thick and lumpy.

5 Leave over low heat until chocolate melts, stirring often with wooden spoon. Switch off heat.

6 Arrange fruit on skewers on a serving plate. Spoon chocolate over fruit on skewers with the teaspoon. Eat while the chocolate is still runny.

Choco Fruit Sticks

Apple Crunchies

Serves 2

These baked apples make a great dessert.

Time to make: 30 minutes

INGREDIENTS

2 large cooking apples (Rome Beauties
   are good)
2 teaspoons chopped hazelnuts
4 teaspoons golden raisins
2 teaspoons clear honey
$\frac{2}{3}$ cup whipping cream
1 teaspoon butter or margarine, softened

UTENSILS

1 apple corer
1 small knife
Measuring spoons
1 small bowl
1 heatproof dish
1 pastry brush
1 mixing bowl
1 hand whisk
Oven gloves or pot holders
1 heatproof pad
2 plates

1 Rinse apples under cold running water. Ask an adult to help you remove cores from apples with an apple corer. Cut the skin in a line around the middle of the apple using a sharp knife.

2 Ask an adult to help you switch oven to 400°F. Put nuts, golden raisins, honey, and 2 tablespoons of cream into small bowl. Mix well.

3 Put butter or margarine into heatproof dish and spread over bottom and side with pastry brush. Stand apples in dish. Fill centers with nut and raisin mixture.

4 Carefully put dish in oven and bake apples for 20 minutes. Meanwhile, pour rest of cream into mixing bowl. Whip until stiff with hand whisk.

5 Switch off oven. Take out dish of apples with oven gloves or pot holders. Stand on heatproof pad. Put apples onto 2 plates. Top each one with whipped cream.

TIP
If liked, dot tops with extra golden raisins.

Apple Crunchies

◆NOTES◆

◆NOTES◆

Kids' Parties
Made Easy

Series Consultant: **Sonia Allison**

GREAT COOKING VALUE

Introduction

Fun and games go hand-in-hand as does party food with flair and there is no shortage of sparkling ideas in this book. Tempt the kids with a Sneaky Snake, Double Deckers, Mini Pizzas, Potato Posies, and a whole lot more besides, including chilled thirst quenchers for hot sunny days and warming drinks for winter. You may be kept busy in the kitchen but you will be well rewarded by the looks of delight on the faces of gleeful children as they tuck in to your creations with gusto!

Written by Dagmar V. Cramm

Raspberry Fluff

Serves 10

Light and cool, ideal for a birthday dessert. A child's age made from fruit makes a spectacular finishing touch.

Preparation time: about 45 minutes, plus 2 hours chilling

CRUST
19 graham crackers
¼ cup sugar
½ teaspoon cinnamon
¼ cup margarine

FILLING
1 envelope raspberry-flavored gelatin
⅔ cup boiling water
16-ounce can raspberries in syrup
¾ cup undiluted evaporated milk, chilled
   overnight
1 tablespoon lemon juice
Fresh raspberries for decoration
1 tablespoon rolled porridge oats
Fresh mint leaves for decoration

1 To make crust, crush crackers and put into mixing bowl. Toss in sugar and cinnamon. Melt margarine. Add to cracker mixture and mix well with fork. Press cracker crumbs over base and side of 9-inch glass pie plate. Chill for 1 hour to set.

2 Mix gelatin and water in a saucepan and melt over low heat. Add ¼ cup syrup from can of fruit. Let cool, then chill until just starting to thicken and set. The gelatin should have the consistency of unbeaten egg white.

3 Drain raspberries thoroughly, reserving remaining syrup for drinks or fruit salads. Whip evaporated milk and lemon juice together in mixing bowl until fluffy and very thick.

4 Gradually whisk thickened gelatin into evaporated milk mixture then quickly and gently fold in raspberries. Spoon into crumb crust and chill for about 2 hours until set and firm.

5 Before serving, decorate top edge of pie with fresh raspberries and side with oats. Arrange more raspberries in shape of child's age and decorate with mint leaves. Cut into portions with a wet knife to stop gelatin mixture from sticking.

Nutritional value per portion:
about 310 calories
Protein: 13g
Fat: 14g
Carbohydrate: 31g

Raspberry Fluff

Double Deckers

Makes 4

Marvelous little treats cakes to delight any child.

Preparation time: about 20 minutes

1 ready-made gingerbread or chocolate
  slab cake
2/3 cup heavy cream
1 teaspoon vanilla extract
1 teaspoon finely grated lemon zest
3 tablespoons cherry jelly or jam
2 teaspoons powdered sugar

1 Put cake onto board, and cut lengthwise into 4 long strips. Using a 2½-inch
round pastry cutter, cut out 2 rounds from
each strip of cake.

2 Pour cream into mixing bowl, add
vanilla and whip until cream is thick.

3 Fold in lemon zest and jelly or jam,
gently stirring with large spoon until well
combined.

4 Sandwich rounds of cake together, in
pairs, with cream mixture.

5 Sift over powdered sugar just before
serving.

TIP
Try making these with different cakes and
fillings. A mixture of strawberries and
whipped cream makes a very good filling.

Nutritional value per serving:
about 450 calories
Protein: 10g
Fat: 28g
Carbohydrate: 39g

Double Deckers

Fruit Patty Puffs

Makes 24

Puff pastry cases with a light creamy filling and delicious fruit topping.

Preparation time: about 35 minutes

24 medium-size frozen patty shells
1 egg, beaten
⅔ cup heavy cream
⅔ cup cream cheese, softened at room
   temperature
1 tablespoon milk
2 tablespoons superfine sugar
4 cups mixed fresh summer fruits
1 package glaze mix (see Tip)

1 Put all the frozen patty shells onto
2 ungreased baking sheets, placing
them 1 inch apart. Brush rims with beaten
egg and bake as directed on packaging.

2 Transfer cooked patties to cooling racks
and cut off tops. Push down soft centers
gently with back of teaspoon. Cool pastry
shells completely.

3 To make filling, place cream in mixing
bowl and whip until thick. In separate
bowl, beat cheese with milk until smooth.
Fold in cream alternately with sugar.

4 Spoon equal amounts of filling into
patty shells then cover with soft fruit.
Finally, spoon over glaze, made up as
directed on package.

VARIATIONS

For alternatives to patty shells, try the
following:
1 Ready-made puff pastry cases in
assorted shapes as shown in picture.
2 Ready-made or home-made
meringue nests.

TIP

Can't locate glaze mix? Make your own by
mixing 1 cup sugar, 1 cup water and
3 tablespoons cornstarch in a pan. Cook
over a low heat, stirring, until thick. Off heat,
stir in ¼ cup strawberry-flavored gelatin
powder. Cool slightly before using.

Nutritional value of each patty puff:
about 120 calories
Protein: 5g
Fat: 6g
Carbohydrate: 14g

Fruit Patty Puffs

Berry Gelatin Mold

Serves 6

Children will love this impressive molded fruit gelatin.

Preparation time: about 40 minutes , plus 5 hours setting

½ package raspberry-flavored gelatin
½ package strawberry-flavored gelatin
½ package pineapple-flavored gelatin
2 cups mixed fresh raspberries and
  strawberries

1 Mix the raspberry and strawberry gelatin in a large liquid measure.

2 Make mixture up to 2 cups with boiling water. Stir until dissolved, then pour into mixing bowl.

3 Leave gelatin to stand until cold then cover with plate and chill until just starting to thicken and set.

4 Make pineapple gelatin as directed on the package. Pour into shallow dish and chill until set.

5 Meanwhile rinse fruit, drain thoroughly and set aside a strawberry half for decoration. Stir fruit into half-set berry gelatin then spoon into medium-size, wetted mold. Cover loosely with non-stick baking parchment and chill for 5 hours until set.

6 Before serving, tip pineapple gelatin onto piece of dampened non-stick baking parchment placed on cutting board. Chop into tiny cubes with wetted round-bladed knife.

7 Unmold fruit gelatin onto serving plate and surround with chopped pineapple gelatin cubes. Decorate with strawberry half and serve in dessert dishes.

Nutritional value per portion:
about 130 calories
Protein: 4g
Fat: negligible
Carbohydrate: 27g

Berry Gelatin Mold

Mini Pizzas

Makes 21

Delicious little morsels for children of all ages.

Preparation time: about 1 hour

BASE
1 package (10 ounces) Pizza Base Mix or use
 frozen pizza dough, thawed

TOPPING
2 tablespoons olive oil
¾ cup passata or thick tomato sauce
Garlic salt to taste
Freshly ground black pepper to taste
7 thin slices of salami
7 cherry tomatoes
7 mushrooms
1 small zucchini, thinly sliced
¼ cup diced lean cooked ham
1 cup shredded mozzarella cheese
2 tablespoons chopped fresh parsley

1 Make up pizza base mix as directed on package. Put onto floured work surface and divide into 21 equal-size pieces. Roll out into rounds measuring about 1½ inches in diameter. Put onto large oiled baking sheets. Preheat oven to 425°F.

2 Mix oil and passata or thick tomato sauce. Spread evenly over pizza bases, leaving edges clear. Sprinkle with garlic salt and pepper.

3 Cover 7 pizzas with slices of salami. Halve tomatoes and place on top. Trim mushrooms and put onto next 7 pizzas, stalk-sides up. Finally add zucchini slices and diced ham to remaining 7 Pizzas.

4 Sprinkle shredded mozzarella evenly over pizzas. Bake for about 12 minutes, rearranging position of baking sheets halfway through cooking. Sprinkle with parsley and serve warm.

Nutritional value per pizza:
about 100 calories
Protein: 5g
Fat: 5g
Carbohydrate: 9g

Mini Pizzas

Sneaky Snake

Serves 6

A fun way to arrange party food.

Preparation time: about 25 minutes

1 large cucumber
1 strip of red bell pepper
2 cloves
3½ ounces sliced pumpernickel or whole-
  wheat bread
⅔ cup cream cheese or cheese spread
6-ounce piece of ready-to-eat garlic
  sausage or other cooked sausage
2 cherry tomatoes
5 round smoked cheese slices

1 Cut tail end off cucumber to form a snake's head and make a slit in its narrowest part to resemble mouth. Cut pepper strip into a tongue with a center split running almost to the top to form a forked tongue. Put tongue into snake's mouth then add 2 cloves for eyes. Put onto large serving plate or board.

2 Cut remaining cucumber into slices. Cut pumpernickel or whole-wheat bread into 2-inch rounds with a pastry cutter and spread with soft cheese or cheese spread.

3 Slice sausage and tomatoes. Arrange all prepared ingredients with smoked cheese slices on plate to form a curved snake, starting at head end.

4 Alternate ingredients for color contrast, referring to picture opposite. Allow kids to eat their way through snake with their fingers or let them spear their favorite ingredients on forks.

Nutrition value per portion:
about 260 calories
Protein: 14g
Fat: 18g
Carbohydrate: 12g

Sneaky Snake

Beano Buns

Makes 8

These seeded buns filled with ham and vegetable salad are hard to resist!

Preparation time: about 30 minutes

4 seeded hamburger buns
1 tablespoon margarine

FILLING
4 cherry tomatoes
2 tablespoons scissored fresh chives
4 ounces cooked ham
½ cup drained whole kernel corn
⅔ cup thick sour cream
Salt and pepper
8 lettuce leaves

1 Warm rolls through either in oven, microwave, or under broiler, then cut each one in half.

2 Halve tomatoes and put into mixing bowl. Add chives. Cut ham into narrow strips. Add to bowl with corn and thick sour cream.

3 Stir tomato mixture well and season to taste with salt and pepper.

4 Spread buns with margarine, top with lettuce leaves and equal amounts of salad. Serve directly.

TIPS
1 Chopped and crisply-broiled bacon can replace ham, as can strips of Edam or Gouda cheese.
2 Coarsely chopped unpeeled red apple can be used in place of corn.

Nutritional value per filled bun:
about 210 calories
Protein: 8g
Fat: 8g
Carbohydrate: 28g

Beano Buns

Step-by-step

STRAWBERRY AND LEMON MILK SHAKE

1 Put 1 cup plain yogurt and 1 cup skim milk into blender. Add 3 cups washed and hulled strawberries and blend until smooth.

2 Pour milk shake into 4 tall glasses and add 1 or 2 scoops of lemon sherbet to each.

3 Decorate with whole or halved strawberries speared on sticks. Add a drinking straw.

LEMONADE

4 Finely grate zest of 2 lemons. Cut rind of third lemon into spiral, keeping it in one continous piece.

5 Squeeze juice from fruit. Mix with ⅓ cup clear honey. Add grated zest, cover and let stand for 1 hour to bring out flavors.

6 Strain juice into pitcher and decorate rim with lemon rind spiral. To serve, pour into tall glasses, half filling each. Top up with club soda, and add a drinking straw.

CHILLED MELON PUNCH

7 Halve a small honeyball or Canteloupe melon. Remove seeds and cut out flesh using a melon baller.

8 Put flesh into large bowl. Add 1 cinnamon stick and ⅓ cup unsweetened apple juice. Cover and chill for 1 hour.

9 Remove cinnamon stick. Pour 2 pints ginger ale over melon and stir a round. Pour into tall glasses and add a drinking straw to each.

1

4

7

2

3

5

6

8

9

Fruit Waffles

Serves 6

You can make your own waffles if you have a waffle iron but bought ones are more convenient and taste just as good. If you are unable to find fancy-shaped waffles, like the ones shown in the picture, use square or rectangular ones instead.

Preparation time: about 15 minutes

2 oranges
⅔ cup heavy cream
2 tablespoons superfine sugar
2 kiwi fruit
6 ready-made or home-made waffles

1 Cut skin and pith from oranges and cut into sections, cutting between the skin. Pat slices dry with paper towels and set aside.

2 Whip cream and sugar until thick.

3 Peel kiwi fruit thinly, halve each one lengthwise then cut each half into thin slices.

4 Reheat waffles as directed on package, usually by toasting. Alternatively, warm through in microwave.

5 Put waffles onto 6 plates. Top with whipped cream then decorate with orange and kiwi slices. Serve warm.

TIPS
1 If preferred, use canned peach slices instead of fresh orange sections.
2 Add 2 tablespoons chocolate chips to cream mixture after whipping.

Nutritional value per portion:
about 570 calories
Protein: 15g
Fat: 33g
Carbohydrate: 54g

Fruit Waffles

Funny Face Cake

Serves 12

A quick and easy novelty cake, especially if using a ready-made cake.

Preparation time: about 1 hour

3 squares (3 ounces) semi-sweet chocolate
1¼ cups heavy cream, chilled
2 x 9-inch cake layers
4 tablespoons apricot preserves
3 large chocolate flake bars or 1 cup
   chocolate sprinkles
2 hazelnuts
1 slice of white bread, lightly toasted
1 tablespoon powdered sugar
Red food coloring

1 Break up chocolate and melt in bowl standing over saucepan of gently simmering water. Alternatively, melt in microwave for 1-2 minutes on Medium power. Leave chocolate until just cold but still liquid.

2 Whip cream until very stiff then gradually beat in cooled, melted chocolate. Cover and chill for 30 minutes to firm up.

3 Cut each cake layer in half horizontally then sandwich together again with the apricot preserves and a little of the whipped chocolate cream.

4 Spread remaining cream smoothly over top and side of cake. Crush flake bars and press against side with round-bladed knife. Alternatively, use sprinkles. Using 2 spatulas, carefully lift cake onto center of serving plate.

5 Make eyes with hazelnuts. Cut out a triangular nose and crescent eyebrows from toast. Cut out a ring for the mouth.

6 Mix powdered sugar with a few drops water and color pale pink. Spoon onto ring to make pink lips. Arrange nose, eyebrows and lips on cake. Chill cake before serving.

Nutritional value per portion:
about 310 calories
Protein: 9g
Fat: 15g
Carbohydrate: 35g

Funny Face Cake

Date and Nut Baked Apples

Serves 6

Designed to add a little extra sweetness to those winter parties.

Preparation time: about 45 minutes

Margarine for greasing
6 large fresh dates
½ cup hazelnuts
½ teaspoon cinnamon, plus a little extra
6 red apples
1 cup plain yogurt
½ teaspoon vanilla extract
2 tablespoons clear honey
½ cup heavy cream

1 Preheat oven to 425°F. Lightly grease a baking pan with margarine. Skin dates, cut each in half and remove pits. Chop flesh finely.

2 Slowly dry-fry hazelnuts in a non-stick pan until golden, stirring frequently. Tip nuts into large cloth and rub hard between folds to remove as much skin as possible. Chop nuts and put into mixing bowl. Add dates and cinnamon.

3 Core apples with apple corer and pack hollows with date mixture. Place in prepared baking pan and bake in oven for 15 minutes.

4 Meanwhile, tip yogurt into small mixing bowl and stir in vanilla and honey. Whip cream in separate bowl until thick then gradually fold into yogurt with large metal spoon. Spoon into serving dish, dust with extra cinnamon and serve with apples.

Nutritional value per portion:
about 240 calories
Protein: 2g
Fat: 13g
Carbohydrate: 29g

Date and Nut Baked Apples

Whirligigs

Makes 8

Melt-in-the-mouth!

Preparation time: about 40 minutes

1½ sticks butter, softened
½ cup powdered sugar, sifted
½ teaspoon vanilla extract
1¼ cups plus 2 tablespoons cake flour
2 tablespoons unsweetened cocoa powder
Orange sections for serving

FILLING
⅓ cup heavy cream
2 teaspoons sugar
1 tablespoon chopped shelled pistachios

1 Grease a large cookie sheet. Preheat oven to 325°F.

2 Put butter, powdered sugar and vanilla into mixing bowl and beat until light and creamy.

3 Sift flour and cocoa powder onto plate. Gradually fork into creamed butter mixture until well mixed. Spoon into pastry bag fitted with large star-shaped tip.

4 Pipe 16 whirls of mixture onto prepared sheet. Bake in oven for about 20 minutes until light golden. Cool slightly then gently remove cookies from sheet with knife or spatula and put onto wire cooling rack.

5 Whip cream and sugar until thick. Stir in nuts. Sandwich cookies together in pairs with nut cream. Serve on the day of cooking with orange sections.

TIP
Instead of pistachios, use chopped walnuts or lightly toasted almond flakes.

Nutritional value per pair of cookies:
about 210 calories
Protein: 4g
Fat: 13g
Carbohydrate: 21g

Whirligigs

Party Porcupine

Serves 6

A colorful centerpiece for the party table!

Preparation time: about 1 hour

1 small red or white hard cabbage
7 ounces pepperoni sausage or cocktail franks
10 ounces Gouda or Edam cheese, rind removed or Cheddar
1 cucumber
1 yellow bell pepper
3 small carrots
12 cherry tomatoes
16 cornichons, drained
1 cup cocktail onions

1 Cut a slice off stem end of cabbage so that it stands upright. Wrap in foil and stand on large plate.

2 Cut pepperoni or franks into ½-inch pieces. Cut cheese into 1-inch cubes.

3 Wash and dry cucumber. Cut into 1-inch pieces; cut each piece into fourths. Cut pepper in half, then remove inner white membranes and seeds. Cut flesh into 1-inch squares. Peel carrots, cut each in half lengthwise and cut each half into 1-inch pieces.

4 Thread all prepared ingredients alternately onto toothpicks, interspersing them with tomatoes, cornichons, and onions. Push into cabbage and serve.

Nutritional value per serving:
about 380 calories
Protein: 20g
Fat: 31g
Carbohydrate: 7g

Party Porcupine

Baked Pancake Stack

Serves 6

A savory cheese and egg dish which goes well with coleslaw or a mixed green salad.

Preparation time: about 1 hour

3 large eggs
1½ cups all-purpose flour
1 cup cold milk
½ teaspoon salt
4 tomatoes
8 ounces mozzarella cheese
Sparkling water or club soda
⅔ cup heavy cream or crème fraîche
2 tablespoons scissored fresh chives

1 To make batter, break eggs into large mixing bowl, whisk until foamy then beat in flour alternately with milk. Season with salt.

2 Thinly slice tomatoes. Shred cheese. Preheat oven to 400°F.

3 Add a dash of sparkling water or club soda to batter for extra lightness then use to make six 9-inch pancakes, frying them in a greased skillet.

4 Stack pancakes, as they are cooked, one on top of the other with squares of non-stick baking parchment between each.

5 Fill a well-greased 8-inch springform cake pan with alternate layers of pancakes, cream or crème fraîche, chives, tomatoes and mozzarella, starting with cream or crème fraîche and ending with cheese.

6 Bake in oven for 30 minutes. Unclip sides of pan, cut cake into 6 portions and serve hot.

Nutritional value per portion:
about 450 calories
Protein: 17g
Fat: 29g
Carbohydrate: 32g

Baked Pancake Stack

◆NOTES◆

◆NOTES◆

One Dish
Dinners
Made Easy

Series
Consultant:
Sonia Allison

GREAT COOKING VALUE

Introduction

One dish dinners are the perfect solution to weekday meals when time is at a premium. Beginners will find them a boon and those with small kitchens will appreciate the fact that little is required by way of utensils and cookware.

All the recipes are imaginative and versatile and can be made from fresh and frozen foods as well as storecupboard ingredients and leftovers. The choice of dishes is varied enough to suit all tastes.

Recipe Notes

Use standard spoon and cup measures. All measures are level unless otherwise stated.

Eggs used are large unless otherwise stated.

Calorie counts for average-size servings are set down at the end of each recipe, and are rounded up to the nearest whole number.

Written by Annette Wolter and Johanna Handschmann

Tomato and Mozzarella Bake

Serves 4

Melted mozzarella and baked tomatoes top this delicous bake.

Preparation time: about 30 minutes
Baking time: 30 minutes

1½ pounds beefsteak tomatoes
14 ounces mozzarella cheese
2 onions
2 cloves garlic
6 tablespoons virgin olive oil
4-6 large slices of whole-wheat bread,
    crusts removed
1 teaspoon salt
Freshly ground pepper to taste
2 sprigs of fresh thyme

1 Grease a fairly large fluted pie dish with butter or margarine. Alternatively, brush lightly with oil.

2 Preheat oven to 425°F. Cut tomatoes in half, then in ¼-inch slices. Cut the mozzarella cheese in slices of similar size and thickness. Set tomatoes and cheese aside.

3 Finely chop onions and garlic. Place in a bowl and stir in the olive oil.

4 Cover base of prepared dish with bread slices, trimming them to fit. Moisten with a little of the olive oil mixture, drizzling it over with a teaspoon.

5 Arrange tomato and cheese slices alternately on top of bread as illustrated opposite. Sprinkle with salt and pepper.

6 Spoon rest of oil mixture on top. Bake, uncovered, for 30 minutes.

7 Meanwhile, strip thyme leaves from stalks. Chop fairly finely and sprinkle over tomatoes and cheese on top of bake. Serve at once.

Nutritional value per portion:
360 calories
Protein: 16g
Fat: 21g
Carbohydrate: 25g

Tomato and Mozzarella Bake

Cheese and Asparagus Soufflé

Serves 4

A light and puffy soufflé for early summer when tender asparagus is in season.

Preparation time: about 1 hour
Baking time: 45 minutes

2 pounds thin green asparagus
½ stick butter or margarine
½ cup all-purpose flour
1¼ cups warm milk
4 eggs, separated
1 cup shredded Cheddar cheese
1 teaspoon salt
½ teaspoon mustard powder
Pinch of ground nutmeg

1 Grease or oil a 5 cup straight-sided soufflé dish. Preheat oven to 375°F.

2 Peel asparagus stalks if necessary. Cut tough ends off each stalk, two thirds of the way down from tips. Bring a large skillet of water to a boil, add asparagus, lower heat and simmer for 8 minutes or until tender. Tip into a strainer, rinse under cold running water, then shake dry. Cut each asparagus stalk in half; arrange in prepared soufflé dish.

3 Melt butter or margarine in a small heavy-based saucepan. Stir in flour and cook for 1 minute. Gradually add warm milk, stirring constantly until mixture boils and thickens. When mixture forms a smooth ball, leaving side of pan clean, transfer it to a bowl.

4 Gradually beat in egg yolks, one at a time, alternately with cheese. Stir in salt, mustard and nutmeg.

5 In a grease-free bowl, whisk egg whites until stiff; fold into egg yolk and cheese mixture with a large spoon.

6 When smooth and evenly combined, gently pour over asparagus in dish.

7 Bake for 45 minutes or until well risen and golden. Serve at once.

TIP
Do not open oven door while soufflé is baking or it will collapse.

Nutritional value per portion:
480 calories
Protein: 25g
Fat: 29g
Carbohydrate: 29g

Cheese and Asparagus Soufflé

Jansson's Temptation

Serves 4

Potatoes and anchovies combine in this tasty Swedish dish.

Preparation time: about 45 minutes
Baking time: 50-60 minutes

1¾ pounds mealy potatoes
2 large onions
½ stick butter or margarine
Freshly ground black pepper to taste
2 x 2-ounce cans anchovy fillets in oil,
   drained, oil reserved
1¼ cups heavy cream
3 tablespoons soft white bread crumbs
½ cup chopped, fresh parsley

1 Grease or oil an oval baking dish.
Preheat oven to 375°F.

2 Cut potatoes in ¼-inch slices, then in
¼-inch wide strips. Thinly slice onions;
separate slices into rings.

3 Sizzle half the butter or margarine in a
large skillet, add onions and stir-fry
gently until they soften and begin to look
transparent.

4 Cover bottom of prepared dish with
half the potato strips then season with
pepper. Top with all the onions, followed by
the anchovy fillets. Drizzle anchovy oil over
the top and season with more pepper.

5 Arrange remaining potato strips on top
of anchovy fillets as illustrated opposite.
Drizzle cream over bake.

6 Sprinkle with soft bread crumbs. Cut
remaining butter or margarine into
flakes and dot over bread crumb topping.
Bake for 50-60 minutes, until the top is
golden and crisp, and the potato strips are
tender. Serve at once, garnished with the
chopped parsley.

Nutritional value per portion:
500 calories
Protein: 12g
Fat: 30g
Carbohydrate: 44g

Jansson's Temptation

Pasta Twists with Mushrooms and Tomatoes

Serves 4

A made-in-minutes main course with vegetarians in view.

Preparation time: about 40 minutes
Baking time: 20 minutes

2 cups dried whole-wheat pasta spirals
2 teaspoons olive oil
1 onion
2½ cups mushrooms
4 tablespoons corn oil
4 large tomatoes
3½ ounces process cheese slices
4 tablespoons minced fresh parsley
Salt
Freshly ground black pepper
⅓ cup heavy cream

1 Grease a fairly deep casserole. Preheat oven to 400°F.

2 Bring a large saucepan of lightly salted water to a boil. Add pasta, with olive oil, and cook for about 10 minutes or until just tender. Drain pasta; set aside.

3 Chop onion. Wipe mushrooms clean; slice them thinly.

4 Heat half the corn oil in a large skillet. Add onion and sauté for 3-4 minutes until softened and pale gold. Stir in rest of corn oil. When hot, add mushrooms. Sauté for 3 minutes more.

5 Cut a small cross in each tomato. Put into heatproof bowl. Cover with boiling water. Let stand for 1 minute. Rinse under cold water. When cool enough to handle, slip off skins. Slice tomatoes.

6 Layer prepared dish with pasta, sautéed onions and mushrooms, sliced tomatoes, half the cheese and half the parsley, sprinkling salt and pepper between the layers.

7 Trickle in the cream, top with remaining cheese slices and bake, uncovered, for 20 minutes. Garnish with rest of parsley and serve at once.

TIP
For non-vegetarians, serve with broiled bacon or chipolata sausages.

Nutritional value per portion:
1100 calories
Protein: 37g
Fat: 84g
Carbohydrate: 36g

Pasta Twists with Mushrooms and Tomatoes

Eggplant Moussaka

Serves 4-6

A popular specialty from Greece.

Preparation time: about 1 hour
Baking time: 40 minutes

2 pounds eggplants
4 teaspoons salt
5 tablespoons virgin olive oil
1 onion, chopped
2 cloves garlic, crushed
1 pound ground lamb
2 tablespoons tomato paste
2 tablespoons water
1 teaspoon sugar
1/4 teaspoon freshly ground black pepper
4 tablespoons soft white bread crumbs
1/2 cup ricotta cheese
2 egg yolks
3 1/2 ounces feta cheese, thinly sliced
2 tablespoons dried oregano
2 tablespoons butter or margarine, flaked

1 Grease or oil a large oval gratin dish. Preheat oven to 400°F.

2 Cut unpeeled eggplants into 1/2-inch rounds. Spread out in a single layer on a large board or on a work surface lined with paper towels. Sprinkle with 3 teaspoons of the salt. Leave for 15 minutes to draw out bitter juices.

3 Tip eggplant rounds into a strainer, rinse thoroughly under cold running water and wipe dry with paper towels.

4 Heat 2 tablespoons of the oil in a large skillet until sizzling. Fry eggplant rounds, a few at a time, until golden brown on both sides, turning once. Remove with turner and use half the rounds to cover bottom of dish, reserving remainder for topping.

5 Add rest of oil to pan. When hot, sauté onion and garlic until soft and golden.

6 Add ground lamb. Stir-fry until browned, then stir in tomato paste, measured water and sugar. Add ground pepper with remaining salt.

7 Spread on top of eggplants in dish then cover with reserved eggplant rounds. Sprinkle with bread crumbs.

8 Stir ricotta and egg yolks together in a small bowl; spread over bread crumbs. Top with feta, oregano and butter or margarine flakes. Bake for about 40 minutes. Serve at once.

Nutritional value per portion:
570 calories
Protein: 27g
Fat: 43g
Carbohydrate: 18g

Eggplant Moussaka

Piquant Cheese Bakes

Serves 4

Millet is the mystery ingredient in these delicious individual cheese bakes.

Preparation time: about 40 minutes
Baking time: 20-25 minutes

2 cups millet
4 cups water
2 vegetable bouillon cubes
¼ teaspoon salt
½ teaspoon soy sauce
1 tablespoon chopped mixed fresh herbs
   (fennel, dill, parsley, marjoram)
2 tablespoons shredded fresh basil
1 cup shredded Cheddar cheese
½ stick butter or margarine
½ cup sour cream
4 eggs

1 Grease or oil four 5-inch individual baking dishes. Preheat oven to 400°F.

2 Put millet and measured water into large saucepan. Crumble in bouillon cube and add salt. Bring to a boil, stirring. Stir in soy sauce, lower heat and cover the pan. Simmer for about 20 minutes or until all the liquid has been absorbed.

3 Drain millet mixture, then tip it into a bowl and add mixed herbs and basil, forking in gently.

4 Fork two-thirds of the shredded cheese into the millet with butter or margarine and sour cream.

5 Divide mixture equally among the 4 prepared dishes. Beat eggs until frothy. Spoon equally over top of bakes then sprinkle with rest of cheese.

6 Bake for 20-25 minutes until top of each bake is golden brown and crisp. Serve hot, straight from the oven.

TIP
Millet is not widely available, so use buckwheat groats or bulgur wheat instead, if you like. Try Monterey Jack instead of Cheddar, or use Parmesan. The recipe is suitable for vegetarians; use rennet-free cheeses where applicable.

Nutritional value per portion:
620 calories
Protein: 24g
Fat: 30g
Carbohydrate: 63g

Piquant Cheese Bakes

Polenta and Bacon Hotpot

Serves 4

An original shepherds' dish from the Abruzzi region of Italy.

Preparation time: about 50 minutes
Baking time: 30 minutes

1 quart vegetable stock
1½ cups yellow corn meal
Salt
2 large onions
6 bacon slices, rind removed
1 tablespoon virgin olive oil
1 cup grated Pecorino or Parmesan cheese
½ cup chopped pitted green olives
4 tablespoons fresh white bread crumbs
2 tablespoons butter or margarine, flaked

1 Bring stock to a boil in a large, non-stick saucepan. Lower heat slightly. Add corn meal and salt to taste then stir constantly for 2 minutes over a moderate heat until mixture thickens.

2 Half cover pan with lid to prevent splattering, lower heat and continue to cook corn meal for 30 minutes, stirring 3 or 4 times with a wooden spoon. Let cool.

3 Preheat oven to 425°F. Chop onions and bacon fairly finely. Heat oil in a skillet. Add onions and bacon and sauté over a moderate heat, stirring occasionally, until onions are pale golden brown. Remove pan from heat.

4 Grease or oil a fairly deep heatproof oval dish. Spread the bottom with half the corn meal and half the cheese.

5 Top with onion and bacon mixture and dot with olives. Cover smoothly with rest of corn meal. Mix remaining cheese with bread crumbs, sprinkle over corn meal and dot with flakes of butter or margarine.

6 Bake, uncovered, for 30 minutes until golden brown. Serve at once, with a homemade tomato sauce and a green salad, if you like.

Nutritional value per portion:
710 calories
Protein: 20g
Fat: 43g
Carbohydrate: 61g

Polenta and Bacon Hotpot

Macaroni Cheese with Ham and Zucchini

Serves 4

A stylish version of a well-loved classic.

Preparation time: about 35 minutes
Baking time: 20 minutes

2½ cups dried elbow macaroni (total
    weight about 14 ounces)
1 teaspoon olive oil
2 zucchini
6 tablespoons milk
¼ teaspoon salt
7-ounce slice of country-cured ham
1 onion
1 tablespoon corn oil
⅔ cup plain yogurt
2 eggs
½ cup shredded Gouda or Edam cheese
2 tablespoons butter or margarine, flaked

1 Grease a fairly large heatproof dish.
Preheat oven to 400°F.

2 Bring a large saucepan of lightly salted
water to a boil. Add macaroni, with
olive oil, and cook for about 7 minutes or
until just tender. Take care not to overcook.
Drain macaroni in a strainer; set aside.

3 Trim zucchini, but do not peel them.
Dice finely.

4 Bring milk to a boil in a small saucepan.
Add zucchini, with salt; simmer, half
covered, for 2-3 minutes or until tender. Set
pan aside.

5 Dice ham. Cut onion into fairly small
pieces.

6 Sizzle oil in a large skillet. Add ham and
onion and sauté fairly briskly until ham is
cooked and onion is golden brown. Off
heat, add macaroni. Stir in zucchini, with
milk in which they were cooked.

7 Transfer to prepared dish. Mix yogurt
with eggs in a small bowl. Spread over
macaroni mixture. Sprinkle with cheese; top
with flakes of butter or margarine. Bake,
uncovered, for about 20 minutes until
golden. Serve at once.

TIP

Use lean cooked ham instead of cured ham
if you prefer. Do not sauté it with the onion,
but add it with the cooked zucchini.

Nutritional value per portion;
760 calories
Protein: 29g
Fat: 43g
Carbohydrate: 63g

Macaroni Cheese with Ham and Zucchini

Ham-wrapped Belgian Endives in Cheese Sauce

Serves 4

This version of one of Belgium's most renowned dishes is unusual in that it contains chicken.

Preparation time: about 40 minutes
Baking time: 15-20 minutes

4 large heads of Belgian endive
1 tablespoon lemon juice
2 teaspoons sugar
1 pound boneless, skinless chicken breasts
2 tablespoons butter or margarine
⅔ cup hot chicken stock
2 teaspoons cornstarch
¼ teaspoon ground nutmeg
⅔ cup heavy cream
Salt
Freshly ground black pepper
4 slices of lean cooked ham
2 egg yolks
4 tablespoons shredded Gouda cheese

1 Preheat oven to 400°F. Grease or oil an oval baking dish.

2 Break off and throw away damaged or bruised outer leaves from endives, then cut a cone-shaped core out of base of each to prevent bitterness.

3 Bring a saucepan of lightly salted water to a boil, add the endives with the lemon juice and sugar, and cook for 20-25 minutes until just tender. Drain.

4 Cut chicken into bite-size pieces. Heat butter or margarine in a skillet. Add chicken and cook over a moderate heat, stirring often, for 6 minutes. Pour in stock.

5 Mix cornstarch and nutmeg in a bowl. Stir in 3 tablespoons of the cream until smooth. Season with salt and pepper, then add to chicken mixture. Bring to a boil, stirring constantly.

6 Cover bottom of prepared dish with chicken mixture. Wrap ham around endives and arrange on top of chicken mixture.

7 In a small bowl, beat rest of cream smoothly with egg yolks.

8 Pour over endives, then sprinkle with cheese. Bake, uncovered, for about 15-20 minutes until hot and bubbling.

Nutritional value per portion:
430 calories
Protein: 35g
Fat: 30g
Carbohydrate: 5g

Ham-wrapped Belgian Endives
in Cheese Sauce

Pork and Mixed Vegetable Casserole

Serves 4

A colorful pork dish that tastes as good as it looks.

Preparation time: about 1 hour
Baking time: 45 minutes

14 ounces pork tenderloin, trimmed
2 onions
2 green bell peppers
2 beefsteak tomatoes
2 tablespoons corn oil
2 cups drained canned or thawed frozen
   whole kernel corn
2 large potatoes
1 teaspoon salt
½ teaspoon paprika
½ teaspoon dried rosemary
6 tablespoons sour cream
Freshly ground black pepper
1 egg
½ cup shredded Cheddar cheese
4 tablespoons soft white bread crumbs

1 Grease or oil a fairly deep, round ovenproof dish. Preheat oven to 400°F. Cut pork in 1-inch cubes.

2 Chop onions. Cut peppers in half, remove inner fibers and seeds, then cut flesh in 1½-inch squares. Dice tomatoes.

3 Heat oil in large skillet. Add pork, onions, peppers and tomatoes. Stir-fry, over a moderate heat, for about 15 minutes or until onions are golden brown and pork is tender. Transfer to prepared dish, then sprinkle over whole kernel corn.

4 Thinly slice potatoes and arrange on top of pork and vegetables,

5 Put all remaining ingredients, except cheese and bread crumbs, into a bowl; beat well together. Pour over potatoes. Sprinkle with cheese and bread crumbs.

6 Bake, uncovered, for 45 minutes until potatoes are tender and cheese topping is golden.

Nutritional value per portion:
670 calories
Protein: 29g
Fat: 41g
Carbohydrate: 45g

Pork and Mixed Vegetable Casserole

Beef and Cauliflower Crisp

Serves 4

Tender cauliflower flowerets combine with ground beef in a simple supper dish.

Preparation time: about 40 minutes
Baking time: 1 hour

1 cauliflower, trimmed
1 pound beefsteak tomatoes, blanched
   (see step 5, page 10)
1 large slice of bread
1 onion
2 tablespoons corn oil
1 pound lean ground beef
Salt
Freshly ground black pepper
1 egg, beaten
$\frac{1}{2}$ cup grated Parmesan cheese
1 tablespoon whole-wheat bread crumbs
2 tablespoons melted butter or margarine
3 tablespoons chopped fresh parsley

1 Grease or oil a deep heatproof dish. Preheat oven to 425°F.

2 Divide cauliflower into small neat flowerets, then blanch tomatoes (see step 5, page 10), remove skins and slice. Place bread in a shallow bowl with water to cover. Chop onion roughly.

3 Heat oil in large skillet. Add onion and sauté over a moderate heat, stirring occasionally until golden brown.

4 Add ground beef and fry until browned and crumbly. Add salt and pepper to taste; set pan aside and cool slightly.

5 Drain bread, squeezing out excess water. Add bread to pan with egg; mix well. Arrange cauliflower flowerets over bottom of dish. Spoon meat mixture on top, then cover with tomato slices.

6 Mix cheese with bread crumbs; sprinkle over tomatoes. Drizzle melted butter or margarine over the top.

7 Cover securely with or oiled aluminum foil and bake for 1 hour. Garnish with parsley. Serve hot, with crusty bread, rice or pasta, if you like.

TIP
Try this with broccoli flowerets for a delicous change.

Nutritional value per portion:
570 calories
Protein: 39g
Fat: 39g
Carbohydrate: 18g

Beef and Cauliflower Crisp

Oriental Rice Pots

Serves 2

Leftover rice gets an exciting new lease of life.

Preparation time: about 45 minutes
Baking time: 12 minutes

2 cups cooked long-grain brown rice,
    cooled
2 cups cauliflower flowerets
1 teaspoon lemon juice
½ cup light cream
2 teaspoons semolina or rice flour
4 teaspoons golden raisins
1 tablespoon mild curry paste
1 teaspoon corn oil
2 tablespoons roughly chopped blanched
    almonds or cashews
1 banana

1 Preheat oven to 400°F and then butter 2 individual heatproof dishes. Tip rice into a mixing bowl; break up any clumps gently with a fork.

2 Bring a saucepan of lightly salted water to a boil. Add cauliflower flowerets and lemon juice. Lower heat and simmer for about 10 minutes, until flowerets are just tender. Using a slotted draining spoon, lift flowerets onto a plate. Set aside ⅔ cup of the cooking water in a separate saucepan. Stir in cream. Discard all the remaining cooking water.

3 In a bowl, mix semolina or rice flour to a smooth paste with about 2 tablespoons of the liquid in the pan. Return mixture to pan, whisking well. Stir in 3 teaspoons of the golden raisins.

4 Bring golden raisin mixture to a boil, stirring constantly, then lower heat. Half cover pan. Simmer for 5 minutes, then stir in curry paste. Remove pan from heat.

5 Heat oil in a small sauté pan. Add nuts and cook gently until golden. Slice banana thinly.

6 Fill prepared dishes with alternate layers of rice, cauliflower flowerets and banana slices. Add half the nuts. Coat evenly with sauce, then sprinkle with the remaining nuts and golden raisins. Bake for 12 minutes to heat through. Serve.

Nutritional value per portion:
670 calories
Protein: 14g
Fat: 40g
Carbohydrate: 67g

Oriental Rice Pots

Zucchini Soufflés

Serves 2

A perfect after-theatre treat for two.

Preparation time: about 30 minutes
Baking time: 15 minutes

1 large zucchini (about 7 ounces)
1 tablespoon butter
2 tablespoons all-purpose flour
6 tablespoons warm milk
3 tablespoons heavy cream
2 eggs, separated
⅓ cup shredded Emmental or Gouda
  cheese
½ teaspoon dried thyme
Salt
Freshly ground black pepper

1 Butter 2 individual soufflé dishes. Preheat oven to 400°F.

2 Trim zucchini, then shred it. Place it in a saucepan over a gentle heat and simmer for about 5 minutes until all the natural juices have evaporated. Stir once or twice.

3 Meanwhile, melt butter in a small heavy-based saucepan. Stir in flour and cook for 1 minute. Gradually add warm milk and cream, stirring constantly until mixture boils and thickens. When mixture forms a smooth ball, leaving side of pan clean, transfer it to a bowl.

4 Gradually beat in egg yolks, one at a time, alternately with cheese and thyme. Stir in zucchini and add salt and pepper to taste.

5 In a grease-free bowl, whisk egg whites until stiff; fold into zucchini mixture with a large metal spoon.

6 Divide soufflé mixture among prepared dishes. Bake for 15 minutes until risen and golden. Serve at once.

Nutritional value per portion:
330 calories
Protein: 17g
Fat: 25g
Carbohydrate: 12g

Zucchini Soufflés

Potato Bake with Sautéed Onions

Serves 2

A tasty potato casserole laced with sautéed onions and apple.

Preparation time: about 45 minutes
Baking time: 15 minutes

1 pound mealy potatoes, peeled, halved
   or quartered if large
2 tablespoons corn oil
2 onions, sliced and separated into rings
1 eating apple
$\frac{2}{3}$ cup heavy cream
1 egg, beaten
Salt
Pinch of ground nutmeg
$\frac{1}{2}$ cup shredded Gruyère or grated
   Parmesan cheese
2 tablespoons sunflower seeds or
   sesame seeds

1 Grease or oil a heatproof dish.
Preheat oven to 450°F.

2 Bring a large saucepan of lightly salted
water to a boil. Add potatoes and cook
until soft.

3 Meanwhile heat oil in a skillet. Add
onion rings; sauté for about 10 minutes,
stirring occasionally, until golden brown.
Set pan aside.

4 Peel, quarter and core apple. Cut into
fairly thin slices.

5 Drain potatoes, return to dry pan and
mash finely. Add cream and egg. Beat
until mixture is smooth and creamy, then
season with salt and nutmeg.

6 Spoon half the potato mixture onto the
bottom of the prepared dish. Smooth
the surface. Cover with half the onions, all
the apple and half the cheese.

7 Spread with remaining potato mixture,
then with rest of onions and cheese.
Sprinkle with sunflower or sesame seeds and
bake for 15 minutes. Serve at once.

Nutritional value per portion:
840 calories
Protein: 24g
Fat: 60g
Carbohydrate: 53g

Potato Bake with Sautéed Onions

◆NOTES◆

◆NOTES◆

◆NOTES◆

◆NOTES◆

Pasta

Made Easy

Series
Consultant:
Sonia Allison

Introduction

The type and varieties of pasta available are enormous but here we show you a small selection.

In general, the fourteen or so varieties listed in the book should be adequate for most culinary purposes.

Recipe Notes

Use standard spoon and cup measures. All measures are level unless otherwise stated.

Eggs used are large unless otherwise stated.

Calorie counts for average-size servings are set down at the end of each recipe, and are rounded up to the nearest whole number.

Written by Annette Wolter

Spaghetti alla Carbonara

Serves 4

A classic combination of spaghetti with cream, bacon, and cheese.

Preparation time: about 15 minutes
Cooking time: about 15 minutes

2 quarts boiling water
1½ teaspoons salt
2 tablespoons olive oil, plus 1 teaspoon
12 ounces spaghetti
6 bacon slices, rinds removed
2 cloves garlic
3 eggs
4 tablespoons whipping cream
½ cup grated Pecorino or Parmesan cheese
Salt and pepper to taste

1 Have ready a serving dish, keeping it warm in a low oven until the spaghetti is ready.

2 Pour boiling water into a large saucepan. Add salt and 1 teaspoon oil. Bring to a boil. Ease in spaghetti without breaking. As it softens, it will yield to gentle pressure and settle in a coil in the bottom of the pan. Stir well to separate.

3 Cook pasta, uncovered, for 7-10 minutes, until spaghetti is 'al dente' or just tender to the bite. Let stand for 1 minute.

4 Meanwhile chop bacon roughly. Peel garlic and cut each clove lengthwise into 4 strips.

5 Heat remaining oil in a second large saucepan. Add garlic and sauté gently until golden brown. Remove pan from heat.

6 Tip bacon into the saucepan and stir-fry until crisp and golden. Take pan off the heat, leaving bacon where it is.

7 Thoroughly drain spaghetti, and add to pan of garlic-flavored oil and bacon.

8 Beat eggs, cream and cheese together. Season to taste with salt and pepper and pour over the spaghetti. Return pan to a medium heat.

9 Cook and toss gently with 2 spoons until egg mixture thickens slightly and clings to the spaghetti. Do not over-heat or the mixture will scramble.

10 Transfer pasta to the warm serving dish and eat straight away. A simple green salad goes well with the richness of this dish.

Nutritional value per portion:
740 calories
Protein: 25g
Fat: 39g
Carbohydrate: 73g

Spaghetti alla Carbonara

Fettucine with Bacon and Cheese

Serves 4

Flat pasta ribbons with bacon and peas makes a perfect midweek meal.

Preparation time: about 10 minutes
Cooking time: about 15 minutes

6 bacon slices, rinds removed
2 quarts boiling water
1½ teaspoons salt
1 tablespoon olive oil, plus 1 teaspoon
12 ounces wide fettucine
⅔ cup whipping cream
10-ounce package frozen peas

1 Using kitchen shears, cut bacon into narrow strips.

2 Pour boiling water into a large saucepan. Add salt and 1 teaspoon oil and bring back to a boil. Lower in the fettucine and stir well to separate.

3 Cook pasta, uncovered, for 7-10 minutes until 'al dente' or just tender to the bite. Let stand for 1 minute.

4 Meanwhile, heat remaining tablespoon of olive oil separately in a large pan until sizzling. Add bacon and cook over a medium heat until crisp and golden brown, stirring occasionally.

5 Mix in cream and peas, cover and simmer for 3-4 minutes, stirring the mixture occasionally.

6 Drain fettucine, add to pan of bacon mixture and toss with 2 spoons over a low heat until piping hot.

7 Transfer to a warm serving dish and accompany with broiled or panfried tomatoes.

Nutritional value per portion:
710 calories
Protein: 21g
Fat: 33g
Carbohydrate: 82g

Fettucine with Bacon and Cheese

Spaghetti Bolognese

Serves 4

An internationally-famed classic from Bologna, in Northern Italy.

Preparation time: 20 minutes
Cooking time: about 1 hour

2-ounce piece of Parmesan cheese
1 onion
1 carrot
2 celery stalks
2 beefsteak tomatoes
3 tablespoons butter
1 tablespoon tomato paste
1 pound lean ground beef
⅔ cup meat stock
1 clove
1 bay leaf
Salt and pepper to taste
2 quarts boiling water
1½ teaspoons salt
1 teaspoon olive oil
12 ounces spaghetti
⅔ cup red wine

1 Grate Parmesan into a small serving bowl. Set aside.

2 Peel and chop onion and carrot or mince the onion and shred the carrot. Cut celery on the bias in thin strips. Peel tomatoes and chop.

3 Melt butter in a saucepan. Add the onion, carrot, and celery and sauté for about 5 minutes until light golden brown.

4 Stir in chopped tomatoes, tomato paste and the ground beef. Stir-fry for 10 minutes.

5 Pour in meat stock, then add clove, bay leaf, and seasoning. Bring to a boil, lower heat and cover. Simmer for about 45 minutes, stirring occasionally.

6 To cook spaghetti, pour boiling water into a large saucepan. Add salt and oil. Bring back to a boil. Ease in spaghetti without breaking. As it softens, it will yield to gentle pressure and settle in a coil in the bottom of the pan. Stir well to separate.

7 Cook pasta, uncovered, for 7-10 minutes until 'al dente' or just tender to the bite. Let stand for 1 minute.

8 Meanwhile, add red wine to meat sauce and season with salt and pepper. Leave uncovered and simmer until spaghetti is ready.

9 Drain spaghetti thoroughly. Divide equally among 4 warm plates and top with sauce. Hand round the Parmesan cheese.

Nutritional value per portion:
790 calories
Protein: 40g
Fat: 31g
Carbohydrate: 78g

Spaghetti Bolognese

Fettucine with Tuna Sauce

Serves 4

This supper dish is quick and easy to make using storecupboard ingredients.

Preparation time: about 15 minutes
Cooking time: about 40 minutes

2 cloves garlic
8-ounce can tuna in oil
14-ounce can tomatoes
½ cup fresh parsley
1 tablespoon olive oil, plus 1 teaspoon
1½ teaspoons salt
2 quarts water
12 ounces wide fettucine
Fresh basil leaves for garnish

1 Peel garlic and chop it finely. Drain tuna, reserving oil, and flake fish into large chunks. Drain and chop tomatoes. Chop parsley fairly finely, removing stalks.

2 Pour 1 tablepoon olive oil and oil from can of tuna into a medium-size saucepan. Add garlic and sauté until pale gold.

3 Add the tomatoes and ½ teaspoon salt, then cover and simmer gently for 20 minutes. Add tuna and parsley and continue to simmer for 10 minutes while you cook the pasta.

4 Pour boiling water into a large saucepan. Add remaining teaspoon salt and remaining teaspoon oil and bring back to a boil. Lower in the fettucine. Stir well to separate.

5 Cook pasta, uncovered, for 7-10 minutes until 'al dente' or just tender to the bite. Let stand for 1 minute. Drain and transfer to 4 warm plates. Spoon over tuna sauce and garnish with basil.

Nutritional value per portion:
640 calories
Protein: 32g
Fat: 23g
Carbohydrate: 77g

Fettucine with Tuna Sauce

Whole-wheat Macaroni with Mushroom Sauce

Serves 4

Mushrooms in cream make a wonderful sauce for whole-wheat pasta

Preparation time: about 15 minutes
Cooking time: about 20 minutes

1 onion
2 cloves garlic
2½ cups button mushrooms
1 tablespoon olive oil, plus 1 teaspoon
1¼ cups vegetable stock
2 quarts boiling water
1½ teaspoons salt
12 ounces whole-wheat elbow macaroni
2 tablespoons semi-sweet white wine or
    1 teaspoon lemon juice
2 pinches of herb salt
6 tablespoons sour dairy cream
1 egg yolk
2 tablespoons scissored fresh chives

1 Peel onion and garlic and chop both finely. Trim and clean mushrooms and cut into thin slices.

2 Heat 1 tablespoon oil in a medium-size saucepan. Add onion and garlic and cook fairly gently until pale golden. Stir in mushrooms and sauté for 2 minutes.

3 Add stock to pan, bring to a boil and cover. Simmer gently for 10 minutes.

4 Pour boiling water into a large saucepan. Add salt and remaining teaspoon oil and bring back to a boil. Tip in the macaroni, then stir well to separate.

5 Cook pasta, uncovered, for 6-9 minutes until 'al dente' or just tender to the bite. Stand for 1 minute.

6 Meanwhile, finish the sauce. Purée the mushroom mixture in a blender or food processor. Pour back into saucepan.

7 Add the wine or lemon juice and herb salt. Whisk cream and egg yolk together. Pour into pan. Reheat, stirring, without boiling or egg might curdle.

8 Drain macaroni and tip into a warm serving dish. Spoon over the mushroom sauce, then sprinkle with chives.

Nutritional value per portion:
450 calories
Protein: 19g
Fat: 10g
Carbohydrate: 70g

Whole-wheat Macaroni with Mushroom Sauce

Spaghetti alla Napoletana

Serves 4

This delicious fresh tasting basil and tomato sauce makes a perfect accompaniment to spaghetti.

Preparation time: about 15 minutes
Cooking time: about 25 minutes

1 large onion
½ cup fresh parsley
8 fresh basil leaves
4 tablespoons olive oil, plus 1 teaspoon
2 x 16-ounce cans tomatoes
½ teaspoon ground paprika
1 teaspoon sugar
2½ teaspoons salt
2 quarts boiling water
12 ounces spaghetti
½ cup grated Pecorino or Parmesan cheese

1 Peel the onion and chop it finely. Remove the stalks from the parsley and chop finely with the basil leaves

2 For sauce, pour 4 tablespoons oil into a medium-size saucepan, heat until sizzling, then add onion. Sauté until light golden brown.

3 Add parsley and basil to saucepan with tomatoes. Cook tomatoes until hot, crushing them against side of pan with a wooden spoon.

4 Add paprika, sugar, and 1 teaspoon salt. Bring to a boil, lower heat and cover. Simmer gently for 10 minutes, stirring fairly frequently.

5 Pour boiling water into a large saucepan. Add remaining 1½ teaspoons salt and 1 teaspoon oil.

6 Bring liquid back to a boil. Ease in spaghetti without breaking. As it softens, it will yield to gentle pressure and settle in a coil in the bottom of the pan. Stir well to separate.

7 Cook pasta, uncovered, for 7-10 minutes until spaghetti is 'al dente' or just tender to the bite. Let stand for 1 minute. Drain thoroughly and transfer equal amounts to 4 warm plates.

8 Spoon sauce over spaghetti and hand cheese separately.

Nutritional value per portion:
570 calories
Protein: 20g
Fat: 18g
Carbohydrate: 83g

Spaghetti alla Napoletana

Spinach Fettucine with Cheese Sauce

Serves 4

*This creamy cheese sauce is quick and easy to prepare and goes well
with all types of pasta.*

Preparation time: about 10 minutes
Cooking time: about 10 minutes

2 quarts boiling water
1 teaspoon salt
1½ teaspoons olive oil
12 ounces green fettucine
1¼ cups vegetable stock
7 ounces French Boursin cheese, with or
    without herbs, or other rich creamy cheese
2 teaspoons cornstarch
2 tablespoons white wine
Salt and pepper to taste

1 Pour boiling water into a large pan. Add salt and oil. Bring back to a boil. Lower in the fettucine and stir well to separate the strands.

2 Cook pasta, uncovered, for 7-10 minutes until fettucine is 'al dente' or just tender to the bite. Let stand for 1 minute.

3 Heat the vegetable stock until it just comes to a boil. Put the cheese into a bowl and mash finely with a fork. Gradually work in the stock.

4 Return to saucepan. Mix cornstarch with wine until smooth. Add to the cheese and stock mixture.

5 Slowly bring to a boil, stirring all the time. Simmer for 1 minute, then season. Remove from heat and cover.

6 Drain fettucine thoroughly. Transfer to 4 warm plates and spoon sauce over.

TIP
Try this with Bel Paese, or use a blue cheese, such as Roquefort.

Nutritional value per portion:
480 calories
Protein: 15g
Fat: 19g
Carbohydrate: 56g

Spinach Fettucine with Cheese Sauce

Spaghetti al Pesto

Serves 4

Brilliantly-colored green with basil, this is a simple pasta dish enhanced with pesto, which is sold in jars in delicatessens and specialty food stores. A recipe for home-made pesto for keen cooks is included here.

Preparation time: about 15 minutes
Cooking time: about 15 minutes

1 cup fresh basil leaves
3 cloves garlic
½ cup pignoli (pine nuts)
1 cup grated Parmesan Cheese or Romano
6 tablespoons olive oil, plus 1 teaspoon
Salt and pepper to taste
2 quarts boiling water
1½ teaspoons salt
12 ounces spaghetti
Fresh basil sprig for garnish

1 Chop basil leaves very finely and put into a bowl.

2 Peel garlic and crush on top of basil.

3 Chop pignoli (pine nuts) finely and add to basil and garlic with grated cheese. Gradually beat in 6 tablespoons of the olive oil.

4 Season to taste with salt and pepper, cover and set aside.

5 Pour water into a large saucepan. Add salt and remaining 1 teaspoon oil. Bring back to a boil. Ease in spaghetti without breaking. As it softens, it will yield to gentle pressure and settle in a coil in the bottom of the pan. Stir well to separate.

6 Cook pasta, uncovered, for 7-10 minutes until spaghetti is 'al dente' or just tender to the bite. Drain off water, leaving about 2 tablespoons behind in the saucepan, with the spaghetti.

7 Mix in pesto and toss thoroughly with 2 spoons.

8 Transfer to a warm dish to serve and garnish with basil sprig.

Nutritional value per portion:
860 calories
Protein: 24g
Fat: 44g
Carbohydrate: 77g

Spaghetti al Pesto

Twistetti with Tomato Sauce

Serves 4

A rustic Mediterranean dish of tomatoes, olives, anchovies, and pasta.

Preparation time: about 15 minutes
Cooking time: about 25 minutes

3 cloves garlic
8 drained canned anchovy fillets, in oil
1 cup pitted olives
3 tablespoons olive oil, plus 1 teaspoon
16-ounce can chopped tomatoes
1 tablespoon drained capers
½ teaspoon paprika
Salt to taste
2 quarts boiling water
1½ teaspoons salt
12 ounces spiral pasta

1 Peel garlic and crush into a medium-size saucepan. Chop anchovies fairly finely. Chop olives coarsely. Add both to pan with 3 tablespoons of the olive oil.

2 Sauté over medium heat until garlic turns pale golden. Stir in tomatoes, capers, paprika, and salt.

3 Bring to a boil, lower heat and cover. Simmer gently for 20 minutes, stirring fairly frequently.

4 After sauce has been cooking for 10 minutes, pour boiling water into a large saucepan. Add salt and remaining oil. Bring back to a boil. Tip in the pasta and stir well to separate.

5 Cook pasta, uncovered, for 6-9 minutes until `al dente' or just tender to the bite. Let stand for 1 minute, then drain and put in a warm serving dish.

6 Spoon over sauce and serve .

Nutritional value per portion:
620 calories
Protein: 19g
Fat: 26g
Carbohydrate: 78g

Twistetti with Tomato Sauce

Summer Spaghetti

Serves 4

A delicate, creamy sauce speckled with zucchini and ham.

Preparation time: about 30 minutes
Cooking time: about 20 minutes

3 medium-size zucchini
2 cloves garlic
1 onion
1 tablespoon olive oil, plus 1 teaspoon
14-ounce piece of country-cured ham
1¼ cups vegetable stock
Salt and pepper to taste
Pinch of dried oregano
2 quarts boiling water
1½ teaspoons salt
12 ounces spaghetti
5 tablespoons heavy cream or
  crème fraîche

1 Trim both end of zucchini, wash and dry then cut each one lengthwise into narrow strips. Cut strips into small dice.

2 Peel garlic and onion and finely chop both.

3 Heat 1 tablespoon of the oil in a large saucepan until hot and sizzling. Add garlic and onion and cook fairly gently until pale golden.

4 Add zucchini and continue to cook for about 5 minutes. Meanwhile, cut ham into narrow strips. Add to vegetables with stock.

5 Bring to a boil, stirring. Season with salt, pepper and oregano. Lower heat, cover and simmer gently for 10 minutes.

6 Pour boiling water into a second large saucepan. Add salt and remaining teaspoon oil. Bring back to a boil. Ease in spaghetti without breaking. As it softens, it will yield to gentle pressure and settle in a coil in the bottom of the pan. Stir well to separate the strands.

7 Meanwhile, cook pasta, uncovered, for 7-10 minutes until 'al dente' or just tender to the bite. Let stand for 1 minute then drain thoroughly and transfer to a large, warm serving dish.

8 Add cream or crème fraîche to sauce, heat through briefly and pour over spaghetti. Toss with 2 spoons until well-mixed. Serve at once.

Nutritional value per portion:
480 calories
Protein: 17g
Fat: 17g
Carbohydrate: 65g

Summer Spaghetti

Spaghetti with Garlic Oil and Herbs

Serves 4

Strongly flavored with garlic, this is a favorite pasta dish in Southern Italy.

Preparation time: about 25 minutes
Cooking time: about 10 minutes

4 cloves garlic
1 cup fresh parsley
8 fresh basil leaves
6 tablespoons olive oil, plus 1 teaspoon
Salt and pepper to taste
2 quarts boiling water
1½ teaspoons salt
12 ounces spaghetti

1 Peel garlic and crush directly into a small saucepan. Chop parsley, discarding stalks. Finely chop basil.

2 Add 6 tablespoons of the oil to pan of garlic and cook gently until pale golden. Mix in parsley and basil and season well with salt and pepper. Leave over a very low heat while you cook the pasta.

3 Pour boiling water into a large saucepan. Add salt and remaining teaspoon oil. Bring back to a boil. Ease in spaghetti without breaking. As it softens, it will yield to gentle pressure and settle in a coil in the bottom of pan. Stir well to separate.

4 Cook pasta, uncovered, for 7-10 minutes or until spaghetti is 'al dente' or just tender to the bite. Let stand for 1 minute. Drain thoroughly and tip into a warm serving dish.

5 Spoon over the garlic and herb oil and toss with 2 spoons until well mixed.

Nutritional value per portion:
550 calories
Protein: 14g
Fat: 23g
Carbohydrate: 74g

Spaghetti with Garlic Oil and Herbs

Spaghetti Omelet

Serves 4

Children will love this swirly omelet.

Preparation time: about 20 minutes
Cooking time: about 25 minutes

2 quarts boiling water
1½ teaspoons salt
1 teaspoon olive oil
12 ounces spaghetti
3 eggs
⅔ cup whipping cream
1 cup grated Parmesan cheese
Salt and pepper to taste
3 tablespoons butter
1 tablespoon scissored fresh chives

1 Pour boiling water into a large saucepan. Add salt and oil. Bring back to a boil. Ease in spaghetti without breaking. As it softens, it will yield to gentle pressure and settle in a coil in the bottom of the pan. Stir well to separate.

2 Cook pasta uncovered, for 7-10 minutes until 'al dente' or just tender to the bite. Let stand for 1 minute. Thoroughly drain and let cool.

3 To complete, beat eggs and cream together. Stir in two-thirds of the cheese and season with salt and pepper.

4 Melt half the butter in a large, non-stick skillet.

5 Add the spaghetti in an even layer and cook for about 5 minutes over a medium heat until underside is golden.

6 Pour in the egg mixture then cover pan with a lid. Continue to cook slowly for 5 minutes then uncover.

7 Sprinkle the top of the omelet with the remaining cheese then dot with flakes of remaining butter.

8 Stand skillet under a hot broiler, making sure handle is away from source of heat and broil for 1-2 minutes or until top is well-browned.

9 Cut omelet into 4 portions with a non-stick spatula, sprinkle with chives and serve immediately.

Nutritional value per portion:
710 calories
Protein: 28g
Fat: 35g
Carbohydrate: 73g

Spaghetti Omelet

Macaroni with Ham

Serves 4

This dish makes a substantial supper dish served with crusty bread and a mixed salad.

Preparation time: about 15 minutes
Cooking time: about 30 minutes

2 quarts boiling water
1½ teaspoons salt
1 teaspoon olive oil
12 ounces elbow macaroni
6 tablespoons milk
10-ounce package frozen peas
10 ounces cooked ham
1 onion
½ cup fresh parsley
1 tablespoon corn oil
⅔ cup soured cream
2 eggs
Salt and pepper to taste
½ cup shredded Cheddar cheese or
    Monterey Jack
2 tablespoons butter
Chopped fresh parsley for garnish

1 Pour boiling water into a large saucepan. Add salt and olive oil. Bring back to a boil. Tip in the macaroni, then stir well to separate.

2 Cook pasta, uncovered, for 6-9 minutes until 'al dente' or until just tender to the bite. Let stand for 1 minute. Drain.

3 Meanwhile prepare all the remaining ingredients. Bring milk to a boil in a separate pan. Add peas. Cover and cook for 3 minutes.

4 Chop ham coarsely. Peel onion and chop very finely. Chop parsley finely, discarding stalks. Preheat oven to 375°F. Butter a fairly shallow ovenproof dish.

5 Heat corn oil in a pan until hot and sizzling. Add ham and onion and sauté until pale golden. Drain macaroni well and mix into cooked ingredients with parsley. Spoon into ovenproof dish.

6 Beat cream and eggs together and season well with salt and pepper. Pour over macaroni mixture.

7 Sprinkle with cheese then top with flakes of butter.

8 Bake in oven for 15-20 minutes until golden brown and bubbly. Garnish and serve immediately.

Nutritional value per portion:
690 calories
Protein: 33g
Fat: 32g
Carbohydrate: 67g

Macaroni with Ham

◆NOTES◆

◆NOTES◆

Pizzas

Made Easy

Series Consultant:
Sonia Allison

GREAT
COOKING
VALUE

Introduction

Make, bake and eat and you will soon discover there is nothing quite like the real thing; your own freshly-cooked pizza, sizzling with mouth-watering toppings which *you* have created. There is no end to the ingenious toppings you can prepare to make true Italian-style pizzas such as vegetables, fish, mushrooms, cooked ham, cheese, or even nuts. For spicier tastes, add pepperoni or salami, anchovies, olives, cornichons, garlic, and herbs. Have fun!

Recipe Notes

Use standard spoon and cup measures. All measures are level unless otherwise stated.

Rising times for yeast doughs are approximate only. The dough is ready when it has doubled in bulk and springs back when pressed lightly with a floured finger.

Eggs used are large unless otherwise stated.

Calorie counts for average-size servings are set down at the end of each recipe, and are rounded up to the nearest whole number.

Written by Annette Wolter

Pizza with Mozzarella and Basil

Serves 4

A crispy, thin-crusted pizza which is popular all over Italy.

Preparation time: about 40 minutes, plus about 1½ hours for rising dough.

3¼ cups all-purpose flour
1 teaspoon salt
½ ounce compressed yeast or 1 sachet
  fast-rising active dry yeast
1 cup lukewarm water
2 teaspoons olive oil

TOPPING
8 medium tomatoes
9 bacon slices, rind removed
2 onions
13 ounces Mozzarella cheese, sliced
32 black olives
1 teaspoon Italian Seasoning Mix (dried
  herbs)
4 teaspoons olive oil
Freshly ground black pepper to taste
Fresh basil leaves

1 Make dough with flour, salt, yeast, water, and oil as given in step-by-step instructions.

2 Divide risen dough into 4 equal parts on floured work surface. Roll out each piece of dough into a 9-inch round and put onto 4 oiled baking sheets or pizza pans. Fold over edges of dough inward to make raised rims. Leave in warm place while preparing topping. Preheat oven to 425°F.

3 Cover tomatoes with boiling water for 30 seconds, then plunge into cold water and peel away skins. Cut tomatoes in half, remove any pieces of core and slice. Cut bacon into thin strips.

4 Slice onions thinly and separate slices into rings. Cover pizza bases with tomatoes, bacon, and onions, mozzarella, and olives. Sprinkle with Italian seasoning, oil, and pepper.

5 Bake 2 pizzas at a time for about 30 minutes until crisp and golden brown, rearranging position of sheets or pans half way through cooking. Scatter fresh basil leaves over top and serve warm.

Nutritional value per portion:
830 calories
Protein: 31g
Fat: 42g
Carbohydrate: 81g

Pizza with Mozzarella and Basil

Pizza Napoletana

Serves 4

One of the great classic Italian pizzas and inspiration for seemingly endless variations.

Preparation time: about 40 minutes, plus about 1½ hours for rising dough.

3¼ cups all-purpose flour
1 teaspoon salt
½ ounce compressed yeast or 1 sachet
   fast-rising active dry yeast
1 cup lukewarm water
2 teaspoons olive oil

TOPPING
1 pound ripe tomatoes
10 ounces mozzarella cheese,
2 cloves garlic
4 fresh basil sprigs
1 teaspoon dried oregano
3 tablespoons olive oil
salt to taste
Freshly ground black pepper to taste

1 Make dough with flour, salt, yeast, water, and oil.

2 Divide risen dough into 2 equal pieces on floured work surface. Roll out each piece of dough into a 10-inch round and put onto 2 oiled baking sheets, folding edges of dough inward to make raised rims. Leave in warm place while preparing topping. Preheat oven to 425°F.

3 Cover tomatoes with boiling water for 30 seconds, then plunge into cold water and peel away skins. Slice tomatoes. Cut cheese into thin slices. Peel and crush garlic. Rinse basil and pat dry with paper towels. Reserve about 16 leaves for garnish and finely chop remainder.

4 Cover both pizzas with tomatoes and cheese then sprinkle with garlic, chopped basil, and oregano. Spoon oil over pizza, and season with salt and pepper.

5 Bake for about 30 minutes until golden brown and crisp, rearranging position of sheets half way through cooking. Garnish pizza with remaining basil leaves and cut each pizza in half before serving.

Nutritional value per portion:
640 calories
Protein: 29g
Fat: 21g
Carbohydrate: 80g

Pizza Napoletana

Pizza with Mushrooms and Ham

Serves 4

Mushrooms, ham, and cheese form the topping of this substantial pizza.

Preparation: about 45 minutes, plus about 1½ hours for rising dough.

3¼ cups all-purpose flour
1 teaspoon salt
½ ounce compressed yeast or 1 sachet
   fast-rising active dry yeast
1 cup lukewarm water
2 teaspoons olive oil

TOPPING
2 cups button mushrooms
1 center slice, country-cured ham, cut
   ¼-inch thick, rind removed
1 cup shredded Swiss cheese
Salt to taste
Freshly ground pepper to taste
2 tablespoons minced fresh parsley
2 tablespoons olive oil
Fresh parsley sprig for garnish

1 Make dough with flour, salt, yeast, water, and oil.

2 Roll out dough to fit a large, oiled jelly roll pan as shown in step-by-step picture on page 19. Fold edges of dough inward to form a raised rim and leave in warm place while preparing topping. Preheat oven to 425°F.

3 Rinse mushrooms, drain thoroughly and slice thinly. Cut ham into narrow strips. Arrange mushrooms and ham evenly over pizza base, then sprinkle with cheese, salt, pepper, and parsley.

4 Spoon oil over top of pizza and bake in oven for 25-30 minutes until golden brown and crisp. Garnish with fresh parsley and cut pizza into 4 wedges. Serve warm.

Nutritional value per portion:
620 calories
Protein: 22g
Fat: 28g
Carbohydrate: 67g

Pizza with Mushrooms and Ham

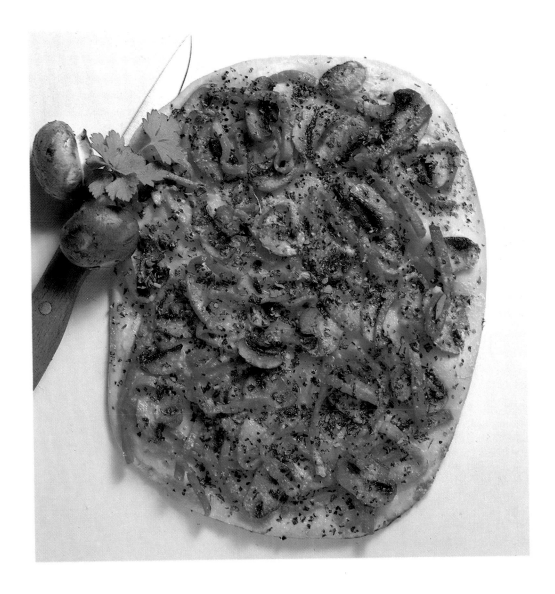

Calzone

Serves 4

Calzone are pizza turnovers and these are filled with one of Italy's most cherished combinations – ricotta cheese and spinach.

Preparation time: about 1 hour, plus about 1½ hours for rising dough.

3¼ cups all-purpose flour
1 teaspoon salt
½ ounce compressed yeast or 1 sachet fast-rising active dry yeast
1 cup lukewarm water
2 teaspoons melted butter or shortening

FILLING

1¼ pounds fresh spinach
1 onion
2 cloves garlic
3 tablespoons olive oil
½ cup ricotta cheese
1 teaspoon salt
Freshly ground pepper to taste
Extra olive oil for brushing

1 Make dough with flour, salt, yeast, water, and melted butter or shortening.

2 Prepare filling while dough is rising. Wash spinach leaves. Put into large saucepan with a little boiling, salted water and boil for 3 minutes. Drain thoroughly, cool and chop.

3 Peel onion and chop finely. Peel garlic and crush. Cook both gently in oil in skillet until soft. Mix in spinach, and ricotta cheese and season with salt and pepper. Preheat oven to 425°F.

4 Put risen dough onto floured work surface and divide into 4 equal parts. Roll out each piece into a 6-inch square. Cover with spinach mixture to within ½ inch of edges. Dampen edges with water then fold each piece of dough in half, pinching edges together to seal.

5 Put folded dough packages onto oiled baking sheet and brush all over with extra oil. Bake in oven for 30 minutes until golden brown and crisp. Serve.

Nutritional value per portion:
760 calories
Protein: 31g
Fat: 34g
Carbohydrate: 83g

Calzone

Seafood Pizza

Serves 4

A luscious mix of mussels, anchovies, mackerel and shrimp.

Preparation time: about 1 hour, plus 1½ hours for rising dough.

3¼ cups all-purpose flour
1 teaspoon salt
½ ounce compressed yeast or 1 sachet fast-rising active dry yeast
1 cup lukewarm water
2 teaspoons olive oil

TOPPING
4 large tomatoes
1 large onion
2 tablespoons olive oil
7 ounces bottled or canned mussels
2-ounce can anchovy fillets in oil
8 ounces smoked mackerel fillets
10 shelled baby shrimp
2 tablespoons drained capers, chopped
½ teaspoon salt
Freshly ground black pepper to taste
2 tablespoons shredded fresh basil
Fresh basil sprig for garnish

1 Make dough with flour, salt, yeast, water, and oil.

2 Roll out risen dough into an oval on a large, oiled jelly roll pan as shown in step-by-step picture on page 19. Fold edges of dough inward to form a raised rim. Leave in warm place while preparing topping. Preheat oven to 425°F.

3 Cover tomatoes with boiling water for 30 seconds, then plunge into cold water, peel away skins and chop finely. Set aside. Peel and chop onion, then sauté onion in half the oil until just beginning to turn golden. Add tomatoes and cook gently, uncovered, until most of the liquid has evaporated, stirring frequently. Cool and spread over pizza base.

4 Drain mussels and anchovies. Chop anchovies and flake mackerel fillets with 2 forks. Arrange over pizza with shrimp and capers. Sprinkle with salt and pepper then spoon over remaining oil.

5 Bake for 30 minutes until golden brown and crisp. Scatter top with shredded basil. Cut into portions and serve immediately garnished with basil.

Nutritional value per portion:
640 calories
Protein: 39g
Fat: 18g
Carbohydrate: 81g

Seafood Pizza

Focaccia

Serves 4

A wonderful flat bread based on a pizza dough but without a topping. This version contains walnuts and is a perfect partner for cheese and celery. Eat while still warm.

Preparation time: about 40 minutes, plus 1¾ hours for rising dough.

3¼ cups all-purpose flour
1 teaspoon salt
½ ounce compressed yeast or 1 sachet
    fast-rising active dry yeast
250ml (8 fl oz/1 cup) lukewarm water
2 teaspoons, plus 2 tablespoons extra
    olive oil
½ cup walnut halves
Fresh sage sprig for garnish

1 Make dough with flour, salt, yeast, water, and 2 teaspoons oil.
While dough is rising, coarsely chop walnuts.

2 After punching down, leave dough on floured work surface and knead in walnuts and half remaining oil. Preheat oven to 450°F.

3 Roll out dough into a large round and use to line a 12-inch oiled pizza pan. Press out dough until it reaches edge of pan and prick all over with fork. Cover with piece of oiled non-stick baking parchment and leave in a warm place for 20 minutes.

4 Brush dough with remaining oil and bake for 15-20 minutes until golden brown and crisp. Serve warm, garnished with sage.

Nutritional value per portion:
430 calories
Protein: 11g
Fat: 16g
Carbohydrate: 58g

Focaccia

Tuna and Artichoke Pizza

Serves 4

This quick-to-prepare pizza makes a good party dish.

Preparation time: about 40 minutes.

¾ cup ricotta or softened cream cheese
⅓ cup milk
½ cup olive oil
3¼ cups all-purpose flour
½ teaspoon salt
1½ teaspoons baking powder

TOPPING

12-ounce can tuna
2 cloves garlic
½ teaspoon salt
3 tablespoons olive oil
1 teaspoon dried thyme
Freshly ground black pepper to taste
2 x 14-ounce cans artichoke hearts
⅔ cup grated Parmesan cheese
3 tablespoons crème fraîche or
   heavy cream
2 egg yolks
2 tablespoons scissored fresh chives
Fresh chives for garnish

1 To make pastry, put ricotta or cream cheese, milk, and oil into mixing bowl and beat until smooth. Sift flour, salt and baking powder into bowl, mix together until well combined. Preheat oven to 400°F.

2 Roll out pastry on floured work surface into a large round and use to line an oiled 12-inch pie pan. Prick the pastry all over with a fork.

3 For topping, drain tuna and separate fish into chunky flakes. Put into mixing bowl. Peel and crush in garlic, then add salt, oil, thyme, and pepper. Mix well and spoon over pizza. Drain artichokes, cut in half and arrange on top of tuna filling.

4 Beat together remaining ingredients and spoon over topping. Bake pizza for 30 minutes until golden brown and crisp. Cut in wedges and serve hot, garnished with chives.

Nutritional value per portion:
1100 calories
Protein: 55g
Fat: 59g
Carbohydrate: 85g

Tuna and Artichoke Pizza

Cornichon and Pepperoni Pizza

Serves 4

A stylish pizza, based mostly on storecupboard ingredients.

Preparation time: about 45 minutes

¾ cup ricotta or softened cream cheese
⅓ cup milk
½ cup olive oil
3¼ cups all-purpose flour
½ teaspoon salt
1½ teaspoons baking powder

TOPPING
2 large onions
⅓ cup olive oil
4 tablespoons tomato paste
½ teaspoon salt
4 cornichons
3½ ounces thinly sliced pepperoni
2 tablespoons drained capers
1 cup grated Parmesan cheese

1 Make pastry with ricotta or softened cream cheese, milk, oil, flour, salt, and baking powder. Preheat oven to 400°F.

2 Roll out pastry on floured work surface into a large round and use to line a 12-inch oiled pizza pan. Prick all over the surface with fork.

3 For topping, peel onions and slice them thinly. Separate slices into rings and sauté in half the oil until light golden brown.

4 Mix remaining oil with tomato paste and salt, then spread over pizza base. Thinly slice cornichons lengthwise into strips and arrange on top of tomato mixture with onions and pepperoni. Dot with capers, then sprinkle with cheese.

5 Bake for 30 minutes until golden brown and crisp. Cut into 4 pieces and serve the pizza hot.

Nutritional value per portion:
1000 calories
Protein: 37g
Fat: 55g
Carbohydrate: 85g

Cornichon and Pepperoni Pizza

Broccoli and Bacon Pizza

Serves 4

An unusual combination of ingredients make a fresh-tasting topping.

Preparation time: about 45 minutes

2 cups all-purpose flour
½ teaspoon salt
1 egg yolk
1 stick butter or shortening
3 tablespoons cold water

TOPPING
1½ pounds young broccoli
2 cloves garlic
6 bacon slices, rind removed
1 tablespoon olive oil
2 egg yolks
½ teaspoon salt
½ cup crème fraîche or heavy cream

1 Make Rich Pie Dough with flour, salt, egg yolk, butter or shortening, and water. Preheat oven to 400°F.

2 Roll out dough into a 10-inch round on floured work surface. Transfer to large, oiled baking sheet and prick all over with fork. Set aside while preparing topping.

3 Wash broccoli, cut into small flowerets. Cook in a pan of boiling, salted water until just tender but still bright green. Drain and let cool completely.

4 Peel and crush garlic. Chop bacon. Sauté both gently in oil until just beginning to color. Arrange over pizza base. Add broccoli.

5 Beat together remaining ingredients and spoon over topping. Bake in oven for 30 minutes until golden brown and crisp. Cut into pieces and serve hot.

Nutritional value per portion:
about 1000 calories
Protein: 29g
Fat: 78g
Carbohydrate: 57g

Broccoli and Bacon Pizza

Whole-wheat Tomato Pizza

Serves 4

A wholesome tomato, mushroom, and cheese pizza.

Preparation time: about 30 minutes

2 cups whole-wheat flour
1 egg yolk
½ teaspoon salt
1 stick butter or shortening
¼ cup cold water

TOPPING
6 tomatoes
1¼ cups small button mushrooms
1 cup (6 ounces) feta cheese
¼ cup olive oil
15 small basil leaves

1 Make Rich Pie Dough with flour, egg yolk, salt, butter or shortening, and water. Preheat oven to 400°F.

2 Roll out dough into a 10-inch round on floured work surface. Transfer to large, oiled baking sheet. Prick all over with fork and set aside while preparing topping.

3 Cover tomatoes with boiling water for 30 seconds, then plunge into cold water and peel away skins. Cut tomatoes into small pieces and spoon over pizza base. Trim and slice mushrooms, with stalks. Crumble cheese. Scatter mushrooms and cheese on top of tomatoes.

4 Spoon oil over pizza and bake for 30 minutes until golden brown and crisp. Garnish with basil. Cut into wedges and serve warm.

Nutritional value per portion:
670 calories
Protein: 23g
Fat: 43g
Carbohydrate: 39g

Whole-wheat Tomato Pizza

Anchovy and Yellow Pepper Pizza

Serves 4

A favorite choice for pizza lovers.

Preparation time: about 40 minutes, plus 1½ hours for rising dough.

3¼ cups whole-wheat flour
1 teaspoon salt
½ ounce compressed yeast or 1 sachet fast-rising active dry yeast
1 cup lukewarm skim milk
2 teaspoons olive oil

TOPPING

6 tomatoes
½ teaspoon salt
2 cloves garlic
1 onion
2 baby yellow peppers
2 tablespoons olive oil
2 celery stalks
4 ounces mozzarella cheese
20 pitted black olives
2-ounce can anchovy fillets in oil

1 Make dough with flour, salt, yeast, milk, and oil and substituting the skim milk for the lukewarm water. Roll out risen dough into a 9-inch square baking pan. Preheat oven to 425°F.

2 Prepare topping. Cover tomatoes with boiling water for 30 seconds, then plunge into cold water and peel away skins. Slice tomatoes, put onto plate and sprinkle with salt. Peel garlic and crush over tomatoes.

3 Peel onion, slice thinly and separate slices into rings. Cut peppers in half, remove inner white membranes and seeds and cut flesh into strips. Sauté onion and peppers in half the oil until just soft.

4 Meanwhile, trim celery and cut into slices. Slice mozzarella thinly. Cover pizza base with tomato and garlic mixture then top with onion and peppers, celery, and mozzarella.

5 Chop olives and sprinkle over pizza with drained anchovies. Spoon over remaining oil. Bake for 30 minutes until golden brown and crisp.

TIP

If you can't locate baby peppers, use 1 yellow bell pepper instead.

Nutritional value per portion:
520 calories
Protein: 19g
Fat: 22g
Carbohydrate: 57g

Anchovy and Yellow Pepper Pizza

Vegetable Pizza with Ham

Serves 4

A lattice of mozzarella gives this pizza an impressive finishing touch.

Preparation time: about 1 hour

¾ cup ricotta or softened cream cheese
⅓ cup milk
½ cup olive oil
3¼ cups all-purpose flour
½ teaspoon salt
1½ teaspoons baking powder

FILLING

6 tomatoes
1 zucchini (about 6 ounces)
1 cup mushrooms
2 ounces Prosciutto
3 tablespoons olive oil
1 tablespoon drained capers
2 pinches of salt
½ teaspoon dried oregano
4 ounces mozzarella cheese
1 tablespoon chopped fresh parsley

1 Make pastry with ricotta or softened cream cheese, milk, oil, flour, salt, and baking powder. Preheat oven to 400°F.

2 Roll out pastry into a large round and use to line an 11-inch greased pie pan. Prick base with fork and set aside while preparing filling.

3 Cover tomatoes with boiling water for 30 seconds, plunge into cold water then peel away skins and slice thinly. Trim zucchini and cut in thin slices. Arrange tomatoes and zucchini over pizza base.

4 Cut mushrooms in thin slices. Cut Prosciutto in narrow strips. Sprinkle over tomatoes and zucchini then spoon half the oil over pizza.

5 Sprinkle with capers, salt, and oregano. Cut cheese in strips and arrange in a criss-cross design on top of pizza. Sprinkle with remaining oil. Bake for 30 minutes until golden brown and crisp. Sprinkle with parsley and serve warm.

Nutritional value per portion:
790 calories
Protein: 29g
Fat: 37g
Carbohydrate: 82g

Vegetable Pizza with Ham

Four Seasons Pizza

Serves 4

Four assorted toppings to appeal to everyone.

Preparation time: about 50 minutes, plus 1½ hours for rising dough.

3¼ cups all-purpose flour
1 teaspoon salt
½ ounce compressed yeast or 1 sachet
   fast-rising active dry yeast
1 cup lukewarm water
2 teaspoons olive oil
Mixed fresh herb sprigs for garnish

TOPPINGS
2 drained canned artichoke hearts
8 mushrooms
4 slices cooked ham
4 ounces mozzarella cheese
8 pitted black olives
2-ounce can anchovy fillets in oil
4 tomatoes
½ teaspoon salt
½ teaspoon dried oregano
7 ounces drained canned or bottled mussels
2 tablespoons olive oil

1 Make dough with flour, salt, yeast, water, and oil following step-by-step instructions.

2 Divide dough into 2 parts on floured work surface and roll out each into a 10-inch round. Put onto oiled baking sheets or pizza pans, folding edges of dough inward to make raised rims. Leave in warm place while preparing toppings. Preheat oven to 400°F.

3 Cut each artichoke into fourths. Trim mushrooms and slice. Cut ham into strips. Shred cheese. Rinse olives and drain. Drain anchovies and cut each in half. Cover tomatoes with boiling water for 30 seconds, plunge into cold water then peel away skins and chop. Put tomatoes into bowl and season with salt and oregano.

4 Score each pizza base into 4 sections. Fill 1 section of both pizzas with mussels and artichokes; 1 section with mushrooms and ham; 1 section with cheese, olives, and anchovies; and last section with seasoned tomatoes.

5 Spoon oil over each pizza. Bake for 35 minutes until golden brown and crisp, rearranging position of sheets or pizza pans halfway through cooking. Cut in portions and serve hot, garnished with herbs.

Nutritional value per portion:
450 calories
Protein: 23g
Fat: 18g
Carbohydrate: 45g

Four Seasons Pizza

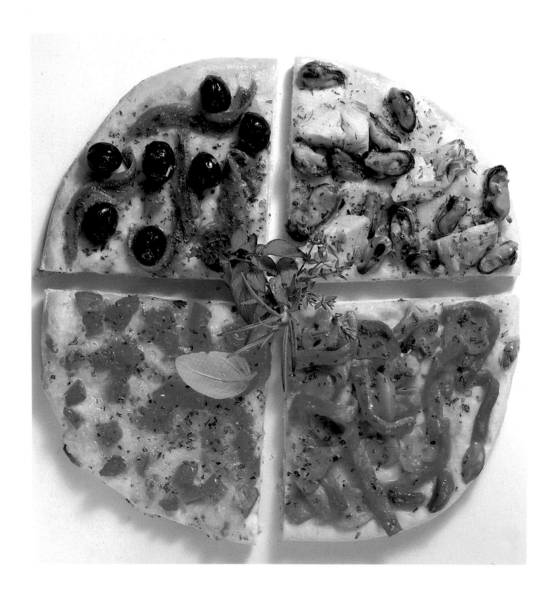

Step-by-step PIZZA DOUGH

For quantities, refer to individual recipes.

1 Sift flour and salt into mixing bowl and make well in center.

2 Crumble in fresh yeast with finger tips. (If using fast-rising active dry yeast, simply stir into flour.

3 Pour in ⅔ cup of the lukewarm water and work in a little flour from edge of well with a wooden spoon. Sprinkle flour on top. Cover bowl with clean dish towel. Set aside for 15-20 minutes in warm place. If using fast-rising yeast, skip this stage and work in all the liquid. (Step 5).

4 The mixture is ready when the compressed yeast starts to bubble or 'sponge'.

5 Add remaining water (or all the water, if using fast-rising yeast) and oil, gradually working in flour.

6 Continue to beat mixture until smooth. Put on floured work surface and knead until dough holds together.This can be done in a food mixer fitted with a dough hook or a food processor with plastic blade attachment.

7 Shape dough into ball on floured work surface and knead for 10 minutes more.

8 Transfer dough to a large, lightly oiled bowl. Sprinkle top with a dusting of extra flour. Cover bowl with a clean dish towel and leave in a warm place for about 1½ hours.

9 Once dough has doubled in bulk return it to floured work surface. Punch down by hitting once with your fist. Knead quickly and lightly until smooth. Use as directed in recipes.

Step-by-step

RICH PIE DOUGH

1 Sift flour and salt onto work surface. Make a well in center and fill with whole egg or egg yolk and water. Add cubes of butter or shortening to rim of flour.

2 Work ingredients together until crumbly. Knead dough lightly until smooth. Shape into ball and wrap in foil. Chill for 30-40 minutes.

3 Roll out dough on lightly floured work surface. If lining pie pan, lift into pan with help of rolling pin.

CHEESE PASTRY WITH OIL

4 Put ricotta or softened cream cheese, milk and oil, into mixing bowl. Mix well together with wooden spoon until smooth.

5 Sift flour, salt, and baking powder over cheese mixture. Stir until it holds together.

6 Using both hands, put onto floured surface and knead until pastry is smooth. Wrap in foil and chill for 40 minutes before using.

SHAPING PIZZAS

7 Divide risen dough into 4 equal-size pieces and roll each out into a 6-inch round. Put onto 2 large oiled baking sheets. Add toppings and bake.

8 To make 1 large pizza, roll out risen dough in an oiled jelly roll pan. Gently pull and stretch edge with fingers to make even shape.

9 For individual small pizzas, roll out risen dough into 6 rounds, cover with topping and bake on large, oiled baking sheet.

◆NOTES◆

◆NOTES◆

Risotto
& Rice Recipes
Made Easy

Series
Consultant:
Sonia Allison

GREAT
COOKING
VALUE

Introduction

Risotto is one of Italy's greatest inventions and one which demands care and constant attention as it cooks gently on the hob. The secret of perfect risotto lies in using Arborio rice or Vialone rice which are short grain varieties, capable of staying whole and 'al dente' while they absorb a surprisingly large amount of liquid.

In Italy, risotto is regarded as a main course in its own right, usually served in soup plates and eaten like a pudding, with a spoon and fork.

Recipe Notes

Use standard spoon and cup measures. All measures are level unless otherwise stated.

Eggs used are large unless otherwise stated.

Calorie counts for average-size servings are set down at the end of each recipe, and are rounded up to the nearest whole number.

Written by Sabine Sälzer

Vegetable Risotto

Serves 4

A colorful mix of vegetables makes this risotto particularly appealing.

Preparation time: about 25 minutes
Cooking time: about 35 minutes

1 medium zucchini
10-ounce wedge of pumpkin or
    summer squash
1 beefsteak tomato
1 onion
2 cloves garlic
4 cups hot chicken or vegetable stock
2 tablespoons olive oil
1¼ cups risotto rice
1 tablespoon dry sherry wine
4 drained canned artichoke hearts
Salt and pepper to taste
2 tablespoons fresh Italian parsley

1 Trim the zucchini and cut into small cubes. Peel pumpkin or squash, remove seeds and cut flesh into fairly arge pieces.

2 Cover tomato with boiling water for 30 seconds, then plunge into cold water and peel away skin. Cut tomato into fourths, remove seeds with a teaspoon and discard. Chop remaining flesh coarsely. Peel onion and garlic and finely chop separately.

3 Bring stock to a boil in a saucepan then leave to simmer over a low heat. Heat oil in a large, heavy-based pan until sizzling and hot. Add chopped onion, sauté gently, without coloring, until it softens and looks semi-transparent. Stir in rice and cook slowly, for 2 minutes, stirring constantly.

4 Add garlic and sherry wine to pan and then gradually add stock in small amounts with a ladle, stirring over a medium heat until every batch of liquid had been absorbed before adding the next. Allow about 20 minutes cooking time.

5 Add remaining stock with the zucchini and pumpkin or squash and continue to cook for a further 10 minutes, stirring constantly. Cut artichoke hearts into fourths, add to risotto and heat through briefly.

6 Season to taste, spoon into warm soup bowls, sprinkle each with chopped tomato and garnish with parsley leaves.

Nutritional value per portion:
310 calories
Protein: 8g
Fat: 5g
Carbohydrate: 60g

Vegetable Risotto

Risotto alla Milanese

Serves 4

Preparation time: 10 minutes
Cooking time: about 30 minutes

1 beef shin bone (optional)
1 onion
4 cups chicken, beef or vegetable stock
½ stick butter
1½ cups risotto rice
1 package saffron strands or powder
½ cup freshly grated Parmesan cheese
Salt and pepper to taste

1 Remove marrow from inside of well-washed shin bone, if using. Cut into small pieces.

2 Peel and finely chop onion. Bring stock to a boil in a saucepan and let simmer over a low heat.

3 Put half the butter into a large, heavy-based saucepan. Add bone marrow, if used, and chopped onion and cook gently without coloring, stirring constantly until onion softens and looks transparent.

4 Sprinkle in rice and mix thoroughly with cooked onion. Add a ladle of boiling stock, making sure enough has been added to cover rice. Heat until risotto just begins to simmer, stirring constantly. As soon as all the liquid has been absorbed, add another ladle of hot stock.

5 Continue adding boiling stock, ladle at a time, until all the stock has been absorbed. Keep mixture over a low heat and stir frequently so that the rice cooks evenly and smoothly.

6 After about 20-25 minutes, soak the saffron strands briefly in hot water or mix saffron powder with 1 tablespoon of hot water.

7 Mix saffron into risotto well and then stir in remaining butter, Parmesan cheese and seasoning. Continue to cook risotto for a further 5 minutes, then remove pan from heat, cover and let stand for 1 minute.

Nutritional value per portion:
480 calories
Protein: 11g
Fat: 24g
Carbohydrate: 61g

Risotto alla Milanese

Risi e Bisi

Serves 4

This is a simple risotto of rice and peas and is eaten in Italy as a main course.

Preparation time: 10 minutes
Cooking time: about 35 minutes

6 bacon slices, rinds removed
1 onion
½ cup fresh Italian parsley
3 tablespoons butter
10-ounce package frozen peas
4 cups meat or vegetable stock
1¼ cups risotto rice
½ cup grated Parmesan cheese
Salt and pepper to taste

1 Cut bacon into small pieces. Peel and chop onion. Finely chop parsley.

2 Put 2 tablespoons butter into a large, heavy-based saucepan and melt until sizzling and hot. Add the bacon, onion, and parsley and cook gently, without coloring, until onion softens and looks semi-transparent.

3 Add the peas and 1 cup of the stock. Bring to a boil, lower heat and simmer gently for 5 minutes.

4 Pour in remaining stock and bring back to a boil. Add the rice and simmer, uncovered, for 25 minutes, stirring frequently.

5 Add remaining butter and half the cheese. Mix in well and season with salt and pepper. Transfer to 4 warm soup bowls, sprinkle with remaining parsley and pass round remaining cheese separately for sprinkling over the top.

Nutritional value per portion:
500 calories
Protein: 17g
Fat: 23g
Carbohydrate: 59g

Risi e Bisi

Cream Risotto with Salmon

Serves 4

This creamy salmon risotto makes a perfect dish for special occasions.

Preparation time: about 10 minutes
Cooking time: about 30 minutes

12-ounce piece of salmon, boned,
    and skinned
1 small lemon
12 fresh basil leaves
4 tablespoons olive oil
1 ¼ cups chicken stock
4 shallots or baby onoins
2 tablespoons butter
1 ¼ cups risotto rice
scant 1 cup white wine
⅔ cup heavy cream
Salt and pepper to taste
4 tablespoons grated Parmesan cheese
Fresh basil sprig for garnish

1 Cut salmon into 1-inch cubes and carefully remove bones with tweezers. Put into a shallow dish.

2 Wash and dry lemon. Grate lemon and then squeeze out the juice. Cut basil leaves into strips.

3 Add lemon rind, juice, half the basil and 2 tablespoons of oil to the salmon and toss gently to mix. Cover and leave to marinate in the refrigerator while preparing remaining ingredients.

4 Pour stock into a saucepan, bring to a boil, then reduce heat and simmer gently. Peel shallots or baby onions; chop them finely. Heat remaining oil in a large, heavy-based pan. Add butter and melt.

5 Mix in shallots or baby onions and cook gently until they are soft, pale creamy-yellow and semi-transparent. Stir in rice until every grain is covered with oil and butter.

6 Pour in wine and cook until it has been absorbed. Gradually add a ladle of simmering stock, making sure enough has been added to cover the rice. Heat until rice mixture just begins to simmer, stirring constantly. As soon as all the liquid has been absorbed, add another ladle of stock. Repeat until all the stock has been added and absorbed. Allow about 25 minutes cooking time.

7 Stir in cream and season to taste. Cover pan and leave over a low heat while cooking fish. Put into a shallow pan with the lemon marinade, bring to a boil, then reduce heat and simmer, uncovered, for 5 minutes.

8 Season risotto and then mix in cheese. Transfer to 4 warm plates, top each with salmon and pan juices and then sprinkle with remaining basil. Garnish with basil sprig and serve.

Nutritional value per portion:
740 calories
Protein: 29g
Fat: 43g
Carbohydrate: 55g

Cream Risotto with Salmon

Ground Beef and Pepper Rice

Serves 4

Ground beef, red bell peppers, and long-grain white rice are the basic ingredients for this wholesome risotto.

Preparation time: about 15 minutes
Cooking time: about 45 minutes

1 each red and green bell peppers
2 onions
3 cups beef stock
2 tablespoons corn oil
2 cloves garlic
12 ounces (1½ cups) lean ground beef
1 cup American easy-cook long-grain
 white rice
2 tablespoons white wine
Salt and pepper to taste
½ teaspoon ground paprika
½ cup fresh Italian parsley
1 tablespoon small capers
1 tablespoon lemon juice
4 tablespoons finely shredded
 Gouda cheese

1 Wash and dry bell peppers and keep separate as they are added to risotto at different times. Cut each into fourths then remove inner white membranes and seeds. Cut into strips and then chop into small pieces. Peel and coarsely chop the onions.

2 Pour stock into a saucepan, bring to a boil and keep hot over a low heat. In a separate large, heavy-based pan, heat oil until sizzling and hot. Add onions and then crush in garlic. Sauté until pale golden and then gradually add ground beef and stir-fry over a fairly high heat until brown and crumbly. Mix in rice.

3 Add the chopped green bell pepper to the meat mixture and continue to cook over a high heat for 2 minutes. Pour in wine.

4 Add the hot stock, ladle at a time. Bring back to a boil and stir well to mix. Cover pan with tight-fitting lid and cook, without stirring, for about 15 minutes until rice is tender and has absorbed most of the liquid.

5 Stir in the red bell pepper then season well with salt, pepper, and paprika. Cover and continue to cook for 10 minutes.

6 Meanwhile wash, dry and finely chop parsley. Stir capers and lemon juice into meat and rice mixture then put onto 4 warm plates. Sprinkle each with parsley and cheese and serve piping hot.

TIP
If preferred, use brown rice, allowing an extra 7 minutes cooking time in step 4.

Nutritional value per portion:
570 calories
Protein: 28g
Fat: 33g
Carbohydrate: 45g

Ground Beef and Pepper Rice

Red Wine Risotto with Mushrooms

Serves 4

Fresh and dried mushrooms add a delicious texture and flavor to this hearty risotto.

Preparation time: about 15 minutes plus soaking time
Cooking time: about 35 minutes

½ ounce dried Chinese
   mushrooms (optional)
6 scallions
3 carrots
4 tablespoons olive oil
1¼ cups risotto rice
1¼ cups chicken or vegetable stock
2¼ cup red wine
½ teaspoon dried thyme
Salt and pepper to taste
1 cup thinly sliced, fresh mushrooms
4 ounces Prosciutto
1½ tablespoons balsamic or red
   wine vinegar
4 tablespoons grated Parmesan cheese

1 If using dried mushrooms, wash them well under cold, running water. Put into bowl, cover with boiling water and let soak for 30 minutes. Trim scallions. Slice green stems and finely chop white part. Peel and shred 1 carrot.

2 Heat 3 tablespoons oil in a large, heavy-based saucepan. Add white parts of scallions with shredded carrot and stir-fry gently until pale golden. Stir in rice.

3 Bring stock to a boil. Add to rice with half the wine then season with thyme, salt, and pepper. Bring back to a boil, then simmer uncovered until all the liquid has been absorbed, stirring frequently.

4 Drain dried mushrooms, if used, and add soaking liquid to rice. Cut mushrooms into small pieces and mix into rice with remaining wine. Simmer, stirring constantly, until all the liquid has been absorbed. Allow about 30 minutes cooking time in total.

5 Set aside a few fresh mushroom slices for the garnish. Chop the rest finely. Cut Prosciutto into fine strips. Peel remaining carrots and cut into matchsticks. Heat remaining oil in a skillet. Add Prosciutto and stir-fry for 1 minute. Add carrot sticks, remaining mushrooms and green parts of scallions. Stir-fry for 1 minute more, then add vinegar and adjust the seasoning to taste.

6 Stir half the cheese into the risotto. Transfer to 4 warm plates and top with fried Prosciutto and vegetable mixture. Scatter with reserved sliced mushrooms and sprinkle with remaining cheese.

Nutritional value per portion:
520 calories
Protein: 14g
Fat: 20g
Carbohydrate: 54g

Red Wine Risotto with Mushrooms

Risotto and Chicken Casserole

Serves 4

A deliciously rich risotto with a hint of spice.

Preparation time: about 15 minutes plus marinating time
Cooking time: about 45 minutes

8 ounces boneless, skinless chicken or
   turkey breasts
3 tablespoons lemon juice
⅓ cup corn oil
Pepper to taste
3 cups chicken stock
1 cup dry white wine
1 bay leaf
1 onion
1¼ cups risotto rice
1 tablespoon mild curry powder
3 zucchini
10 ounces mozzarella cheese
6 tablespoons heavy cream
Salt and cayenne pepper
2 tablespoons butter

1 Cut chicken or turkey breast into thin strips and put into a shallow glass or stoneware dish. Toss with lemon juice, 3 tablespoons oil and pepper to taste. Cover and leave to marinate in the refrigerator for about 2 hours.

2 Bring stock, wine, and bay leaf to a boil in a saucepan. Leave to simmer over a low heat. Peel onion and finely chop. Heat 3 tablespoons oil in a large, heavy-based pan. Add onion and cook gently without coloring until it softens and looks semi-transparent. Mix in rice and cook slowly for 2 minutes, stirring constantly.

3 Stir in curry powder. Gradually add stock and wine, a ladle at a time, and cook over a medium heat until every batch of liquid has been absorbed before adding the next and stirring constantly. Allow about 25 minutes cooking time.

4 Preheat oven to 425°F. Brush an oven-proof dish with remaining oil. Trim zucchini. Shred two zucchini and slice the third thinly. Slice the mozzarella thinly.

5 Stir shredded zucchini and cream into the risotto then season with salt and cayenne. Spread smoothly into oiled dish.

6 Cover with strips of marinated chicken or turkey, then top with zucchini and cheese slices. Add small pieces of butter and bake in oven for 15 minutes. Serve hot.

Nutritional value per portion:
555 calories
Protein: 25g
Fat: 28g
Carbohydrate: 45g

Risotto and Chicken Casserole

Seafood Risotto

Serves 4

A Mediterranean-style risotto, packed with squid and shrimp. The lemon juice and sparkling wine bring out the full flavors of the seafood.

Preparation time: about 20 minutes
Cooking time: about 45 minutes

1 pound fresh squid
2 shallots or baby onions
4 tablespoons olive oil
2 cloves garlic
6 tablespoons sparkling wine or hard cider
3 cups fish or chicken stock
1 1/4 cups risotto rice
10 ounces cooked shrimp
24 shucked mussels, thawed
2 lemons
1 tablespoon butter
Salt and pepper to taste
1/2 cup fresh parsley sprigs

1 Prepare squid. Cut cleaned squid body into slender rings and tentacles into small pieces.

2 Peel shallots or baby onions and chop finely. Heat oil in a large, heavy-based saucepan. Add shallots or onions and cook gently until softened and creamy in color. Gradually add squid and sauté over a fairly high heat for 1 1/2 minutes.

3 Peel garlic and crush into pan. Pour in wine or hard cider then simmer over a low heat for 15 minutes. Meanwhile, simmer stock in separate pan. Mix rice into pan with squid and shallots or onions.

4 Gradually add stock, ladle at a time, to risotto, stirring over a medium heat until every batch of liquid has been absorbed before adding the next. Allow about 25 minutes cooking time.

5 Meanwhile, shell shrimp and put into bowl with the mussels. Sprinkle with juice from one of the lemons. Mix into risotto with butter and seasoning, then reheat briefly, stirring constantly.

6 Transfer risotto to 4 warm plates then garnish with parsley sprigs and lemon wedges cut from second lemon. Serve hot.

Nutritional value per portion:
480 calories
Protein: 34g
Fat: 14g
Carbohydrate: 53g

Seafood Risotto

Tomato Risotto with Chicken Livers

Serves 4

An unsual risotto, perfect for midweek entertaining.

Preparation time: about 20 minutes plus marinating time
Cooking time: about 30 minutes

½ pound chicken livers
2 tablespoons marsala or port
1 tablespoon lemon juice
5 tablespoons olive oil
Salt and pepper to taste
4 fresh sage leaves
1 pound tomatoes
3 cups beef stock
2 celery stalks with leaves attached
1¼ cups risotto rice
2 shallots or baby onions
Salt
2 tablespoons grated Parmesan cheese

1 Rinse chicken livers, trim, then wipe dry with paper towels. Cut livers into cubes and put into a glass or stoneware dish. Beat marsala or port with lemon juice and 2 tablespoons oil together and season well. Cut sage leaves into thin strips and add to marinade. Pour marinade over liver, mix thoroughly then cover and chill for 2 hours.

2 Cover tomatoes with boiling water for 30 seconds, then plunge into cold water, peel away skins and chop finely. Heat stock in a saucepan until simmering. Thinly slice celery, reserving leaves.

3 Heat 2 tablespoons oil until sizzling and hot in a large, heavy-based saucepan. Add celery and sauté until pale golden. Mix in rice and tomatoes, then gradually add stock, ladle at a time, stirring over a medium heat until every batch of liquid has been absorbed before adding the next. Allow about 25 minutes cooking time. Cover and leave over a low heat while preparing remaining ingredients.

4 Peel and chop shallots or baby onions and sauté in a skillet with remaining oil until pale golden. Add liver and marinade, cover and simmer for 3 minutes. Season with salt.

5 Spoon risotto onto 4 warm plates. Top with liver mixture then sprinkle with cheese. Garnish with coarsely chopped celery leaves and fresh sage and fried sage leaves if desired.

Nutritional value per portion:
450 calories
Protein: 21g
Fat: 17g
Carbohydrate: 58g

Tomato Risotto with Chicken Livers

Risotto Gratin with Fennel

Serves 4

A full-flavored dish with an interesting addition of fennel.

Preparation time: about 20 minutes
Cooking time: about 40 minutes

1¼ pounds fennel bulbs
4 cups meat stock
8 ounces garlic salami or
   ready-to-eat sausage
1 onion
3 tablespoons olive oil
1½ cups risotto rice
¾ cup shredded sharp Cheddar cheese
Salt and pepper to taste
1 tablespoon melted butter

1 Trim fennel bulbs and cut each one in half horizontally. Reserve the green fronds for garnishing. Bring stock to a boil in a saucepan. Add fennel, lower heat, cover and simmer for 10 minutes.

2 Meanwhile, thinly slice salami or sausage. Peel and chop onion. Heat 2 tablespoons oil in a large, heavy-based pan. Add salami or sausage and onion and stir-fry over a high heat until onion just begins to color.

3 Mix in rice and gradually add stock, ladle at a time, stirring over a medium heat until every batch of liquid has been absorbed before adding the next. Allow 20 minutes cooking time. Remove fennel from pan with a draining spoon. Add to the rice and cook, stirring, for a further 5 minutes.

4 Preheat oven to 400°F. Brush a fairly large ovenproof dish with remaining oil.

5 Stir half the cheese into the rice then season with salt and pepper. Spoon risotto into dish then top with fennel, cut-sides facing down. Sprinkle with remaining cheese and butter.

6 Bake in oven for 15 minutes until golden and bubbly. Sprinkle with chopped fennel fronds before serving.

Nutritional value per portion:
790 calories
Protein: 24g
Fat: 49g
Carbohydrate: 68g

Risotto Gratin with Fennel

Risotto Pancakes with Herb Yogurt

Serves 4

A perfect choice for vegetarians, these pancakes are served with a delicious herb dressing.

Preparation time: about 20 minutes
Cooking time: about 35 minutes

3 cups vegetable stock
2 celery stalks with leaves attached
3 tablespoons corn oil
1 cup risotto rice
1¼ cups Greek-style yogurt
2 tablespoons lemon juice
Salt and pepper to taste
½ cup fresh dill
1large bunch of fresh chives
8 ounces carrots
½ cup shredded Emmental or
    Gouda cheese
2 tablespoons chopped hazelnuts
2 eggs, separated
4 tablespoons melted butter
scissored fresh chives for garnishing

1 Bring stock to a boil in a saucepan, then cover and leave to simmer over a low heat. Thinly slice celery, reserving leaves.

2 Heat oil in a large, heavy-based pan. Add celery and rice and fry over a high heat for 2 minutes. Lower heat to medium. Gradually add stock, ladle at a time, stirring until every batch of liquid has been absorbed before adding the next. Allow 25 minutes cooking time. Cover and leave over low heat.

3 Tip yogurt into a bowl, add lemon juice, then season with salt and pepper. Chop dill, chives, and celery leaves then stir into yogurt mixture. Cover and chill.

4 Cool risotto. Peel and coarsely shred carrots. Add carrots and cheese to risotto with hazelnuts and egg yolks. Mix in well. Whisk egg whites stiffly then fold into risotto mixture.

5 Heat a small amount of butter in a small skillet. Add sufficient risotto (about 1½ tablespoons) to cover base of pan and spread level. Cook until underside is golden then flip over with turner and cook second side until golden and crisp. Remove from pan.

6 Drain pancake on piece of crumpled paper toweling and keep hot. Repeat with remaining butter and risotto mixture. Garnish with chives and serve hot with the herb yogurt.

Nutritional value per portion:
500 calories
Protein: 14g
Fat: 30g
Carbohydrate: 50

Risotto Pancakes with Herb Yogurt

Lentil Risotto with Feta Cheese

Serves 4

Ring the changes with this fragrant lentil and rice risotto.

Preparation time: 15 minutes plus soaking time
Cooking time: about 45 minutes

½ cup brown lentils
6 cups hot chicken or vegetable stock
1 bay leaf
1 teaspoon dried thyme
Juice of 1 lemon
½ teaspoon aniseeds (optional)
1 onion
4 tablespoons olive oil
1 tablespoon butter
1¼ cups risotto rice
5 ounces (1 cup) feta cheese
4 drained canned or bottled pimentos
Salt and pepper to taste
Sprigs of fresh thyme for garnish

1 Soak lentils in plenty of cold water for 2 hours. Drain thoroughly.

2 Bring stock to a boil in a saucepan. Add bay leaf, thyme, lemon juice, and aniseeds. Cover and leave to simmer over a low heat while preparing all the remaining ingredients.

3 Peel and chop onion. Heat oil and butter in a large, heavy-based saucepan. Add onion and sauté until lightly-colored. Mix in rice thoroughly and keep heat low.

4 Stir in lentils and gradually add stock, ladle at a time, stirring until every batch of liquid has been absorbed before adding the next. Allow about 35-40 minutes cooking time. Cover and keep hot over a low heat.

5 Cut feta cheese into small cubes. Remove any seeds from the pimentos and cut the flesh into thin strips.

6 Season risotto with salt and pepper and gradually fork in two-thirds of the cheese and pimento strips, reheating briefly for 3-4 minutes.

7 Serve on 4 warm plates, garnished with thyme and adding equal amounts of cheese and pimento strips to each.

Nutritional value per portion:
500 calories
Protein: 17g
Fat: 21g
Carbohydrate: 67g

Lentil Risotto with Feta Cheese

Risotto-filled Eggplants

Serves 4

A delicious fish-based risotto with corn makes a wholesome filling for eggplants.

Preparation time: 15 minutes
Cooking time: about 40 minutes

2 large eggplants, total weight about
   1½ pounds
Salt
1 onion
3 cups chicken or vegetable stock
scant ½ cup olive oil
⅔ cup risotto rice
8-ounce can tuna in oil
8-ounce can whole kernel oil
5 ounces mozzarella cheese
½ cup fresh Italian parsley
4 drained canned anchovy fillets in oil
4 tablespoons fresh white bread crumbs
Salt and pepper to taste
extra oil for drizzling

1 Trim eggplants and cook, uncovered, in boiling salted water for 10 minutes.

2 Drain eggplants, plunge into cold water and leave for 1 minute. Lift out, dry on paper towels and cut in half lengthwise. Remove insides, leaving a ½-inch thick shell. Chop the flesh roughly.

3 Peel and chop onion. Simmer stock in saucepan over a low heat.

4 Heat oil in large, heavy-based pan. Add onion and eggplant flesh and sauté until onion just begins to color. Stir in rice.

5 Gradually add stock, ladle at a time, stirring until every batch of liquid has been absorbed before adding the next. Allow 20 minutes cooking time, then remove pan from heat. Preheat oven to 350°F.

6 Tip tuna and its oil into a bowl and break up into large flakes with a fork. Drain corn and add to bowl. Cut mozzarella into small cubes. Finely chop parsley and drained anchovies. Add to rice with bread crumbs. Season with salt and pepper and stir well with fork to mix.

7 Fill eggplant halves with risotto mixture then arrange in an oiled baking dish. Drizzle remaining oil on top and bake in oven for 15 minutes. Serve hot.

Nutritional value per portion:
550 calories
Protein: 23g
Fat: 28g
Carbohydrate: 47g

Risotto-filled Eggplants

•NOTES•

◆NOTES◆

Salads

Made Easy

Series
Consultant:
Sonia Allison

GREAT
COOKING
VALUE

Introduction

For delicious, healthy salads, choose the freshest vegetables you can find to mix with basics such as pasta, rice, potatoes and grains. Season with fragrant herbs and use good quality oils and vinegars in dressings. Cheeses, sausages, cold cuts, poultry, fish, shellfish and eggs make satisfying additions to any salad and, when pressed for time, turn to the store cupboard or freezer for convenience foods.

Recipe Notes

Use standard spoon and cup measures. All measures are level unless otherwise stated.

Eggs are used large unless otherwise stated.

Calorie counts for average-size servings are set down at the end of each recipe, and are rounded up to the nearest whole number.

Written by Annette Wolter

Tomato and Egg Salad

Serves 4

Use flavorsome ripe tomatoes for this salad.

Preparation time: about 1 hour

12 small potatoes
4 eggs
8 tomatoes
I small onion
1 package corn salad
12 black olives
2 tablespoons tarragon vinegar
Freshly ground black pepper to taste
½ teaspoon salt
2 tablespoons extra virgin olive or corn oil
2 tablespoons scissored fresh chives

1 Scrub potatoes under cold running water. Cook in boiling salted water for 10-15 minutes until tender. Drain and cool completely.

2 Hard-cook eggs for 10 minutes, adding a dash of vinegar to water to hold shells together should eggs crack. Alternatively, make small hole in rounded end of each with egg piercer. When cooked, place eggs under cold running water until cool enough to handle.

3 Slice tomatoes thinly. Peel onion and cut in half, then cut into thin slices and separate slices. Rinse corn salad under cold running water. Drain thoroughly.

4 Peel and thinly slice potatoes. Shell eggs and slice. Arrange rings of potatoes, tomatoes, and eggs on large plate. Garnish with onion rings, corn salad, and black olives.

5 Beat together vinegar, pepper, salt, and oil. Spoon over salad. Sprinkle with scissored chives.

Nutritional value per portion:
about 270 calories
Protein: 11g
Fat: 14g
Carbohydrate: 24g

Tomato and Egg Salad

Salad Niçoise

Serves 4

A famous specialty from the South of France.

Preparation time: about 35 minutes

1 head of Boston or Bibb lettuce
½ cucumber
4 tomatoes
1 onion
8-ounce can tuna in oil
8 drained canned anchovy fillets in oil
24 black olives
1 tablespoon red wine vinegar
2 pinches of salt
¼ cup extra virgin olive oil
Freshly ground white or black pepper
2 generous pinches of herbes de Provence
2 hard-cooked eggs

1 Separate lettuce leaves. Rinse under cold running water. Drain and pat dry with paper towels.

2 Wash and dry cucumber. Slice thinly without peeling. Remove stalks from tomatoes and cut each one into 8 sections. Peel and thinly slice onion. Separate slices into rings.

3 Drain tuna, tip into a bowl and flake flesh with fork. Cut anchovies lengthwise into strips. Rinse olives and drain.

4 Tear lettuce into bite-size pieces. Put into salad bowl with all prepared ingredients and toss together gently.

5 Beat together vinegar, salt, oil, pepper, and herbs. Spoon over salad. Shell eggs and cut each into 8 sections. Top salad with hard-cooked eggs.

Nutritional value per portion:
about 435 calories
Protein: 22g
Fat: 35g
Carbohydrate: 9g

Salad Niçoise

Crunchy Fruit Salad

Serves 4

Serve this salad with whole-wheat bread for a lunch snack or side dish. The maple syrup adds a delicious flavor.

Preparation time: about 45 minutes

2 heads of Belgian endive
1 small banana
1 dessert apple
1 tablesoon lemon juice
2 oranges
2 pinches of salt
2 teaspoons maple syrup
1 teaspoon Dijon mustard
½ cup plain low-fat yogurt
¼ cup heavy cream or crème fraîche
¼ cup hazelnuts

1 Remove any damaged or bruised outer leaves from endives and discard. Wash heads under cold running water, drain and wipe dry with paper towels. Cut a wedge-shaped piece out of base of each to remove bitter core.

2 Halve endives and cut into neat ½-inch thick slices. Peel banana, cut in half lengthwise and thinly slice. Quarter unpeeled apple, remove core and cut into thin wedges. Put endives, banana, and apple into mixing bowl and toss with lemon juice.

3 Peel oranges with sharp knife and remove white pith. Remove sections of orange, cutting in between membranes holding fruit together. Do this over bowl to catch juice. Add orange sections and juice to endive mixture. Toss well to mix and spoon into salad bowl.

4 Beat together all remaining ingredients except nuts. Pour over salad and toss gently to mix.

5 Coarsely chop hazelnuts and sprinkle over salad before serving.

Nutritional value per portion:
about 180 calories
Protein: 4g
Fat: 9g
Carbohydrate: 22g

Crunchy Fruit Salad

Greek Country Salad

Serves 4

A happy reminder of sunny holidays in Greece.

Preparation time: about 40 minutes

1 clove garlic
1 large green bell pepper
1 large onion
½ cucumber
2 large tomatoes
2 tablespoons lemon juice
½ teaspoon salt
½ teaspoon sugar
¼ cup olive oil
5 ounces (1 cup) feta cheese
½ cup marinated black olives
Pinch of dried oregano
Sprigs of fresh basil

1 Peel garlic and halve lengthwise. Rub cut sides against side of salad bowl.

2 Wash bell pepper. Wipe dry with paper towels. Halve and remove inner white membranes and seeds. Cut flesh into narrow strips. Peel onions and slice. Separate slices into rings.

3 Wash and dry unpeeled cucumber and cut into small pieces. Quarter tomatoes and cut each piece in half. Put all prepared vegetables into salad bowl.

4 Beat lemon juice with salt and sugar. Gradually whisk in oil. Pour over salad and toss well to mix. Cut cheese into bite-size pieces. Add to salad with olives and sprinkle with oregano. Cover and let stand at room temperature for 20 minutes before serving. Garnish with basil sprigs.

Nutritional value per portion:
about 315 calories
Protein: 8g
Fat: 25g
Carbohydrate: 14g

Greek Country Salad

Potato and Caraway Salad

Serves 4

Caraway seeds add a delicious, sharp aniseed flavor to this vegetable salad.

Preparation time: about 45 minutes

1½ pounds potatoes
1 teaspoon caraway seeds
⅔ cup vegetable stock
6 scallions
1 red-skinned dessert apple
2 small zucchini
2 tablespoons cider or white wine vinegar
3 tablespoons corn oil
Pinch of brown sugar
Salt to taste
3 tablespoons sesame seeds, toasted

1 Scrub potatoes and cook in boiling salted water with caraway seeds for 20-25 minutes until tender. Drain and cool. Bring vegetable stock to a boil and keep warm over low heat.

2 Trim and wash scallions, cutting away most of the green ends. Chop them very finely.

3 Quarter unpeeled apple, remove core and cut flesh into small pieces. Trim zucchini and cut into small pieces.

4 Peel potatoes and slice. Put into large mixing bowl with prepared vegetables and fruit. Stir in warm stock.

5 Beat together vinegar, oil, sugar, and salt. Add to potatoes and toss gently to mix. Spoon into salad bowl and sprinkle with toasted sesame seeds.

Nutritional value per portion:
about 295 calories
Protein: 8g
Fat: 10g
Carbohydrate: 44g

Potato and Caraway Salad

Salad Provençal

Serves 4

A beautiful salad which looks even better with a garnish of bright blue borage flowers.

Preparation time: about 30 minutes

1 head of Boston lettuce
1 head of radicchio
1 package fresh chervil or parsley
4 fresh borage leaves or 2 sorrel or spinach
    leaves
4 tablespoons garlic croûtons
2 hard-cooked eggs
2 tablespoons red wine vinegar
1 teaspoon Dijon mustard
½ teaspoon salt
Freshly ground black pepper to taste
⅓ cup extra virgin olive oil

1 Separate lettuce and radicchio into leaves. Rinse under cold running water and drain thoroughly. Pat dry with paper towels and tear into bite-size pieces. Put salad leaves into mixing bowl.

2 Rinse chervil or parsley. Repeat with borage, sorrel, or spinach leaves. Drain thoroughly and chop coarsely. Add to mixing bowl. Finely chop croûtons and add to salad in bowl.

3 Shell eggs and chop. Set aside.

4 Beat together all remaining ingredients and add to salad. Toss ingredients gently to mix and spoon into salad bowl. Sprinkle with chopped eggs.

Nutritional value per portion:
about 200 calories
Protein: 7g
Fat: 16g
Carbohydrate: 7g

Salad Provençal

Chicken and Avocado Salad

Serves 2

This salad makes a unusual appetizer for four.

Preparation time: about 1 hour

2 boneless, skinless chicken breasts
2 tablespoons corn oil
½ teaspoon salt
1 large ripe avocado
3 tablespoons lemon juice
1 large orange
2 small red onions
Pinch of cayenne pepper
½ teaspoon sugar
Freshly ground black pepper to taste
Extra salt to taste
3 tablespoons extra virgin olive oil
baby mustard greens and garden cress

1 Wash chicken breasts and pat dry with paper towels. Cut into ½-inch wide strips with a sharp knife.

2 Heat corn oil in skillet until hot. Add chicken and sauté over a fairly high heat for 4 minutes or until cooked through. Sprinkle with salt and remove to plate lined with paper towels.

3 Peel avocado, starting at pointed end. Halve lengthwise by cutting all the way round with knife. Twist avocado apart and remove stone. Cut flesh into small strips and put into mixing bowl. Sprinkle avocado with 1 tablespoon lemon juice to prevent browning. Add chicken to bowl.

4 Peel orange and remove white pith. Cut orange into slices, then cut each slice into quarters. Add to bowl with avocado and chicken.

5 Peel and slice onions. Separate slices into rings and add to avocado and chicken. Spoon into salad bowl.

6 Beat remaining lemon juice with cayenne, sugar, black pepper, salt, and oil. Sprinkle over salad and garnish with baby mustard greens and garden cress before serving.

Nutritional value per portion:
about 400 calories
Protein: 25g
Fat: 30g
Carbohydrate: 8g

Chicken and Avocado Salad

Mixed Grain Salad

Serves 4

A healthy, fiber-rich salad.

Preparation time: about 1 hour 20 minutes, plus overnight soaking

1 cup mixed grains such as wheatberries, whole rye, oat groats, barley, buckwheat, or brown rice
1 teaspoon herb or garlic salt
2 cups (about 4 ounces) corn salad
1 red apple
1 teaspoon lemon juice
2 tablespoons tarragon vinegar
1 teaspoon maple syrup or honey
½ teaspoon salt
Freshly ground white pepper to taste
1 tablespoon corn oil
1 cup cottage cheese
2 teaspoons wheat germ

1 Rinse grains under cold running water. Drain. Tip into bowl and cover with cold water. Cover with clean dish towel and let grains soak overnight.

2 Pour grains and water into saucepan. Add herb or garlic salt. Bring to a boil for 10 minutes, then cover and cook gently for 1 hour over a low heat, stirring occasionally and adding extra boiling water if grains seem to be drying out. Remove pan from heat and set aside until grains are cold.

3 Wash corn salad and pat leaves dry with paper towels. Separate into small bunches.

4 Quarter, core and chop apples. Sprinkle with lemon juice to prevent browning.

5 Drain grains, spoon into mixing bowl then add corn salad and apple.

6 Beat vinegar with syrup or honey, salt, pepper, oil, and cottage cheese. Add to salad and toss well to mix. Spoon into salad bowl and sprinkle with wheat germ.

Nutritional value per portion:
about 315 calories
Protein: 15g
Fat: 14g
Carbohydrate: 32g

Mixed Grain Salad

Chicken and Corn Salad

Serves 4

Based on chicken and corn, this salad has a delicious piquant grapefruit dressing.

Preparation time: about 25 minutes

2 skinned cooked chicken breasts
1 green or red bell pepper
1 dessert apple
2 tablespoons lemon juice
12-ounce can whole kernel corn, drained
¼ cup grapefruit juice
½ teaspoon salt
½ teaspoon sugar
2 tablespoons corn oil

1 Cut cooked chicken into ½-inch wide strips. Wash and dry bell pepper, cut in half and remove inner white membranes and seeds. Finely chop flesh. Quarter and core apple. Finely chop flesh and sprinkle with 1 tablepoon lemon juice to prevent browning.

2 Tip corn into mixing bowl and add chicken, pepper, and apple.

3 Beat remaining lemon juice with grapefruit juice, salt, sugar, and oil. Check for taste, adding more sugar if necessary. Pour over salad and toss well. Spoon into salad bowl and serve.

Nutritional value per portion:
about 295 calories
Protein: 27g
Fat: 8g
Carbohydrate: 29g

Chicken and Corn Salad

Vegetable and Ham Salad

Serves 4

Easily put together with frozen vegetables.

Preparation time: about 30 minutes

⅔ cup water
1½ teaspoons salt
2 pounds frozen mixed vegetables
8 ounces lean cooked ham
4 tomatoes
1 cup diced Cheddar or Edam cheese
6 tablespoons mayonnaise
About 3 tablespoons milk
½ teaspoon salt
½ teaspoon freshly ground pepper
2 teaspoons paprika

1 Bring water and pinch of salt to a boil. Add frozen vegetables and cook until tender, following the directions on the package. Drain thoroughly and let cool. Tip into mixing bowl.

2 Cut ham into small dice. Put tomatoes in a heatproof bowl and pour over some boiling water. Leave for 1 minute. Drain and peel. Slice tomatoes and cut flesh into strips. Add ham, cheese, and tomatoes to cooked vegetables.

3 Beat mayonnaise with just enough milk to make a smooth, creamy sauce. Mix in salt, pepper and paprika.

4 Transfer salad to salad bowl then spoon over mayonnaise sauce.

Nutritional value per portion:
about 550 calories
Protein: 26g
Fat: 33g
Carbohydrate: 37g

Vegetable and Ham Salad

Whole-wheat Pasta Salad with Salami

Serves 4

A host of flavors are combined in this unusual pasta salad.

Preparation time: about 30 minutes

3 quarts water
1½ teaspoons salt
1 teaspoon corn oil
2 cups whole-wheat pasta shapes
3 small pieces of preserved ginger in syrup
4 ounces salami
½ cucumber
2 tablespoons red wine vinegar
½ teaspoon salt
4 tablespoons mayonnaise
5 tablespoons plain low-fat yogurt
1 teaspoon sugar
1 teaspoon lemon juice
Drop of hot pepper sauce
baby mustard greens and garden cress,
   for garnish

1 Bring water, salt, and oil to a brisk boil in a large saucepan. Add pasta and cook uncovered for about 12 minutes until *al dente* or just tender. Drain pasta, rinse under cold running water, drain again thoroughly and cool completely. Tip into mixing bowl.

2 Rinse ginger and pat dry with paper towels. Cut into small cubes. Cut salami into strips. Cut unpeeled cucumber into ½-inch pieces. Add ginger, salami, and cucumber to bowl of pasta.

3 Mix vinegar with salt and spoon over salad. Mix mayonnaise with all remaining ingredients except garnish, and spoon over salad. Top salad with baby mustard greens and garden cress.

Nurtitional value per portion:
about 410 calories
Protein: 15g
Fat: 18g

Whole-wheat Pasta Salad with Salami

Rice Salad with Celery and Orange

Serves 4

A luscious salad, packed with vitamins.

Preparation time: about 40 minutes

2 cups water
½ teaspoon salt
1¼ cups long grain white rice
4 celery stalks
2 drained canned pineapple rings
2 oranges
1 small head of Belgian endive
1 package fresh basil
Juice from 1 medium pink grapefruit
2 teaspoons lemon juice
1 tablespoon corn oil
4 tablespoons plain low-fat yogurt
⅓ cup heavy cream
½ teaspoon sugar
Fresh basil, for garnish

1 Bring water and salt to a boil in large saucepan. Add rice and stir around with fork. Cover and simmer gently for about 15 minutes until grains are tender and water has been absorbed. Alternatively, follow package directions for cooking times. Drain rice if necessary, tip into mixing bowl and let cool.

2 Remove and discard tough outer strings from each celery stalk, see pages 18-19. Rinse celery under cold running water then drain and slice thinly.

3 Drain pineapple rings on paper towels and cut into small pieces.

4 Peel oranges and remove white pith. Remove sections with sharp knife, cutting in between membranes. Work over bowl to catch juice. Set bowl aside.

5 Remove any damaged or bruised outer leaves from endive and wash gently under cold running water. Wipe dry with paper towels and cut a wedge-shaped piece out of base. Halve endive lengthwise then cut each half into strips from top to bottom.

6 Add celery, pineapple pieces, orange sections, and endive to rice. Rinse basil and shake dry.

7 Combine reserved orange juice with grapefruit juice, lemon juice, oil, and yogurt. Whip cream with sugar until thick and combine with yogurt mixture. Add to rice salad and toss thoroughly to mix. Garnish with finely shredded basil leaves.

Nutritional value per portion:
about 315 calories
Protein: 7g
Fat: 8g
Carbohydrate: 57g

Rice Salad with Celery and Orange

Tuna and Tomato Salad

Serves 2

*This bright and cheerful Mediterranean salad makes a delicious snack
served with rye bread.*

Preparation time: about 45 minutes

2 medium-size potatoes
Salt to taste
10-ounce package frozen peas
3 tomatoes
2 onions
8-ounce can tuna in brine
2 tablespoons red wine vinegar
½ teaspoon salt
Freshly ground white pepper to taste
Pinch of sugar
3 tablespoons corn oil
A few fresh chives

1 Scrub potatoes and cook in boiling salted water until tender. Drain and set aside to cool.

2 Meanwhile, bring second pan of water to a boil, then add peas; salt to taste. Boil for 3 minutes, drain thoroughly and cool.

3 Cut each tomato into eighths. Peel onions and chop coarsely. Drain tuna, tip into a bowl and separate flesh into small chunks with fork.

4 For dressing, beat together vinegar, salt, pepper, sugar, and oil.

5 Peel and cube potatoes and put into mixing bowl. Add dressing with peas, tomatoes, onions, and tuna. Toss well to mix. Spoon into salad bowl.

6 Rinse chives, drain and chop finely. Sprinkle over salad.

Nutritional value per portion:
about 435 calories
Protein: 26g
Fat: 24g
Carbohydrate: 29g

Tuna and Tomato Salad

Sausage Salad

Serves 4

Quick and easy to make, this salad makes an ideal midweek meal.

Preparation time: about 30 minutes

10-ounce piece of luncheon meat or
    ready-to-eat garlic sausage
8 ounces Cheddar or Edam cheese
1 red bell pepper
1 dill pickle
1 onion
1 tablespoon wine vinegar
2 tablespoons ketchup
2 tablespoons mayonnaise
3 tablespoons thick sour cream
mustard baby greens and garden cress

1 Cut luncheon meat or garlic sausage and cheese into ½-inch cubes. Put both into mixing bowl.

2 Halve bell pepper lengthwise, remove inner white membranes and seeds and dice flesh finely. Cut dill pickle into cubes. Peel onion and chop. Add pepper, dill pickle, and onion to bowl of meat or sausage and cheese.

3 Beat vinegar with ketchup, mayonnaise and sour cream. Add to salad and toss well to mix.

4 Spoon into salad bowl and sprinkle with baby mustard greens and garden cress.

Nutritional value per portion:
about 500 calories
Protein: 23g
Fat: 42g
Carbohydrate: 6g

Sausage Salad

◆NOTES◆

◆NOTES◆

Spaghetti
Made Easy

Series Consultant: **Sonia Allison**

◆NOTES◆

Spaghetti with Broccoli

Spaghetti e Broccoli

Serves 4

An unusual combination of pasta with broccoli and anchovies which works well.

Preparation time: about 1 hour

5 cloves garlic
5 canned anchovy fillets, drained
1kg (2lb) broccoli
2 litres (3½ pints/8 cups) water
1½ teaspoon salt
90ml (3fl oz/ ⅓ cup) olive oil
1 small dried red chilli (hot capsicum)
500g (1lb) spaghetti

1 Peel garlic. Finely chop with anchovies. Wash broccoli and break into small florets. Thinly slice stalks.

2 Bring water and salt to boil in large saucepan. Add broccoli and cook, uncovered, for 5 minutes. It should still be firm and bright green. Lift out of pan with draining spoon and transfer to plate. Reserve cooking water and leave it in saucepan.

3 Heat oil in small pan. Add garlic, anchovies and chilli and simmer gently, uncovered, for 15 minutes. Remove and discard chilli.

4 Bring pan of broccoli water to boil. Lower in spaghetti, gradually pushing it down as it softens. Stir and cook for 4 minutes.

5 Add broccoli florets and sliced stalks to saucepan of spaghetti. Continue to cook for 8-10 minutes until spaghetti is just tender or al dente, stirring occasionally. Alternatively, follow packet instructions for cooking times. Drain spaghetti and broccoli thoroughly. Return to saucepan and stand over low heat.

6 Mix anchovy and garlic mixture into spaghetti and toss with 2 forks until well combined. Lift spaghetti out on to warm serving plates and serve straight away.

Nutritional value per portion:
570 cal.

Spaghetti with Broccoli

Spaghetti e Broccoli

Spaghetti with Mushrooms

Spaghetti al Funghi

Serves 4

A fragrant mushroom sauce complements the spaghetti.

Preparation time: 1 hour

1 medium onion
1 clove garlic
375g (12oz) chestnut or brown cap mushrooms
60g (2oz) butter or margarine
60ml (2fl oz/¼ cup) olive oil
60ml (2fl oz/¼ cup) Marsala or medium sherry
Salt to taste
Freshly milled white pepper to taste
2 pinches dried thyme
Pinch freshly grated nutmeg
100ml (3½ fl oz/½ cup) single (light) cream
2 litres (3½ pints/8 cups) water
1½ teaspoons salt
½ teaspoon olive oil
500g (1lb) spaghetti
6 sprigs fresh parsley
100g (3½ oz) freshly grated Parmesan cheese

1 Peel onion and thinly slice. Peel and finely chop garlic. Trim mushrooms and rinse under cold water. Pat dry with absorbent kitchen paper and cut into fairly thin slices.

2 Melt half the butter or margarine in a frying pan with the oil. Add onions and garlic. Sauté for 10 minutes over moderate heat until onions are soft but still pale, stirring frequently. Mix in mushrooms and continue to cook over a low heat for 10 minutes.

3 Pour Marsala or sherry into pan. Season with salt and pepper and add thyme and nutmeg. Simmer, uncovered, for 10 minutes. Gradually stir in cream and simmer, uncovered, for a further 10 minutes, stirring occasionally.

4 In a large saucepan, bring water, salt and oil to the boil. Lower spaghetti into water, gradually pushing it down as it softens. Cook, uncovered, for about 10-12 minutes until pasta is just tender or al dente, stirring occasionally. Alternately, follow packet instructions for cooking times. Drain thoroughly.

5 Meanwhile, wash, dry and finely chop parsley. Add to mushroom sauce with remaining butter or margarine and cook gently until hot, stirring constantly.

6 Tip spaghetti into warm serving dish. Add mushroom sauce and toss with 2 forks until well combined. Serve straight away. Pass cheese separately.

Nutritional value per portion:
690 cal.

Spaghetti with Mushrooms

Spaghetti al Funghi

Spaghetti with Leek Sauce

Spaghetti con Porri

Serves 4

Vegetarians will love this dish of spaghetti with a leek and tomato sauce.

Preparation time: about 1 hour

1 medium carrot
1 stick celery
6 medium leeks
396g (14oz) can tomatoes
3 tablespoons olive oil
45g (1½ oz) butter or margarine
125ml (4fl oz/½ cup) dry white wine
Salt to taste
Freshly milled black pepper to taste
½ teaspoon dried marjoram
2 litres (3½ pints/8 cups) water
1½ teaspoon salt
½ teaspoon olive oil
500g (1lb) spaghetti
6 sprigs fresh parsley
100g (3½ oz) freshly grated Parmesan
   cheese

1 Peel carrot and grate. Trim and wash celery and pat dry with absorbent kitchen paper. Finely chop celery. Cut away and discard roots and green parts of leeks. Slit leeks lengthwise, almost to root end, with sharp knife and wash under cold running water to remove grit. Shake dry and cut into thin slices.

2 Drain tomatoes. Rub through fine sieve and reserve juice.

3 Heat oil and butter or margarine in saucepan. Add carrot and celery and sauté for 5 minutes. Stir in leeks, cover pan and cook gently for 10 minutes. Pour in wine. Heat briskly until it evaporates. Add sieved tomatoes. Season with salt, pepper and marjoram. Cover and simmer gently for about 7-10 minutes or until sauce thickens, stirring occasionally. Mix in reserved tomato juice.

4 In large suacepan, bring water, salt and oil to the boil. Lower spaghetti into water, gradually pushing it down as it softens. Cover pasta and cook for about 10-12 minutes until just tender or al dente, stirring occasionally. Alternately, follow packet instructions for cooking time.

5 Wash and dry parsley and finely chop. Add to leek sauce. Drain spaghetti. Put into warm serving dish. Spoon leek sauce over top. Toss thoroughly with 2 forks. Serve straight away. Pass cheese separately.

Nutritional value per portion:
690 cal.

Spaghetti with Leek Sauce

Spaghetti con Porri

Spaghetti with Peppers (Capsicums)

Spaghetti con Peperoni

Serves 4

This dish sums up the tastes of Southern Italy.

Preparation time: about 1¼ hours

625g (1¼ lbs) mixture of red and yellow
   peppers (capsicums)
4 cloves garlic
6 sprigs fresh parsley
315g (10oz) ripe tomatoes
125ml (4fl oz/½ cup) olive oil
Salt to taste
Freshly milled white pepper to taste
½ teaspoon sugar
2 litres (3½ pints/8 cups) water, plus 3-5
   tablespoons extra
1½ teaspoons salt
½ teaspoon olive oil
500g (1lb) spaghetti
1 tablespoon white wine vinegar

1 Halve peppers (capsicums). Remove inner white membranes and seeds. Wash halves thoroughly and pat dry with absorbent kitchen paper. Chop finely, either by hand or in food processor.

2 Peel garlic. Wash parsley and shake dry. Chop garlic and parsley. Put tomatoes into large bowl. Cover with boiling water. Leave to stand for 3 minutes then drain. Cover with cold water. Peel tomatoes when cool enough to handle and coarsely chop.

3 Heat oil gently in saucepan. Add garlic and parsley and sauté slowly for 5 minutes. Stir in chopped peppers (capsicums) and sauté for 10 minutes.

4 Stir in tomatoes. Season with salt, pepper and sugar. Cover and simmer gently for about 10 minutes or until sauce becomes very thick, stirring frequently to prevent tomatoes sticking to pan and adding 3-5 tablespoons water if necessary.

5 In large saucepan, bring water, salt and oil to the boil. Lower spaghetti into water, gradually pushing it down as it softens. Cook pasta for 10-12 minutes until just tender or al dente, keeping pan uncovered and stirring occasionally. Alternately, follow packet instructions for cooking times.

6 Mix vinegar into pepper (capsicum) sauce. Adjust seasoning to taste. Bring sauce just to the boil. Spoon into warm serving dish. Drain spaghetti, add to sauce and toss thoroughly with 2 forks. Serve straight away.

Nutritional value per portion:
550 cal.

Spaghetti with Peppers (Capsicums)

Spaghetti con Peperoni

Spaghetti with Garlic and Oil

Spaghetti all'aglio e Olio
Serves 4
A much-loved and widely eaten Italian favorite from South of the country.

Preparation time: about 30 minutes

2 litres (3½ pints/8 cups) water
1½ teaspoons salt
1 teaspoon olive oil
500g (1lb) spaghetti
5 cloves garlic
6 large sprigs fresh parsley
90ml (3fl oz/⅓ cup) olive oil
2cm (½in) piece of dried red chilli (hot capsicum)
100g (3½ oz) freshly grated Pecorino or Parmesan cheese

1 In large saucepan, bring water, salt and oil to the boil. Lower spaghetti into water, pushing it down as it softens. Cook for about 10-12 minutes until just tender or al dente keeping pan uncovered and stirring occasionally. Alternately, follow packet instructions for cooking times.

2 Meanwhile, peel and crush garlic. Wash parsley, shake dry and finely chop.

3 Warm a deep serving dish in the oven or under the grill.

4 Heat oil in small pan. Add garlic and chilli (hot capsicum) and sauté gently until garlic turns pale golden. Remove pan from heat.

5 Drain spaghetti. Tip into warm serving dish. Reserve 2 tablespoons cooking water.

6 Pour garlic and chilli (hot capsicum) oil on top of spaghetti. Add reserved water. Toss thoroughly with 2 forks. Sprinkle with chopped parsley. Serve straight away. Pass cheese separately.

Nutritional value per portion:
870 cal.

Spaghetti with Garlic and Oil

Spaghetti all' aglio e Olio

Spaghetti Sicilian Style

Spaghetti alla Siciliana

Serves 4

This thick sauce has a very Mediterranean flavour.

Preparation time: about 1 hour

1 large yellow or red pepper (capsicum)
1 medium aubergine (eggplant)
375g (12oz) ripe tomatoes
10 black olives, stoned
1 tablespoon capers, drained
2 cloves garlic
5 canned anchovy fillets,drained
5 fresh basil leaves
75ml (2½ fl oz/⅓ cup) olive oil
Salt to taste
Freshly milled pepper to taste
2 litres (3½ pints/8 cups) water
1½ teaspoons salt
1 teaspoon olive oil
500g (1lb) spaghetti
3 tablespoons freshly grated Pecorino or
   Parmesan cheese

1 Quarter pepper (capsicum). Remove inner white membranes and seeds. Wash quarters and wipe dry with absorbent kitchen paper. Cut into narrow strips. Trim aubergine (eggplant). Wash and dry and cut aubergine (eggplant) into 1cm/½ in cubes.

2 Put tomatoes into large bowl. Cover with boiling water. Leave to stand for 1 minute or until skins split. Drain. Cover with cold water. Peel when cool enough to handle and coarsely chop.

3 Thinly slice olives. Finely chop capers. Peel garlic and finely chop with anchovies. Lightly rinse basil and pat dry with absorbent kitchen paper.

4 Heat 75ml (2½ fl oz/⅓ cup) oil in saucepan. Add aubergine (eggplant) cubes, tomatoes, garlic and anchovies. Cook gently for 10 minutes, stirring frequently.

5 Stir in pepper strips, basil leaves, olives and capers. Season with salt and pepper. Cover and simmer gently for 20 minutes, stirring occasionally.

6 After 10 minutes, bring water, salt and oil to the boil in large saucepan. Lower in spaghetti, gradually pushing it down as it softens. Cook pasta for 10-12 minutes until just tender or al dente, keeping pan uncovered and stirring occasionally. Alternatively, follow packet instructions for cooking times. Drain. Tip into warm serving dish. Add vegetable and tomato sauce with cheese. Toss thoroughly with 2 forks. Serve straight away.

Nutritional value per portion:
710 cal.

Spaghetti Sicilian Style

Spaghetti alla Siciliana

Spaghetti with Prawns and Green Peas

Spaghetti con Gamberetti e Piselli

Serves 4

Quick and easy to prepare, this colourful dish is ideal for informal entertaining.

Preparation time: about 45 minutes

220g (7oz) frozen peas
250g (8oz) frozen peeled prawns
3 shallots
60g (2oz) butter or margarine
3 tablespoons virgin olive oil
60ml (2fl oz/¼ cup) vegetable stock
2 litres (3½ pints/8 cups) water
1½ teaspoons salt
500g (1lb) spaghetti
30ml (6tsp) brandy
Salt to taste
Freshly milled white pepper to taste
155ml (5fl oz/⅔ cup) single (light) cream
1 egg yolk

1 Thaw peas and prawns. Peel shallots and thinly slice.

2 Melt butter or margarine and 2 tablespoons oil until hot. Add shallots and sauté over low heat until soft but still pale, stirring frequently. Stir in peas and cook for 5 minutes. Add vegetable stock, cover and simmer gently until peas are just tender but still bright green.

3 Rinse and drain prawns.

4 In large saucepan, bring water, salt and remaining oil to the boil. Lower spaghetti into water, gradually pushing it down as it softens. Cook pasta for about 10-12 minutes until just tender or al dente, keeping pan uncovered and stirring occasionally. Alternatively, follow packet instructions for cooking times. Warm serving dish.

5 Add prawns to peas in pan. Pour in brandy and season with salt and pepper. Bring to the boil then lower heat. Stir in cream. Cover and simmer slowly for 5 minutes.

6 Drain spaghetti and tip into a warm serving dish. Remove peas and prawns from heat. Stir in egg yolk. Adjust seasoning to taste. Pour over spaghetti. Toss with 2 forks. Serve straight away.

Nutritional value per portion:
760 cal.

Spaghetti with Prawns and Green Peas

Spaghetti con Gamberetti e Piselli

Spaghetti with Mussels

Spaghetti con le Cozze

Serves 4

Mussels and tomatoes are ideal partners in this simple dish.

Preparation time: about 1¼ hours

1kg (2lb) fresh mussels
60ml (2fl oz/¼ cup) water
2 cloves garlic
6 sprigs fresh parsley
396g (14oz) can peeled tomatoes
75ml (2½ fl oz/⅓ cup) olive oil
2 pinches cayenne pepper
Salt to taste
2 litres (3½ pints/8 cups) water
1½ teaspoons salt
1 teaspoon olive oil
500g (1lb) spaghetti

1 Brush mussels clean under cold running water. Discard any which are open or have broken shells. Pull away beards, then cut off with scissors. Put mussels into large saucepan with 60ml (2fl oz/¼ cup) water. Cover and steam for 10 minutes or as soon as shells have opened. Shake pan frequently to cook mussels evenly. Discard any which remain closed.

2 Peel garlic. Wash parsley and shake dry. Finely chop with garlic. Rub tomatoes and their juice through sieve.

3 Heat 75ml (2½ fl oz/⅓ cup) oil in pan until hot. Add garlic and parsley and sauté gently for 5 minutes, stirring. Mix in sieved tomatoes.

4 Strain cooking liquid from mussels through fine mesh sieve. Add to tomato mixture. Season with cayenne pepper and salt. Cook gently, uncovered, until three-quarters of the liquid has evaporated, leaving a semi-thick sauce. Warm serving dish.

5 In large saucepan, bring water, salt and oil to the boil. Lower spaghetti into water, gradually pushing it down as it softens. Cook pasta for 10-12 minutes until just tender or al dente, keeping pan uncovered and stirring occasionally. Alternatively, follow packet instructions for cooking times.

6 Meanwhile, take mussels out of their shells and heat through for 2 minutes in tomato mixture. Drain spaghetti. Tip into serving dish. Add tomato and mussel mixture. Toss thoroughly with 2 forks. Sprinkle with extra chopped parsley if liked. Serve straight away.

Nutritional value per portion:
710 cal.

Spaghetti with Mussels

Spaghetti con le Cozze

Spaghetti with Tuna and Mascarpone

Spaghetti con Tonno e Mascarpone

Serves 4

A luxurious spaghetti dish which is surprisingly easy to make.

Preparation time: about 45 minutes

198g (7oz) can tuna in oil
5 canned anchovy fillets, drained
6 sprigs fresh parsley
2 litres (3½ pints/8 cups) water
1½ teaspoon salt
½ teaspoon olive oil
60g (2oz) butter or margarine, softened
220g (7oz) Mascarpone cheese
1 teaspoon lemon juice
Salt to taste
Freshly milled white pepper to taste
2 tablespoons dry white wine
500g (1lb) spaghetti
Fresh parsley for garnishing

1 Drain tuna and mash flesh with fork. Finely chop anchovies. Wash, shake dry and finely chop parsley.

2 Bring water, salt and oil to boil in large saucepan. Warm serving dish.

3 In small bowl, beat butter or margarine with wooden spoon until smooth then stir in tuna and anchovies. Gradually beat in Mascarpone cheese. Season with lemon juice, salt and pepper. Continue to beat until mixture is smooth, gradually adding the wine.

4 Lower spaghetti into the pan of water, gradually pushing it down as it softens. Cook for 10-12 minutes until just tender or al dente, keeping pan covered and stirring occasionally. Alternatively, follow packet instructions for cooking times. Drain spaghetti thoroughly and return to pan.

5 Add the tuna mixture and parsley to the pasta and toss thoroughly with 2 forks. Spoon into warm serving dish and garnish with a sprig of parsley and an extra anchovy fillet, if liked. Serve straight away.

Nutritional value per portion:
760 cal.

Spaghetti with Tuna and Mascarpone

Spaghetti con Tonno e Mascarpone

Spaghetti with Bacon and Eggs

Spaghetti alla Carbonara

Serves 4

A well-loved favorite of pasta with bacon and eggs.

Preparation time: about 40 minutes

4 cloves garlic
155g (5oz) bacon
2 litres (3½ pints/8 cups) water
1½ teaspoon salt
1 tablespoon olive oil
30g (1oz) margarine or dripping
500g (1lb) spaghetti
3 eggs
60g (2oz) freshly grated Pecorino or
    Parmesan cheese
Salt to taste
Freshly milled pepper to taste
1 tablespoon chopped fresh chives

1 Peel garlic and thickly slice. Cut bacon into tiny squares.

2 In large saucepan, bring water, salt and oil to the boil. Lower spaghetti into pan of boiling water, gradually pushing it down as it softens. Cook for 10-12 minutes until tender or al dente, keeping pan uncovered and stirring occasionally. Alternatively, follow packet instructions for cooking times.

3 Meanwhile, melt margarine or dripping in small pan until hot. Add garlic and sauté until light golden brown. Remove from pan with fork. Add bacon to pan and sauté fairly briskly until crisp. Keep warm over low heat.

4 Break eggs into bowl and beat until foamy. Mix in cheese. Season with salt and pepper.

5 Drain spaghetti. Return to pan and stand over low heat.

6 Remove bacon from pan with draining spoon and add to spaghetti.

7 Pour in egg mixture and remove pan from heat. Toss with 2 forks until egg thickens and coats each strand of spaghetti. Sprinkle each portion with chives. Serve straight away.

Nutritional value per portion:
860 cal.

Spaghetti with Bacon and Eggs

Spaghetti alla Carbonara

Spaghetti with Bacon and Courgettes

Spaghetti con Guanciale e Zucchini

Serves 4

This is a fresh-tasting summery spaghetti dish.

Preparation time: about 45 minutes

500g (1lb) small courgettes (zucchini)
396g (14oz) can peeled tomatoes
220g (7oz) bacon
1 large onion
2 cloves garlic
6 sprigs fresh parsley
2 tablespoons olive oil
Salt to taste
Freshly milled pepper to taste
2 litres (3½ pints/8 cups) water
1½ teaspoon salt
1 teaspoon olive oil
500g (1lb) spaghetti
100g (3½ oz) freshly grated Parmesan
   cheese
Fresh parsley for garnishing

1 Top and tail courgettes (zucchini). Wash thoroughly and wipe dry. Cut each courgette (zucchini) lengthwise into 4 strips. Chop strips into small pieces.

2 Drain tomatoes through a sieve. Coarsely chop and reserve juice.

3 Coarsely chop bacon. Peel and chop onion. Peel garlic. Wash parsley, shake dry and finely chop with garlic.

4 Heat 2 tablespoons oil in saucepan. Add bacon and sauté until crisp. Add onion, garlic and parsley and sauté gently for 5 minutes, stirring.

5 Add courgettes (zucchini) and tomatoes to pan. Season with salt and pepper. Cover and simmer gently for 20 minutes, stirring frequently. Pour in reserved tomato juice and mix in well. Leave over low heat.

6 In large saucepan, bring water, salt and oil to the boil. Lower spaghetti into water, gradually pushing it down as it softens. Cook pasta for about 10-12 minutes until tender or al dente, keeping pan uncovered and stirring occasionally. Alternatively, follow packet instructions for cooking times.

7 Drain spaghetti. Tip into warm serving dish. Add vegetable sauce and toss with 2 forks until well combined. Serve straight away. Pass cheese separately and garnish with sprig of parsley.

Nutritional value per portion:
760 cal.

Spaghetti with Bacon and Courgettes

Spaghetti con Guanciale e Zucchini

Spaghetti Bolognese

Spaghetti alla Bolognese

Serves 4

The best known spaghetti dish of all time.

Preparation time: about 1¾ hours.

1 small onion
1 small carrot
1 stick celery
60g (2oz) bacon
396g (14oz) can tomatoes
60ml (2fl oz/¼ cup) olive oil
15g (½ oz) butter or margarine
375g (12oz) lean minced beef
60ml (2fl oz/¼ cup) dry red wine
75ml (2½ fl oz/¼ cup) meat stock
Salt to taste
Freshly milled pepper to taste
1 bay leaf
2 pinches freshly grated nutmeg
2 litres (3½ pint/8 cups) water
1½ teaspoon salt
½ teaspoon olive oil
500g (1lb) spaghetti
75g (2½ oz) freshly grated Parmesan cheese

1 Peel onion and carrot. Wash celery. Finely chop all three vegetables either by hand or in food processor. Finely chop bacon.

2 Drain tomatoes through a sieve. Mash with fork and reserve juice.

3 Heat oil and butter or margarine in saucepan until hot. Add vegetables and bacon and sauté over moderate heat for 10 minutes, stirring frequently.

4 Add beef to pan and cook briskly with vegetables for about 5 minutes, stirring constantly until meat is broken up and crumbly. Add wine and stock. Bring to boil then pour in reserved tomato juice.

5 Season with salt, pepper, bay leaf and nutmeg and stir thoroughly. Cover and simmer over low heat for 1 hour, stirring frequently to prevent sticking. Remove bay leaf.

6 In large saucepan, bring water, salt and oil to the boil. Lower spaghetti into water, gradually pushing it down as it softens. Cook pasta for about 10-12 minutes until just tender or al dente, keeping pan uncovered. Alternatively, follow packet instructions for cooking times. Drain.

7 Lift spaghetti out on to 4 warm serving plates. Add equal amounts of meat sauce to each. Sprinkle with fresh chopped parsley if liked and serve hot. Pass cheese separately.

Nutritional value per portion:
860 cal.

Spaghetti Bolognese

Spaghetti alla Bolognese

Spaghetti with Chicken Livers

Spaghetti al Fegatini

Serves 4

An economical meal which is quick and easy to prepare.

Preparation time: about 30 minutes

1 medium onion
220g (7oz) chicken livers
2 egg yolks
1 teaspoon lemon juice
Salt to taste
60g (2oz) butter or margarine
2 litres (3½ pints/8 cups) water
1½ teaspoons salt
½ teaspoon olive oil
500g (1lb) spaghetti
75ml (2½ fl oz/¼ cup) port
75ml (2½ fl oz/¼ cup) single (light) cream
Freshly milled pepper to taste
1 tablespoon chopped fresh chives

1 Peel onion and coarsely chop.

2 Wash livers and pat dry with absorbent kitchen paper. Cut into 1cm/½in pieces, removing fat and small strands of gristle.

3 Beat egg yolks in small bowl with lemon juice and salt.

4 In large frying pan or casserole dish, melt butter or margarine. Add onions and sauté gently until soft but still pale.

5 Bring water, salt and oil to the boil in large saucepan. Lower spaghetti into water, pushing it down as it softens. Cook pasta for 10-12 minutes until just tender or al dente, keeping pan uncovered and stirring occasionally.

6 After spaghetti has been cooking for 5 minutes, add livers to pan of onions and stir-fry briskly for 2-3 minutes.

7 Add port to pan and when liquid bubbles, stir in cream.

8 Drain spaghetti thoroughly.

9 Add spaghetti to pan of liver and onions. Season with salt and pepper. Toss with 2 forks. Spoon on to warm serving plates. Sprinkle each with chives.

Nutritional value per portion:
740 cal.

Spaghetti with Chicken Livers

Spaghetti al Fegatini

Spaghetti with Chicken Sauce

Spaghetti con Noce di Pollo

Serves 4

Cooked with herbs and vegetables, this sauce makes a light supper.

Preparation time: 1 hour

1 large onion
1 stick celery
1 medium carrot
6 sprigs fresh parsley
2 boned chicken breasts, about 375g (12oz),
   skin removed
1 tablespoon olive oil
30g (1oz) butter or margarine
125ml (4fl oz/½ cup) dry white wine
2 teaspoons tomato purée (paste)
125ml (4fl oz/½ cup) chicken stock
Salt to taste
Freshly milled pepper
1 bay leaf
2 litres (3½ pints/8 cups) water
1½ teaspoons salt
½ teaspoon olive oil
500g (1lb) spaghetti
2 tablespoons freshly grated Parmesan
   cheese.

1 Peel onion. Wash celery thoroughly. Peel carrot. Finely chop all three vegetables, either by hand or in food processor. Wash parsley, shake dry and chop. Rinse chicken under cold running water and pat dry with absorbent kitchen paper. Cut chicken into 1cm/½in wide strips. Cut strips into small squares.

2 Heat oil with half the butter or margarine in saucepan until hot. Add vegetables and parsley and cook gently for 10 minutes, stirring frequently.

3 Add chicken to pan and cook for 4-5 minutes. Pour in wine then boil quickly until it evaporates. Mix tomato purée (paste) smoothly with chicken stock and pour into pan. Season with salt and pepper. Add bay leaf. Bring to boil then lower heat. Cover and simmer gently for 15 minutes.

4 In large saucepan, bring water, salt and oil to the boil. Lower spaghetti into water, gradually pushing it down as it softens. Cook pasta for 10-12 minutes until just tender or al dente, keeping pan uncovered and stirring occasionally. Alternatively, follow packet instructions for cooking times.

5 Meanwhile, uncover chicken sauce and continue to cook fairly briskly until spaghetti is ready, stirring frequently. Remove bay leaf from sauce.

6 Drain spaghetti. Tip into warm serving dish. Add remaining butter or margarine and cheese. Top with chicken sauce and toss with 2 forks. Serve straight away.

Nutritional value per portion:
600 cal.

Spaghetti with Chicken Sauce

Spaghetti con Noce di Pollo

•NOTES•

◆NOTES◆

Toasted
Snacks
Made Easy

Series Consultant: **Sonia Allison**

GREAT COOKING VALUE

Introduction

Toasted snacks are easy, convenient and marvellously versatile. Bread is a staple that is seldom missing from the kitchen, and pantry and refrigerator will furnish a wide variety of delectable fillings for all occasions and appetites.

One of the greatest advantages of these snacks is the speed with which they can be prepared, either to satisfy the hunger pangs of small children, or to make speedy sophisticated starters, lunches or light suppers. Whether bread, bun or bagel-based, toasted snacks allow for ingenuity and artistry and also give the cook ample opportunity to experiment.

Recipe Notes

All spoon measures are level:
1 tablespoon = 15ml spoon:
1 teaspoon = 5ml spoon.

Follow EITHER metric or Imperial measures and NEVER mix in one recipe as they are not interchangeable.

Eggs used are a medium size unless otherwise stated.

Written by Cornelia Adam

Gorgonzola Cheese Toasts

Serves 2

A sophisticated snack for a summer lunch.

Preparation time: about 20 minutes

1 zucchini about 125g (4oz)
90g (3oz) smoked salmon or Parma ham
30g (1oz) butter or margarine
2 slices white or wholewheat bread
1 clove garlic
2 egg yolks
Salt
Freshly milled black pepper
Pinch of grated nutmeg
1 tablespoon roughly chopped fresh basil
   leaves
100g (3½ oz) Gorgonzola cheese

1 Top and tail zucchini, then slice thinly. Slice salmon or ham into thin strips.

2 Melt half the butter or margarine in a frying pan, add the courgette slices and fry over low heat for 5 minutes, turning and stirring frequently. Using a slotted spoon, transfer courgette slices to a plate. Set pan aside.

3 Toast bread. Peel garlic and cut in half lengthwise. Rub one side of each toast slice with cut sides of garlic.

4 Spread toast with rest of butter or margarine. Top with courgette slices and salmon or ham.

5 Beat egg yolks in small bowl; season with salt, pepper and nutmeg. Stir in half the basil.

6 Reheat butter in frying pan over gentle heat. Add egg mixture and cook, stirring with a wooden spoon, until scrambled.

7 Spoon scrambled egg equally over both slices of toast. Crumble Gorgonzola on top.

8 Heat the topped toast under a hot grill until cheese melts, sprinkle with rest of basil and serve.

Nutritional value per portion:
520 cal
Protein: 19g
Fat: 43g
Carbohydrate: 13g

Gorgonzola Cheese Toasts

Sausage Toasts with Vegetables

Serves 2

A winning combination that appeals to young and old.

Preparation time: about 20 minutes

1 small stick celery
1 baby carrot
110g (3½ oz) pork or beef
1 egg yolk
1 clove garlic, crushed
Salt
Freshly milled black pepper
2 large slices wholewheat bread
2 teaspoons softened butter or margarine
60g (2oz) Cheddar cheese, grated, or
  2 processed cheese slices
Chervil leaves or mustard and cress to
  garnish

1 Preheat oven to 400°F.
Brush a baking sheet lightly with oil.
Finely chop celery. Cut carrot into fine
matchsticks.

2 Put sausagemeat into a bowl. Work in
egg yolk, garlic and prepared vegetables. Add salt and pepper to taste.

3 Toast bread, spread thinly with
butter or margarine, then with meat
mixture.

4 Transfer to prepared baking sheet and
top with cheese. Bake for 20-25 minutes
until top is bubbling and sausagemeat
mixture is cooked through.

5 Sprinkle with chervil or mustard and
cress and serve at once.

TIP
Instead of using all sausagemeat, try a
mixture of equal quantities of sausagemeat
and finely diced cooked ham. Add a little
chutney, if liked.

Nutritional value per portion:
450 cal
Protein: 21g
Fat: 29g
Carbohydrate: 26g

Sausage Toasts with Vegetables

Welsh Rarebit

Serves 2

A British speciality that has become an international favorite.

Preparation time: about 15 minutes

155g (5oz) Cheddar cheese
1 teaspoon plain flour
2 tablespoons beer
1 teaspoon softened butter or margarine
1/4 teaspoon Worcestershire sauce
1/2 teaspoon prepared English mustard
1 egg yolk
Pinch grated nutmeg
Pinch paprika
2 slices white bread
Parsley or coriander sprig, to garnish

1 Grate cheese into a bowl. Add flour, stout, softened butter or margarine, Worcestershire sauce, mustard and egg yolk. Stir in nutmeg and paprika, mixing well.

2 Toast bread, then spread evenly with cheese mixture, taking it right to the edges.

3 Transfer to a foil-lined grill pan and cook under a hot grill until cheese topping is golden brown and bubbly.

4 Transfer each slice to a plate, garnish with parsley or coriander and serve at once.

TIPS
Top each slice of toast with a poached egg to make Buck Rarebit or add 4 grilled slices of bacon for Yorkshire Rarebit.
For a variation which young children will relish, substitute milk for the beer and fruit chutney for the Worcestershire and mustard.

Nutritional value per portion:
400 cal
Protein: 23g
Fat: 28g
Carbohydrate: 13g

Welsh Rarebit

Lemony Tuna Toasts with Capers

Serves 2

Italy was the inspiration for this delicious snack.

Preparation time: about 15 minutes

200g (7oz) can tuna in brine
2 teaspoons small capers, rinsed and
    drained
1 1/2 teaspoons finely grated lemon rind
2 teaspoons lemon juice
Salt
Freshly milled black pepper
10cm (4 in) length of cucumber
2 slices white bread
2 teaspoons softened butter or margarine
75g (2 1/2 oz) Mozzarella cheese, sliced
Lemon balm or parsley, to garnish

1 Drain tuna thoroughly, tip into a shallow bowl and divide into flakes with 2 forks.

2 Stir in capers, lemon rind and lemon juice. Add salt and pepper to taste.

3 Peel cucumber and slice thinly.

4 Toast bread and spread with butter or margarine. Cover with cucumber slices then sprinkle with salt and pepper to taste.

5 Divide tuna mixture between toast slices, then cover centres with Mozzarella.

6 Transfer to foil-lined grill pan and heat under a hot grill until cheese melts. Serve at once, garnished with lemon balm or parsley.

TIP

For a special occasion starter, pile the mixture on slices of toasted French bread, grill as instructed and serve on a bed of mixed salad leaves.

Nutritional value per portion:
430 cal
Protein: 27g
Fat: 23g
Carbohydrate: 21g

Lemony Tuna Toasts with Capers

Tomato and Mozzarella Toasts

Serves 2

Tomato, Mozzarella and basil are a famous combination, usually served as a salad but delicious as a toasted snack.

Preparation time: about 20 minutes

2 long oblong crusty rolls
1 clove garlic
2 tablespoons virgin olive oil
1 beefsteak tomato
155g (5oz) Mozzarella cheese
Salt
Freshly-milled black pepper
Basil leaves, to garnish

1 Preheat oven to 425°F. Cut rolls in half lengthwise. Crush garlic in a small bowl; stir in oil. Brush mixture over cut sides of rolls. Place in a foil-lined grill pan and brown under a hot grill.

2 Cut a small cross in tomato. Put into a heatproof bowl. Cover with boiling water. Leave to stand for 1 minute. Rinse under cold water. When cool enough to handle, slip off skin. Cut tomato in half. Remove seeds with a teaspoon then cut remaining flesh into narrow strips.

3 Slice Mozzarella. Arrange on halved rolls, alternately with tomato slices. Sprinkle with salt and pepper to taste.

4 Place on foil-lined baking sheet. Bake for 7-10 minutes until cheese has melted.

5 Garnish with basil and serve at once.

TIP
Make pizza rolls by interleaving strips of anchovy fillet between the tomato slices and Mozzarella. Sprinkle with chopped basil before baking.

Nutritional value per portion:
360 cal
Protein: 19g
Fat: 21g
Carbohydrate: 20g

Tomato and Mozzarella Toasts

Ham and Oyster Mushroom Rolls

Serves 2

An imaginative snack with a delicious combination of flavors.

Preparation time: about 15 minutes

200g (7oz) oyster mushrooms
110g (3½ oz) cooked ham, trimmed
155g (5 oz) Mozzarella cheese
1 tablespoon virgin olive oil
Salt
Freshly milled black pepper
2 dinner rolls
2 tablespoons herb butter (bought) or
   see Tips
½ teaspoon dried thyme or 1 tablespoon
   chopped fresh thyme leaves, to garnish

1 Trim mushrooms. Remove woody pieces of stalks and cut flesh into strips. Cut ham into strips. Slice cheese.

2 Heat oil in a frying pan, add mushrooms and fry fairly briskly until all the liquid has been absorbed and the mushrooms are tender and golden brown.

3 Remove pan from heat and stir in ham strips. Add salt and pepper to taste.

4 Cut rolls in half. Spread cut sides with herb butter. Place in a foil-lined grill pan and brown under a hot grill.

5 Divide mushroom mixture evenly between rolls, piling it up in the center.

6 Arrange cheese slices on top; heat rolls under the grill until cheese melts and starts to bubble. Transfer rolls to individual plates, sprinkle with thyme and serve at once.

TIPS

• To make a small pot of herb butter, mix 60g (2oz) softened butter with 2 teaspoons chopped parsley, 1 teaspoon chopped thyme and 1 teaspoon snipped chives. Add salt and pepper to taste.

• As an alternative to the Mozzarella topping, spoon sour cream on to each portion of mushrooms; top with snipped chives.

Nutritional value per portion:
450 cal
Protein: 23g
Fat: 30g
Carbohydrate: 24g

Ham and Oyster Mushroom Rolls

Toasted French Bread with Sardines and Cheese

Serves 4

A colorful appetizer, suitable for any time of year.

Preparation time: about 15 minutes

1 small red pepper
1 small seeded French loaf
4 teaspoons herb butter (bought) or see
  Tips, page 530
125g (4oz) can sardines or pilchards in oil,
  drained
Salt
Freshly milled black pepper
90g (3oz) Gouda cheese. coarsely grated
Paprika for dusting

1 Cut pepper in half, removing inner fibres and seeds. Cut flesh into narrow strips, then cut one third of the strips into small dice. Place strips and dice in separate bowls and set aside.

2 Cut loaf in half lengthwise, cut each half into 4 pieces and spread with the herb butter. Transfer to foil-lined grill pan and toast until golden.

3 Remove any skin and bones from sardines or pilchards, carefully cut them in half and arrange on top of toast with pepper strips.

4 Sprinkle toast pieces with salt and pepper to taste. Add grated cheese. Replace toast under the grill and heat until cheese melts and starts to bubble.

5 Serve on individual plates, garnished with reserved diced pepper. Dust melted cheese lightly with paprika.

TIP
A mild cheese is best for this snack. Use Edam or a mild Cheddar if preferred.

Nutritional value per portion:
400 cal
Protein: 24g
Fat: 27g
Carbohydrate: 20g

Toasted French Bread with Sardines and Cheese

Mexicali Toasts

Serves 2

A fiery treat from Central America.

Preparation time: about 40 minutes

1 ripe avocado
1 tablespoon lemon juice
1 small onion
1 clove garlic
2 tablespoons finely chopped fresh parsley
Pinch dried thyme
1 egg, beaten
4 tablespoons fresh white breadcrumbs
3-4 drops Tabasco sauce or to taste
1 teaspoon Worcestershire sauce
2 large slices white bread
Salt
Freshly milled black pepper

1 Line a baking sheet with foil. Preheat oven to 425°F.

2 Peel avocado as you would peel a pear, starting at the pointed end. Cut in half and remove stone. Scoop flesh into a mixing bowl, add lemon juice and mash finely.

3 Grate onion and crush garlic. Add both to avocado with parsley, thyme, egg, breadcrumbs, Tabasco and Worcestershire sauce, adjusting the quantity of Tabasco to personal taste. Mix well.

4 Toast bread. Spread slices with avocado mixture. Season with salt and pepper.

5 Transfer topped toast slices to baking sheet; heat through in the oven for 5 minutes. Garnish with flat parsley and red chillies, if liked, and serve at once.

TIP
Omit the Tabasco sauce if preferred and substitute 1 red chilli, seeded and very finely chopped. When chopping the chilli take care to avoid touching any part of your face, especially the eyes, or irritation may occur. Wash your hands thoroughly after handling the chilli.

Nutritional value per portion:
430 cal
Protein: 9g
Fat: 28g
Carbohydrate: 32g

Mexicali Toasts

Criss Cross Chicken and Avocado Snacks

Serves 2

An elegant and sophisticated avocado treat.

Preparation time: about 30 minutes

2 tablespoons butter or margarine
1 boneless, skinless chicken breast, cut
   into 2 slices
Salt
Freshly milled black pepper
1 small ripe avocado
Lemon juice
6 diagonally cut slices of French bread
3 tablespoons cream cheese
60g (2oz) Edam, Gouda or Emmental
   cheese, sliced
about 2 tablespoons snipped chives

1 Melt butter or margarine in a frying pan. Add chicken. Fry gently for 8-10 minutes or until cooked through, turning pieces twice.

2 Transfer chicken pieces to a board, season with salt and pepper, then cut against the grain into thin diagonal slices.

3 Peel, halve and stone avocado. Cut flesh into semi circular slices, the same thickness as the chicken. Place in a bowl and sprinkle with lemon juice.

4 Put bread in foil-lined grill pan and toast on both sides under a hot grill.

5 Spread toast with cream cheese; top with alternate slices of chicken and avocado. Sprinkle with more salt and pepper.

6 Cut cheese into strips; arrange in a criss cross pattern on top of the chicken and avocado. Return to the hot grill until the cheese starts to melt.

7 Sprinkle with chives and serve at once.

TIP
Use mayonnaise instead of cream cheese if preferred.

Nutritional value per portion:
690 cal
Protein: 32g
Fat: 47g
Carbohydrate: 37g

Criss Cross Chicken and Avocado Snacks

Broccoli Meringue Toasts

Serves 2

A tasty snack for vegetarians with healthy appetites.

Preparation time: about 25 minutes

185g (6oz) broccoli
1 egg
75g (2½ oz) Gorgonzola or Stilton cheese
Salt
Freshly milled black pepper
½ teaspoon dried marjoram
2 teaspoons lemon juice
2 slices white bread
2 teaspoons softened butter or margarine
2 teaspoons tomato purée (paste)
1 tablespoon sunflower seeds

1 Preheat oven to 425°F.
Trim broccoli and divide into small flow-erets. Bring a saucepan of lightly salted water to the boil, add broccoli and cook for 3 minutes. Drain, refresh under cold running water, then drain again thoroughly.

2 Separate egg, putting yolk into one bowl and white into another. Crumble cheese into yolk. Add salt and pepper to taste, then stir in marjoram and 1½ teaspoons of the lemon juice. Mash until well mixed.

3 Add rest of lemon juice to egg whites and beat stiffly; fold into cheese mixture with a metal spoon.

4 Toast bread. Spread with butter or margarine, then with tomato purée (paste). Top with broccoli, then pile cheese meringue mixture on top and sprinkle with sunflower seeds.

5 Transfer to foil-lined baking sheet. Bake for 10 minutes until puffy and golden. Serve straight away.

TIPS
•Use Cambozola cheese instead of Gorgonzola or Stilton for a milder flavor.
•Toasted almonds or pine nuts make a delicious topping in place of the sunflower seeds.

Nutritional value per portion:
380 cal
Protein: 19g
Fat: 24g
Carbohydrate: 22g

Broccoli Meringue Toasts

Stir-fried Liver and Apple on Toast

Serves 2

Serve this simple supper dish with a fresh green salad.

Preparation time: about 25 minutes

1 small onion
1 Golden Delicious apple
1 clove garlic
45g (1½ oz) butter or margarine
185g (6oz) chicken livers, trimmed
Salt
Freshly milled black pepper
1/2 teaspoon dried marjoram
2 slices wholewheat bread
2 heaped tablespoons grated Cheddar
    cheese
2 tablespoons snipped chives

1 Finely chop onion. Peel, quarter and core apple. Grate coarsely into a bowl. Crush garlic.

2 Heat 2 tablespoons butter or margarine in frying pan. Add onion, apple and garlic. Stir fry gently for 3 minutes.

3 Slice livers thinly. Add to pan and continue to stir fry mixture for a further 3 minutes or until livers are cooked through.

4 Stir in salt and pepper to taste; add marjoram.

5 Toast bread, spread with remaining butter or margarine and put into a foil-lined grill pan.

6 Top with liver mixture, sprinkle with cheese and place under a hot grill until cheese melts. Serve immediately, sprinkled with chives.

TIP
Substitute 90g (3oz) thinly sliced mushrooms for the apple, if preferred. Add Worcestershire sauce to taste.

Nutritional value per portion:
480 cal
Protein: 27g
Fat: 28g
Carbohydrate: 29g

Stir-fried Liver and Apple on Toast

Salami and Olive Baguettes

Serves 2

Perfect for a teenage party or picnic.

Preparation time: about 15 minutes

155g (5oz) sliced Italian salami or see Tip
60g (2oz) drained stuffed green olives
Salt
Freshly milled black pepper
½ teaspoon dried oregano
2 tablespoons chopped fresh parsley
155g (5oz) piece of goats' cheese
1 small French loaf
30g (1oz) butter or margarine, softened

1 Preheat oven to 400°F.
Cut salami into small squares and put into a bowl. Slice olives thinly and add. Season with the salt and pepper. Stir in dried oregano and fresh parsley.

2 Remove rind from cheese and cut into 6 slices.

3 Cut loaf in half lengthwise; toast cut sides under hot grill until golden brown. Spread with butter or margarine.

4 Place buttered toasted bread halves on foil-lined baking sheet; top with salami mixture.

5 Arrange cheese on top as illustrated opposite. Bake for about 8 minutes until cheese starts to melt. Transfer to individual platters or wrap in several layers of foil for taking to a picnic. Serve as soon as possible.

TIP
Use sliced pepper salami or garlic sausage instead of Italian salami if preferred.

Nutritional value per portion:
930 cal
Protein: 30g
Fat: 72g
Carbohydrate: 37g

Salami and Olive Baguettes

Mushroom Toasts with Camembert

Serves 2

A gourmet snack which would make a superb starter.

Preparation time: about 20 minutes

60g (2oz) rindless bacon
1 teaspoon corn oil
110g (3½ oz) mushrooms
2 green scallions
15g (½ oz) parsley
2 slices wholewheat bread
1 tablespoon softened butter or margarine
125g (4oz) Camembert cheese
Freshly-milled black pepper

1 Chop bacon. Heat oil in a frying pan, add bacon and fry over moderate heat, stirring occasionally, for 3-4 minutes.

2 Trim mushrooms, leaving stalks in place. Slice thinly, add to bacon and stir fry for 3 minutes.

3 Trim green scallions and slice thinly. Chop parsley. Add both to bacon mixture. Mix well and stir fry for 1 minute. Remove pan from heat.

4 Toast bread and spread slices with butter or margarine. Put into foil-lined grill pan and top with the fried mixture.

5 Slice Camembert into wide strips; arrange on top of toast as illustrated opposite, then sprinkle with pepper. Place under a hot grill until the cheese melts and becomes runny. Serve at once.

TIP
Cut the tops off 4 small plain or wholemeal rolls and set aside as lids. Hollow out the centres of the rolls, discarding the crumbs, then fill with the mushroom mixture. Top with Camembert, grill as in main recipe, then replace lids.

Nutritional value per portion:
520 cal
Protein: 20g
Fat: 40g
Carbohydrate: 21g

Mushroom Toasts with Camembert

Pan-toasted Sandwiches

Serves 1-2

One of the simplest snacks, popular the world over.

Preparation time: about 15 minutes

1 egg
1 egg yolk
2 tablespoons milk
Salt
Fresh black pepper
2 large slices white bread
90g (3oz) firm cheese (Cheddar, Red
   Leicester, Gruyère), sliced
3 tablespoons corn or sunflower oil
5 tablespoons French dressing
2 tablespoons chopped fresh or freeze-dried
   basil

1 Beat whole egg, yolk and milk together
in a shallow dish or enamel plate.
Season with salt and pepper.

2 Sandwich bread slices together with
cheese; cut in half diagonally to make
2 triangular sandwiches.

3 Add the sandwich triangles to the
beaten egg and milk mixture; leave to
soak for 5 minutes, turning once.

4 Heat the oil in a frying pan. Fry the
sandwiches for about 4 minutes over
moderate heat, turning once.

5 Remove from the pan, drain the sandwiches on absorbent kitchen paper,
transfer to a plate or platter, and serve.

6 Mix the dressing with the basil in a small
bowl. Serve with the sandwiches.

TIP
If preferred, accompany with tomato
ketchup instead of French dressing.

Nutritional value per portion:
500 cal
Protein: 15g
Fat: 44g
Carbohydrate: 12g

Pan-toasted Sandwiches

Wok Cooking

Made Easy

Series Consultant:
Sonia Allison

GREAT COOKING VALUE

Introduction

The wok originated in China and is a wide-topped, bowl-shaped metal pan designed for stir-frying small pieces of food in oil or fat over high heat.

Because the frying technique is brisk, all ingredients should be prepared ahead of time and cut into smallish squares or strips, all roughly the same size for even cooking. To retain valuable food nutrients, vegetables should be lightly stir-fried until tender but still crisp in texture and never over-cooked. A half rack, which clips over the wok, is available from speciality kitchen shops and is useful for draining as the pictures in the book show. If no similar rack is available, drain food to be reheated on absorbent kitchen paper. Finally, a useful tip: use chopsticks for stirring.

Written by Cornelia Adam

Recipe Notes

All spoon measures are level:
1 tablespoon = 15ml spoon;
1 teaspoon = 5ml spoon.

Follow EITHER metric or Imperial measures and NEVER mix in one recipe as they are not interchangeable.

Eggs used are a medium unless otherwise stated.

Lamb with Peppers and Beans

Serves 4

A classic stir-fry combination, well-laced with soy sauce and sherry.

Preparation time: about 25 minutes
Cooking time: 10 minutes

500g (1lb) green beans
Boiling water
Salt to taste
2 medium red peppers (capsicums)
2 medium green peppers (capsicums)
2 medium onions
500g (1lb) boneless fillet of lamb
30g (1oz) fresh parsley
3 tablespoons sunflower or corn oil
4 cloves garlic
60ml (2fl oz/¼ cup) soy sauce
1 tablespoon medium sherry
90ml(3 fl oz/⅓ cup) chicken stock

1 Top and tail beans and remove side strings if necessary. Cut into 1cm (½ in) pieces. Cook beans in boiling salted water for 5 minutes, keeping saucepan two-thirds covered. Drain in a colander. Refresh by rinsing under cold, running water.

2 Halve peppers (capsicums). Remove inner white membranes and seeds. Cut flesh into 1cm (½ in) diamond shapes.

3 Peel and quarter onions. Cut into thin strips.

4 Using a sharp knife, cut lamb into same-sized strips as onions.

5 Wash parsley and shake dry. Coarsely chop.

6 Heat oil in wok until very hot, but not smoking. Add lamb. Stir-fry briskly for 2 minutes. Remove from wok with ladle. Drain on rack or on absorbent kitchen paper.

7 Crush garlic directly into remaining oil in wok. Add beans, peppers and onions. Stir-fry for 3 minutes.

8 Sprinkle soy sauce, sherry and stock over stir-fried ingredients. Return lamb to wok. Reheat until piping hot, stirring. Mix in parsley. Adjust seasoning to taste.

9 Serve with rice, small new potatoes or pasta.

Nutritional value per portion:
480 cal
Protein: 32g
Fat: 34g
Carbohydrate: 14g

Lamb with Peppers and Beans

Fried Fish with Rice and Mixed Vegetables

Serves 4

Use favorite fresh or frozen white fish fillets for this unusual stir-fry dish.

Preparation time: about 25 minutes
Cooking time: 15 minutes   *favourite*

220g (7oz/1⅓ cups) long-grain white rice
500ml (16 fl oz/2 cups) boiling water
Salt to taste
2 bulbs fennel
155g (5oz) frozen peas
1 large onion
2 green shallots
750g (1½ lb) skinned white fish fillets, thawed
   if frozen
Fresh lemon juice
2 tablespoons plain flour
2 eggs
3 tablespoons sunflower or corn oil
2 tablespoons medium sherry
3 tablespoons soy sauce
Fresh pepper

1 Cook rice in boiling, salted water for 20 minutes. Keep pan tightly covered and heat moderate to prevent water boiling over.

2 While rice is cooking, cut fennel into thin strips. Tip peas on to plate. Peel and quarter onion and cut into thin slices. Trim green shallots and thinly slice.

3 Cut fish into 3.5cm (1½ in) squares. Sprinkle with lemon juice and salt. Tip flour on to piece of non-stick baking paper. Add fish. Coat each piece thoroughly. Beat eggs in bowl until frothy. Add fish and stir until well-covered with egg. Drain on a plate.

4 Heat oil in wok until very hot, but not smoking. Add fish, piece by piece, and stir-fry until golden brown all over. Drain on rack or on absorbent paper towel.

5 Add onion slices to remaining oil in wok. Stir-fry for 3 minutes. Add fennel and peas and stir-fry for 5 minutes. Add green shallots and stir-fry for 1 minute.

6 Sprinkle stir-fried ingredients with sherry, soy sauce and pepper. Add salt to taste. Mix in rice, drained if necessary. Top with fried fish cubes. Reheat until hot. Stir carefully, taking care not to break up fish.

Nutritional value per portion:
500 cal
Protein: 46g
Fat: 11g
Carbohydrate: 52g

Fried Fish with Rice and Mixed Vegetables

Pork with Mushrooms

Serves 4

*Look for dried cloud ear mushrooms in Oriental food shops. Or if preferred,
use other dried mushrooms instead.*

Preparation time: about 25 minutes
Cooking time: 12-15 minutes

30g (1oz) dried cloud ear mushrooms or
   other dried mushrooms
Boiling water
500g (1lb) pork
Salt to taste
Fresh black pepper to taste
4 teaspoons cornflour
155g (5oz) fresh spinach leaves
155g (5oz) fresh bean sprouts
1 medium onion
15g (½ oz) fresh chives
3 tablespoons soy sauce
2 tablespoons white wine vinegar
125ml (4fl oz/½ cup) chicken stock
60ml (2fl oz/¼ cup) sunflower or corn oil
1 tablespoon blanched almonds, cut into
   slivers.

1 Rinse mushrooms. Put into bowl. Cover with boiling water and leave for 30 minutes to soak. Tip into sieve. Rinse under cold, running water. Drain thoroughly and cut into small pieces.

2 Cut pork into 1cm (½ in) strips across the grain. Lightly season with salt and pepper. Sprinkle with 2 teaspoons cornflour and rub well into flesh with fingers.

3 Wash spinach leaves thoroughly to remove grit. Drain well and tear leaves into strips.

4 Rinse bean sprouts under cold, running water. Drain.

5 Peel and finely chop onion. Snip chives into small pieces with kitchen scissors.

6 Mix remaining cornflour with soy sauce, vinegar and stock in small bowl until smooth.

7 Heat oil in wok until very hot, but not smoking. Add pork. Stir-fry briskly for about 3 minutes or until golden brown. Add almonds. Stir-fry with pork for further 1 minute. Remove pork and almonds from wok with ladle and drain on absorbent paper towel.

8 Add onion, spinach, bean sprouts and mushrooms to remaining oil in wok. Stir-fry over moderate heat for 4 minutes. Return pork and almonds to wok. Add cornflour mixture and bring to boil, stir-frying continually. Simmer for 2 minutes over low heat. Mix in chives. Adjust seasoning to taste. Serve with rice or pasta.

Nutritional value per portion:
360 cal
Protein: 27g
Fat: 25g
Carbohydrate: 7g

Pork With Mushrooms

Chicken with Wild Rice

Serves 4

Wild rice adds a delicious nutty flavor to this chicken stir-fry.

Preparation time: about 50 minutes
Cooking time: 8-10 minutes

250g (8oz/1½ cups) wild rice
1 litre (1¾ pints/4 cups) boiling water
Salt to taste
500g (1lb) boneless chicken breasts, skinned
1 small onion
2cm (¾ in) fresh root (green) ginger
3 tablespoons snipped fresh chives
90ml (3fl oz/⅓ cup) soy sauce
1 tablespoon dry sherry
1 small cucumber
155g (5oz) fresh or frozen peas
1 medium red pepper
2 eggs
60ml (2 fl oz/¼ cup) sunflower or corn oil

1 Wash rice. Tip into saucepan with boiling water and salt to taste, cover and simmer for 45-50 minutes until grains split open and are tender. Drain if necessary.

2 Cut chicken breasts into thin strips. Transfer to bowl.

3 Peel and finely chop onion. Peel ginger and finely chop. Mix onion and ginger together and combine with chicken. Sprinkle mixture with chives, soy sauce and sherry. Cover and leave to marinate for 30 minutes, stirring occasionally.

4 Peel cucumber, halve lengthwise and remove seeds. Cut flesh into small cubes. Shell peas or thaw frozen ones. Halve pepper . Remove inner white membranes and seeds. Cut into small cubes. Beat eggs until frothy.

5 Lift chicken out of marinade with draining spoon. Heat oil in wok until hot, but not smoking. Add chicken and stir-fry briskly for 1 minute. Add prepared vegetables. Stir-fry with chicken for 2 minutes. Take all ingredients out of wok and put on to plate lined with absorbent paper towel. Keep warm.

6 Pour eggs into wok. Scramble lightly, stirring continuously, with chop sticks or wooden spoon. Add chicken and vegetables. Reheat for 1 minute. Moisten with soy mixture. Add rice. Continue to stir-fry for about 3 minutes until piping hot. Adjust seasoning to taste. Serve straight away.

Nutritional value per portion:
430 cal
Protein: 47g
Fat: 19g
Carbohydrate: 44g

Chicken with Wild Rice

Chicken with Asparagus

Serves 4

Low in calories, this dish makes an excellent choice for slimmers.

Preparation time: about 15 minutes
Cooking time: 10 minutes

250g (8oz) asparagus spears
Boiling water
Salt to taste
220g (7oz) snow peas
500g (1lb) boneless chicken breasts, skinned
Fresh pepper
2 teaspoons cornflour
3 shallots or pickling onions
3 tablespoons sunflower or corn oil
125ml (4 fl oz/½ cup) chicken stock
1 tablespoon medium sherry
2 tablespoons soy sauce
Freshly grated nutmeg to taste
6 sprigs flat parsley

1 Cut woody ends off asparagus. Cut spears into 2.5cm (1in) pieces. Cook asparagus in boiling salted water for 2 minutes. Drain and rinse under cold water straight away to retain fresh green color.

2 Top and tail snow peas. Cut into diamond shapes.

3 Cut chicken breasts into thin strips. Season lightly with salt and pepper. Transfer to round dish. Sprinkle with cornflour and rub well into flesh with fingers.

4 Peel and finely chop shallots or onions.

5 Heat oil in wok until hot, but not smoking. Add chicken and stir-fry briskly for 1 minute. Remove from wok. Drain on rack or absorbent kitchen paper.

6 Add shallots or onions, asparagus and snow peas to remaining oil in wok. Stir-fry briskly for 1-2 minutes. Add chicken, stock, sherry and soy sauce. Mix thoroughly, cover and simmer for 3 minutes. Return chicken to wok and stir in well. Adjust seasoning to taste. Flavor lightly with nutmeg. Cover and simmer for 2 minutes.

7 Wash parsley. Take leaves off stalks. Mix into stir-fry.

8 Serve with boiled new potatoes.

Nutritional value per portion:
1000 cal
Protein: 33g
Fat: 8g
Carbohydrate: 11g

Chicken with Asparagus

Mixed Vegetables with Tofu

Serves 4

A colorful, fiery-flavored stir-fry, perfect for vegetarians.

Preparation time: about 1 hour
Cooking time: 10 minutes

250g (8oz) firm tofu
3 cloves garlic
5 green shallots
125ml (4fl oz/½ cup) vegetable stock
90ml (3fl oz/⅓ cup) soy sauce
250g (8oz) broccoli
1 large red pepper
1 large yellow pepper
1 medium fresh green chilli
3 tablespoons sunflower or corn oil
Salt to taste
Fresh pepper

1 Drain tofu if necessary and cut into 1½ cm (¾ in) pieces. Put on to plate and crush garlic directly over top.

2 Trim spring onions (green shallots) and slice thinly. Sprinkle over tofu with stock and soy sauce. Cover and leave to marinate for 1 hour, stirring occasionally.

3 Divide broccoli into small florets. Cut stalks into thin slices. Halve peppers. Remove inner white membranes and seeds. Cut flesh into thin strips. Repeat with chilli, wearing rubber gloves to prevent skin burns.

4 Heat oil in wok until hot, but not smoking. Stir in chilli. Lift tofu out of marinade with draining spoon and add to wok. Reserve marinade. Fry tofu briskly until pieces start to turn brown, gently turning. Remove tofu and chilli to bowl.

5 Add pepper strips to remaining oil in wok with broccoli florets and chopped stalks. Stir-fry for 3 minutes. Spoon reserved marinade and green shallots into wok. Bring to boil, stirring, and cook gently for further 3 minutes. Return tofu to wok. Season lightly with salt and pepper and heat through for 2 minutes.

6 Serve with rice or pasta.

Nutritional value per person:
150 cal
Protein: 8g
Fat: 9g
Carbohydrate: 9g

Mixed Vegetables with Tofu

Turkey Curry with Celery and Carrots

Serves 4

Unlike most curries, this one takes just minutes to cook.

Preparation time: 15 minutes
Cooking time: 7 minutes

1 medium head celery
315g (10oz) small carrots
500g (1lb) turkey breast fillet
3 tablespoons sunflower or corn oil
Fresh pepper
3 teaspoons curry powder
3 tablespoons soy sauce
125ml (4 fl oz/½ cup) chicken stock
1 tablespoon seedless raisins
Salt to taste

1 Separate celery into sticks, reserving leaves. Remove and discard tough outer strings from each with vegetable knife or peeler. Cut celery into very thin slices. Coarsely chop leaves.

2 Cut carrots into thin slices.

3 Skin turkey breast if necessary. Cut flesh into thin strips.

4 Heat oil in wok until hot, but not smoking. Add turkey breast strips and stir-fry briskly until they start to turn golden. Sprinkle with pepper and curry powder.

5 Add celery and carrots to wok and mix well with turkey. Moisten with soy sauce and stock. Stir in raisins. Simmer for 3 minutes. Adjust seasoning. Sprinkle with chopped celery leaves.

6 Serve with rice or vermicelli noodles.

Nutritional value per portion:
220 cal
Protein: 32g
Fat: 8g
Carbohydrate: 6g

Turkey Curry with Celery and Carrots

Beef Fillet with Bean Sprouts

Serves 4

Strips of beef combined with bean sprouts and spinach.

Preparation time: 20 minutes
Cooking time: 8 minutes

500g (1lb) fillet of beef
1/2 teaspoon cornflour
60ml (2fl oz/¼ cup) sunflower or corn oil
2 cloves garlic
90ml (3fl oz/⅓ cup) soy sauce
155g (5oz) fresh bean sprouts
100g (3½ oz) fresh young spinach
Salt to taste
Fresh black pepper to taste
125ml (4 fl oz/½ cup) chicken stock
1 tablespoon medium sherry

1 Cut beef fillet into very thin slices across grain. Sprinkle with cornflour.

2 Heat oil in wok until very hot, but not smoking. Add beef, slice by slice, and stir-fry briskly until browned. Remove from wok with ladle. Drain on rack or on absorbent kitchen paper.

3 Crush garlic into bowl with garlic press. Add soy sauce and mix in meat. Cover and leave to marinate.

4 Rinse bean sprouts under cold, running water. Drain thoroughly.

5 Wash spinach thoroughly to remove grit and drain. Pull leaves off stalks.

6 Add bean sprouts to remaining oil in wok and stir-fry for 1 minute. Add spinach to wok and stir-fry for 2 minutes. Lightly season with salt and pepper. Moisten with stock and sherry.

7 Add beef to wok with soy sauce and ginger mixture and mix in well. Bring to boil and cook for 1 minute. Adjust seasoning to taste.

8 Serve with mixture of brown and wild rice, cooked separately then forked together.

Nutritional value per portion:
260 cal
Protein: 26g
Fat: 14g
Carbohydrate: 4g

Beef Fillet with Bean Sprouts

Chinese Leaves with Ham

Serves 4

The perfect dish for using leftover cooked ham.

Preparation time: 15 minutes
Cooking time: 7 minutes

1 small leek
315g (10oz) cabbage
345g (11oz) cooked ham
2 cloves garlic
2cm (¾ in) fresh root (green) ginger
60ml (2fl oz/¼ cup) sunflower or corn oil
Salt to taste
Fresh pepper
1 tablespoon medium sherry
2 teaspoons cornflour
125ml (4 fl oz/½ cup) vegetable stock
3 tablespoons soy sauce

1 Trim leek, slit lengthwise and wash thoroughly under cold, running water to remove grit and mud between layers. Shake dry. Cut into thin rings.

2 Separate cabbage. Wash each leaf thoroughly under cold, running water and drain. Cut leaves into thin strips, discarding stalks.

3 Cut ham into thin strips, removing any fat and gristle.

4 Crush garlic on to plate with garlic press. Peel, slice and finely chop ginger.

5 Heat oil in wok until hot, but not smoking. Add ham, garlic and ginger and stir-fry for 1 minute.

6 Mix in leek and strips of Chinese leaves and stir-fry for 5 minutes. Season lightly with salt and pepper. Moisten with sherry.

7 Mix cornflour with stock and soy sauce until smooth. Add to vegetables in wok. Bring to boil. Reheat until piping hot, stirring. Adjust seasoning to taste.

8 Serve straight away with rice or rice noodles.

Nutritional value per portion:
290 cal
Protein: 19g
Fat; 20g
Carbohydrate: 5g

Chinese Leaves with Ham

Chicken Livers with Mushrooms

Serves 4

Use either fresh or dried shiitake mushrooms for this impressive stir-fry.

Preparation time: about 25 minutes
Cooking time: 12 minutes

250g (8oz) fresh shiitake mushrooms or 100g
   (3½ oz) dried mushrooms
Boiling water for dried mushrooms
500g (1lb) chicken livers
2 teaspoons cornflour
Pinch of salt
Fresh pepper
½ teaspoon sugar
2 tablespoons medium sherry
75ml (2½ fl oz/⅓ cup) soy sauce
1 medium onion
345g (11oz) small zucchini
60ml (2 fl oz/¼ cup) sunflower or corn oil
30g (1oz) blanched almonds, cut into slivers
75ml (2½ fl oz/⅓ cup) chicken stock

1 Wipe fresh mushrooms clean with soft cloth or absorbent kitchen paper. Cut into thin strips. If using dried mushrooms, put into bowl, cover with boiling water and leave to soak for 30 minutes. Drain and wipe dry. Cut into strips, discarding stems.

2 Wash and dry livers. Cut into small pieces and toss with cornflour in bowl.

3 Make marinade by mixing together salt, pepper, sugar, sherry and soy sauce. Mix marinade into livers, cover and leave to stand for 10 minutes.

4 Peel and halve onion. Cut each half into thin slices. Top and tail zucchini and slice very thinly with sharp knife or on side of grater.

5 Heat oil in wok until hot, but not smoking. Add almonds and stir-fry until just beginning to brown, watching carefully as they quickly burn. Add onion, zucchini and mushrooms and stir-fry for 5 minutes. Remove from wok with draining spoon and put into bowl.

6 Lift livers out of marinade. Add to remaining oil in wok. Stir-fry briskly for 3 minutes. Mix in vegetables and almonds. Add stock and marinade. Bring to boil, then simmer for 1 minute. Adjust seasoning to taste.

7 Serve with rice or vermicelli noodles.

Nutritional value per portion:
310 cal
Protein: 31g
Fat: 16g
Carbohydrate: 8g

Chicken Livers with Mushrooms

Rice noodles with Prawns

Serves 4

This stir-fry is delicious eaten cold and makes a wonderful buffet dish.

Preparation time: 10 minutes
Cooking time: 5 minutes

100g (3½ oz) rice or vermicelli noodles
Boiling water
250g (8oz) celery sticks
2 green shallots
250g (8oz) carrots
1 fresh green chilli
60ml (2fl oz/¼ cup) sunflower or corn oil
3 cloves garlic
315g (10oz) cooked peeled prawns, thawed
  if frozen
2 tablespoons medium sherry
3 tablespoons soy sauce
90ml (3 fl oz/⅓ cup) vegetable stock
Pinch of salt
Pinch of sugar

1 Put noodles into large bowl, cover with boiling water and leave to stand for 5 minutes. Tip into colander and rinse under cold, running water. Using kitchen scissors, snip noodles into short lengths. Drain thoroughly.

2 To prepare celery, cut off green leaves and reserve. Remove and discard tough outer strings from each celery stick with kitchen knife. Slice celery thinly. Coarsely chop leaves.

3 Trim green shallots. Cut into 1cm (½ in) pieces.

4 Halve carrots lengthwise. Cut each half into thin slices.

5 Wearing rubber gloves, slit chilli lengthwise. Remove seeds with knife and finely chop flesh.

6 Heat oil in wok until hot. Crush garlic directly into hot oil. Add celery, green shallots and carrots. Stir-fry for 1 minute.

7 Mix in noodles and prawns. Stir-fry for 1 minute. Add sherry, soy sauce, stock, salt, sugar and chopped chilli and mix thoroughly. Heat through until piping hot. Sprinkle with chopped celery leaves and serve straight away.

Nutritional value per portion:
290 cal
Protein: 20g
Fat: 11g
Carbohydrate: 25g

Rice noodles with Prawns

Pork with Broccoli

Serves 4

A colorful combination of vegetables and pork.

Preparation time: about 20 minutes
Cooking time: 14 minutes

220g (7oz) carrots
315g (10oz) broccoli
100g (3½ oz) mushrooms
1cm (½ in) fresh root (green) ginger
500g (1lb) pork
Salt to taste
Fresh black pepper to taste
1 tablespoon cornflour
60ml (2fl oz/¼ cup) sunflower or corn oil
2 cloves garlic
3 tablespoons soy sauce
125ml (4fl oz/½ cup) chicken stock
Pinch of sugar
3 tablespoons snipped fresh chives

1 Cut carrots into very thin slices. Separate broccoli into small florets. Thinly slice broccoli stalks.

2 Wipe mushrooms with absorbent paper towel and trim stalks. Thinly slice. Peel ginger, slice thinly and finely chop.

3 Cut pork into thin slices against grain. Season lightly with salt and pepper. Sprinkle with cornflour. Rub well into pork with finger tips.

4 Heat oil in wok until hot, but not smoking. Add pork. Stir-fry briskly for 1 minute. Remove with draining spoon on to rack or absorbent paper towel.

5 Add carrots, broccoli and mushrooms to remaining oil in wok and stir-fry for 1 minute. Crush garlic directly into the hot oil. Add ginger. Sprinkle with soy sauce and stock and mix in sugar. Cover and simmer for 5 minutes.

6 Return pork to wok and mix thoroughly with vegetables. Cover and simmer for 5 minutes. Sprinkle with chives.

7 Serve with curry-flavored rice.

Nutritional value per portion:
310 cal
Protein: 30g
Fat: 18g
Carbohydrate: 6g

Pork with Broccoli

Minced Beef with Savoy Cabbage

Serves 4

A hearty stir-fry ideal for cold winter months.

Preparation time: about 15 minutes
Cooking time: 15 minutes

315g (10oz) cabbage
1 large onion
250g (8oz) oyster mushrooms
60ml (2fl oz/¼ cup) sunflower or corn oil
3 cloves garlic
500g (1lb) lean minced beef
Salt to taste
Fresh pepper to taste
Paprika to taste
3 tablespoons soy sauce
125ml (4fl oz/½ cup) beef stock
Pinch of sugar

1 Separate cabbage leaves and remove pieces of hard stalk from each. Wash leaves well, drain throughly and shred with sharp knife.

2 Peel and halve onion and cut each half into thin slices.

3 Wipe mushrooms with absorbent paper towel, but do not wash. Cut flesh into thin strips.

4 Heat oil in wok until very hot, but not smoking. Add onion and stir-fry fairly gently until they begin to look transparent. Crush garlic directly into the hot oil.

5 Mix in beef and stir-fry briskly until brown and crumbly. Season generously with salt, pepper and paprika. Remove to bowl with draining spoon.

6 Add cabbage to remaining oil in wok and stir-fry for 4 minutes.

7 Add mushrooms to wok and mix well with cabbage. Stir-fry for 5 minutes. Moisten with soy sauce and stock. Add sugar and adjust seasoning.

8 Return beef to wok and combine with vegetables. Reheat until hot.

9 Serve with long grain rice.

Nutritional value per portion:
380 cal
Protein: 33g
Fat: 26g
Carbohydrate: 7g

Minced Beef with Savoy Cabbage